THE PAST IN PIECES

CONTEMPORARY ETHNOGRAPHY

Kirin Narayan, Series Editor

A complete list of books in the series
is available from the publisher.

THE PAST
IN PIECES

BELONGING
IN THE
NEW CYPRUS

Rebecca Bryant

PENN

UNIVERSITY OF PENNSYLVANIA PRESS

PHILADELPHIA · OXFORD

Published by
University of Pennsylvania Press
Philadelphia, Pennsylvania 19104-4112

Printed in the United States of America
on acid-free paper
10 9 8 7 6 5 4 3 2 1

Library of Congress Cataloging-in-Publication Data
Bryant, Rebecca.
   The past in pieces : belonging in the new Cyprus /
Rebecca Bryant.
      p. cm.—(Contemporary ethnography)
   978-0-8122-4260-7 (hardcover : alk. paper)
   Includes bibliographical references
   1. Nationalism—Cyprus.   2. Turks—Cyprus—Ethnic
identity.   3. Greeks—Cyprus—Ethnic identity.
4. Cyprus—History.   5. Cyprus—Ethnic relations.
I. Title.
DS54.5 .B82   2010
956.9304—dc22   2010004560

CONTENTS

1. Ruins of a former Turkish Cypriot village in the Paphos district.

The Sorrow of Unanswered Questions

THE ROAD SEEMED to wind to nowhere, and drought had parched all the bare hills the same color of new wheat. We pulled into a roadside restaurant that overlooked a tiny village at the base of the Troodos Mountains, on the old road that few people travel any more. We had driven for almost an hour from the Paphos coast, making our way through what had once been Turkish villages. As I drove, my Turkish Cypriot colleague flipped through a book he had brought, *Güney'de Kalan Değerlerimiz*, or *Our Valuable Properties Remaining in the South*, and for each ruined or partially abandoned village, he read to me its history.

"I knew there were some villages here, but I had no idea there were so many," my friend commented. Not only were there more than we had expected, but they were also often in locations that would have made them prime targets of the island's recent real estate boom. Instead, mudbrick walls slumped with the exhaustion of years, and gradually settlements that had been molded from the soil seemed to be returning to it. The remains of mosques lacked minarets, headstones in cemeteries had been broken. In some cases the small villages had been taken over for storage, as farmers from neighboring areas installed pens for animals and used the abandoned roads to stow their tractors.

We finally arrived at a tiny village that had once been the home and hiding place of the Hassanpoullia, an infamous gang of bandits that had become the subject of legend at the beginning of the twentieth century. Unlike many of the other villages through which we had passed, there were signs of life, even in the middle of a summer afternoon. "We have to eat *kleftiko* here," my friend insisted. "I want to be able to say that I ate thieves' kebab in the village of the Hassanpoullia."

We sat in the shade of a bamboo awning outside the restaurant, where the only other customers were an elderly couple and an even more ancient woman who was clearly the mother of one of them. They ate their lunch in relative silence, although the mother would sometimes make an inaudible comment that would be greeted by a shouted reply on the part of the daughter. We were slightly above the village, on an angle that faced the mountains, so a breeze stirred the tablecloths. Cicadas hummed, and occasionally a car passed on the road above. A middle-aged woman with blue eyes and ginger-colored hair brought salad and yogurt. But it was only when she brought the kebab and my friend requested lemons and onion that she realized he was Turkish Cypriot.

"Where are you from?" she asked in Greek, and my friend turned to me for translation.

I told her that he was from Nicosia, and she seemed disappointed. "We used to have Turkish neighbors," she remarked. "A lot of them have come to visit." She also described going to a wedding of some former neighbors in the village where they now live in the north of the island.

The couple at the next table had turned toward us, listening. "It was all the politicians who divided us," the elderly man commented. And he asked again my friend's place of origin, my friend again replying that he was from Nicosia, a city that had long been divided. But it seemed to have little importance to the elderly gentleman, who proceeded to ask what had by then become a familiar question: "*Wouldn't it be better if we could all live mixed again, the way we used to?*" I had heard the same question in many different versions at various points in my research, and my friend's response was a typical one—a slight nod of the head, a reluctant smile.

We said our goodbyes, and as we were leaving, the restaurant's owner pulled us inside to point out old photographs that she had hung above the door. She pointed to some Turkish Cypriots, ancestors of her neighbors who had left for the north. My friend nodded, but we were eager to move on. I could see that he was upset, and when we returned to the car, he remarked in Turkish, "They just have to ask that question, don't they? It's like a denial of our whole past. I wish I could just say, 'No.'" Although my friend had worked for years for reconciliation, he had also grown up in a Nicosia enclave, surrounded by Greek soldiers. And so his belated answer to the old man's question was half-joking, half in anger: "We already live mixed now, don't we?" he asked the windshield. "We can come over here, and they can come to the north."

Although five years had passed since Turkish Cypriot authorities opened the ceasefire line dividing the island, the way in which the elderly Greek man and my Turkish friend imagined the meaning of that partition had changed very little. There were partitions not only of place but also of memory, partitions that now took the form of a long pause between the old man's question and my friend's soliloquous answer. But it was now a past visible in pieces, in the chance encounters and fragments of memory that formed what people had begun to call the "new Cyprus."

INTRODUCTION

A Prelude to Mourning

O N APRIL 23, 2003, to the surprise of much of the world, the border that divides Cyprus opened. The ceasefire line that partitions the island had been impenetrable to most Cypriots since 1974, so international media heralded the opening of the checkpoints as a momentous event that echoed the fall of the Berlin Wall. As in the moment of that wall's collapse, cameras captured the rush of Cypriots across the line to visit homes unwillingly abandoned three decades earlier. It was a euphoric moment, one filled with the tears of return to lost homes and the laughter of reunions. Old friends were found and new ones made, and many Cypriots reveled in the simple freedom of being able to stroll in streets that had long been forbidden to them.

This book explores why the momentous event of the opening of the checkpoints has not led the island any closer to reunification, indeed in many ways has driven the two communities farther apart. My research took place at a crucial moment, beginning not long after the opening and continuing intensively over a period of about two years, during which time Cypriots not only had to grapple with their newfound, complex freedom, but also had to confront a plan to reunify the island that divided people within their own communities, even within their own families. Almost exactly a year after the checkpoints' opening, in April 2004, Cypriots were called to vote on a UN-sponsored plan in separate referenda. While Turkish Cypriots ultimately decided to accept it, Greek Cypriots chose overwhelmingly to reject it. A week after that fateful referendum, the Greek Cypriot-controlled Republic of Cyprus would join the European Union as the only recognized government of the island, while the Turkish Republic of Northern Cyprus, the self-proclaimed and unrecognized

2. Upper Ayia Paraskevi neighborhood of Lapithos as it appears today (May 2009).

state in the island's north, would only be acknowledged in Europe as "the areas not controlled by the government of Cyprus." The ceasefire line that divides the island effectively became Europe's border.

The opening brought a period of unexpected change, and I try in this book to unravel its meanings in daily life, showing the ways in which Cypriots made sense of the opening, as well as the political implications of the meanings that they gave to it. In that first year, Cypriots reveled in a newfound freedom and quickly adapted to it. Within a month of the opening, Cypriots were already driving to the "other side" to shop, gamble, work, and lounge at the beach. Many on each side still refused to cross, but even they were confronted by the growing and continuous presence of new others who drove cars with the "other side"'s plates, who spoke among themselves in languages both familiar and long forgotten. And so, in the midst of a seeming normalcy, Cypriots found many of their ideological anchors shaken. Cypriots were quickly confronted with worlds on the "other side" that were different from what they had imagined, and with versions of the past that for three decades had had little voice in the histories of victimization that each side claimed as its own.

They confronted these changes, and often resisted them. And so even as Cypriots adjusted to the practical realities of the open checkpoints, imagination has been much slower to follow suit.

This work, then, represents both an analysis of the importance of institutions in daily life and a meditation on the many meanings of return. Imaginations of life in the "other side" and of an intercommunal past together were made real for many people by institutions that have an important and concrete role to play in daily life. For instance, Greek Cypriot refugees from northern Cyprus still vote in parliamentary elections as though they are resident in their former villages; those villages have "mayors in exile" who, until recently, have had no access to those villages and no contact with the Turkish Cypriot mayors who actually live there and manage them. These institutions represent a denial of the legitimacy of a government in the north, a denial that is also rooted in a particular interpretation of the recent past and the events that divided the island. To say that one does not recognize the Turkish Cypriot mayor of one's village is to say that that mayor is a puppet of an illegitimate occupation regime; to recognize the mayor would be to accept the legitimacy of Turkish Cypriot claims that their government was formed by a community that barely escaped extinction at the hands of their Greek neighbors. It is precisely such institutions, that have made imagination so slow to change in the island.

It is also such institutions that have shaped the many meanings of return. The right of return is, for many Greek Cypriots, part of a universal justice that has heretofore been denied them. But at the same time, as I argue here, the return that Greek Cypriots imagine is not a simple resettling in their homes but primarily entails the reconstruction of lost communities. Indeed, for many Cypriots even the initial moment of euphoria at seeing their homes again was already tainted by the discovery that a "real" return might not be possible. Refugees visited homes and villages that are no longer their own, both in the sense that they are occupied by others, and in the sense that they are not the house or village held in constant remembrance for almost three decades. For the first time, many Cypriots realized that life had gone on in their absence, bringing the village that they had held in memory into a present from which a return to the past looked increasingly unlikely.

Moreover, they have been confronted since the opening of the checkpoints with a Turkish Cypriot refusal to return to their homes, an insistence on remaining where they settled after 1974, and a denial of another meaning of return: namely, a return to wholeness before rupture. Return, I argue here, is about imaginations of a shared past, which one would presumably recreate. Above all else, the opening of the checkpoints fractured those idyllic imaginations of the past, leaving the future uncertain. When the majority of Greek Cypriots rejected reunification after the opening of the checkpoints, it was both a cry against the loss of that imagined and idyllic past, and a prelude to mourning.

While the questions that the book addresses are ones being asked now by most Cypriots, the people whose voices fill its pages and whose lives I have attempted to describe are all in some way associated with the small town of Lapithos (in Turkish, Lapta), in the northern part of the island now under Turkish control. Lapithos was at one time a prosperous mixed town, located in fertile, well-watered land in the Kyrenia district on the northern coast. It is also a town with a violent history: while Turkish Cypriots fled the town in early 1964 and lived in enclaves for ten years, the town's Greek inhabitants fled in 1974 in advance of the Turkish army. It is a town whose local history is both peculiarly its own and representative of many of the events that affected the entirety of the island.

Over the course of about two years, through talking to people and reading their writings and books, and by going back through my own archives, I tried to understand both what happened in the town's past and how Cypriots are reconstructing that past in the present. I had already conceived the project before the border opening as one that would look at the ways in which Cypriots who had once lived together described that former life. With the opening of the checkpoints, I had the chance to see how persons with memories of life together and of specific places that they had lost began to rethink their own relationships to past and place in the present.

As a result, most of the people whose voices appear in this book were born in the mid-1960s or earlier and so have memories—of specific people and places and their life in those places—that were affected by the checkpoints' opening. The experiences of their children or grandchildren were different from their own, reflected in the Annan Plan referendum, when many more Greek Cypriot youth rejected the plan than did their grandparents; among Turkish Cypriots, the results were the reverse. Although the generation that has no experiences of the other deserves study, my aim here has been to see how their parents and grandparents, who do have memories of the other, have found their own memories altered by changes in the political present, and how such changes have in turn affected the political choices that they are now making.

Because much of this book concerns my own search for the past as it is sifted through Lapithiotes' voices in the present, I should say something here about the town's past as I myself reconstructed it. In talking to Lapithiotes, I sifted through pieces of histories, and ones that often contradicted others, and fragments of the past that seemed to fit nowhere. What I pieced together was a picture of the past that included exaggeration, emphasis, broken hopes, resentment, and a fair share of denial. What I pieced together is a history that in my own reconstruction is as partial as in theirs, one in which I can make few claims to certainty, and one in which large holes seem to be papered over with a flimsy patchwork of claims.

What I can say for sure is that the history of Lapithos over the past half century or so is one about which Greek Cypriots and Turkish Cypriots do not agree, and in the ways that they disagree, the history of the town might be seen as a microcosm of the larger Cyprus conflict. The picture that emerged was of a town that was once the largest, wealthiest town in the Kyrenia district and that for almost four hundred years had a Christian majority and a significant Muslim minority. While Greek speakers appear to have arrived in the island around the eleventh century B.C., the island's first substantial Turkish-speaking, Muslim population arrived with the Ottoman conquest of 1571. Large numbers of Muslims who worked for the Ottoman Empire or were loyal to it, including some from Lapithos, left the island when its administration passed to the British in 1878. Changing population figures from the early twentieth century indicate that during the period of British rule, many of the town's wealthy, educated Muslims left for Nicosia and even Anatolia. By the establishment of the Republic of Cyprus in 1960, there was only a small Turkish community of 370 in the town, in comparison to 3,124 Greek Cypriots. Although the large village of Vassilia, immediately to the west, had a Turkish population that fluctuated between a quarter and a half of the total, the small town of Karavas to the east was entirely Greek. While many Lapithos Turks associated themselves with the village of Vassilia, and so in conversation would inflate their numbers to almost 700 to include the Vassilia Turks, many Greek Lapithiotes perceive Karavas as an extension of Lapithos. This would have meant that, in many Greek Cypriots' perceptions, the actual Greek population of Lapithos in 1960 was around 5,500.

Starting near the beginning of the twentieth century, Lapithos became a hub for trades. In the descriptions of older Lapithiotes, one can hear the steady pounding of the carpenter's hammer, the clang of the iron maker's forge, the sharp whine of knives being sharpened, the chit-chit chipping of stone. Traders took Lapithos goods throughout the island, and eventually even exported the women's handiwork to England. Many of these trades depended on the water that was in abundant supply, and on the series of mills that were fed by it. The distribution of the water to the fields was itself an art, and those in possession of its secrets described them to me with pride. In the middle of the century, Cyprus silk became especially profitable, and the Kyrenia range was abundant in mulberry trees. Many people flushed with excitement as they described tending the silkworms, often giving over a room in the house, carefully feeding the creatures mulberry leaves, watching as the worm slowly spun its cocoon. The months of tending the silkworms were ones in which all worked hard, and people helped each other.

Lapithos had a single Turkish neighborhood that occupied a central place in the town, extending from the lower mosque to the upper one. It was near what today is the primary square around the church of Ayios Loukas, the area that contains a grocery, three coffeeshops, a bakery, and a space used for weddings and celebrations. Immediately to the east of the neighborhood are the municipal offices and agricultural cooperative, and the neighborhood winds to the west of those offices, trickling up the hill also to encompass what was the Turkish primary school, a Turkish coffeeshop, an upper mosque, and a street where some of the wealthiest Turkish families lived. The town's Turkish inhabitants had fields and orchards scattered through several quarters, but these were the limited areas where they lived, surrounded on all sides by the six other neighborhoods of the town, almost entirely Greek.

Moreover, during the period when the town's Turkish population was dwindling, its Greek population prospered. And beginning after the First World War, the town began to take on an increasingly Hellenic character, as Lapithiotes sold citrus and silks, or returned from abroad with money and built homes and schools in what I began to think of as Parthenon style: much stone, a few Ionic columns, and a triangle above the front patio. Although it was a rural town, many Lapithiotes of this period were educated and wealthy, with places of standing in the Greek community of the island. Several mentioned to me a tradition of the town—how far back it goes is not certain, but it was certainly in practice in the late 1950s—in which one of the Easter vespers was performed with the participation of the townspeople. While the priest performing the vespers acknowledged the gospel in Greek, townspeople came forward and acknowledged it in German, English, Hebrew, Turkish, French, and other languages. People from surrounding villages would come to observe this performance of linguistic agility.

Lapithos of the early twentieth century, then, had seven neighborhoods, its own mayor and municipality, separate schools for Turks and Greeks, a Greek high school, shops, restaurants, a craft cooperative, and several small hotels. There were Greek and Turkish cinemas, and plays were held in the high school theater. There were musical events, and the town had its poets and artists. There were Greek Lapithiotes who left to work in America, some of whom never returned. By the 1960s, it was common for young men to travel abroad for study, especially to Greece and England. Many of these returned to the island, often to the town. There were doctors and teachers who worked elsewhere in the island but considered Lapithos their home. In general, the sense one gets from Lapithiotes is that although they led an agrarian life, they were townspeople who enjoyed as many of the benefits of a town—such as concerts, theater, and good schools—as anyone of the period could have expected. Lapithiotes remember the town as a "civilized" place.

In the period before everything went awry, Turks were simply a minority in the town, and they were ignored. In fact, for many they simply weren't visible at all. They were encountered in the fields and in the workshops, at weddings and sometimes at festivals. The life and running of the town went on with little attention to them. In that period, the mayor of Lapithos was Feideias Paraskevaidhis, a doctor who had studied in Athens and served on the Albanian front in the Second World War. He would return to become mayor of Lapithos in 1949 and leader of the local branch of the Ethniki Organosis Kyprion Agoniston, or National Organization of Cypriot Fighters, usually known as EOKA. EOKA began an anticolonial guerrilla campaign in 1955 with the aim of *enosis*, or uniting the island with Greece. EOKA imitated other anticolonial struggles, though it was unique in demanding not independence but the right to become part of another country. The guerrilla war it launched against the British occupiers was one of the most intense and determined that the colonial officers had seen, and it depended on the almost unanimous support of the Greek-speaking populace, as well as much reference to the bravery of their ancient Greek ancestors.

It was also a campaign that was intensely anti-Turkish, and in many of its publications EOKA described their Turkish Cypriot neighbors as the remnants of a barbaric invader who now polluted the pure Greek character of the island. Not only did much of the anti-Turkish rhetoric filter down into the language of daily life, but it also shaped quotidian politics in EOKA's demand that the island's "pure" Hellenes avoid commerce and even interaction with their Turkish neighbors. There was considerable local mobilization, and in the period of rebellion between 1955 and 1959, British soldiers would often search Lapithiotes' homes for weapons. Caught up in the ferment of rebellion, it was no doubt difficult for many Greek Lapithiotes to see, or perhaps to care, that their Turkish neighbors felt under threat.

In 1956, not long after the start of the rebellion, Paraskevaidhis was arrested by the British for his involvement in the guerrilla movement. He remained in British prisons for four years, until the amnesty that followed independence, when he again took up his post in the mayoral office. In that year, the town erected in front of the municipal offices a large monument to their own EOKA dead, calling it the "Square of the Heroes." Tassos Papadopoulos, a young minister of labor and EOKA veteran who in 2002 would become president of the Republic of Cyprus, unveiled the monument. The fact that Turks in the village and elsewhere had been opposed to the goals of EOKA was no impediment to rewriting a space at the center of the village with EOKA's name.

But by that time relations in the village had already been spoilt. This is the period that older people mean when they say, "*We got along perfectly fine before politics got in the way.*" It is difficult to understand the register of this remark. What did it mean to get along perfectly fine? What was the substance of those relations, their content, their form? In areas of work, religion seemed to have little importance. Women worked together in the fields, sat in front of their homes and shelled beans together, traded foodstuffs with each other. Men worked together, often sat in the coffeeshops and argued together. A number of people described to me the mid-century practice of rotating the responsibility for halloumi cheese-making among neighbors: a certain number of families would each contribute an amount of milk, and the family making the cheese would redistribute the final product accordingly. These were relationships of shared responsibility and shared work, relationships of necessity. Young Muslim men were often apprenticed to Greek masters, though in the memories of those still living I heard no examples of the opposite being the case. Turkish men were likely to speak Greek, though most of the women that I met knew only a few words.

Many Greek Cypriot women told me, "*We used to work together with the Turks in the fields.*" But those same women who used to work with the Turks in the fields apparently changed towards them in the 1950s. One older Turkish woman told me several times about the change they saw: "*The neighbor Greek women would come in the 50s and 60s, and they'd say, 'You know what we're going to do to the English. We'll take Cyprus, and after that we'll take*

Istanbul. And if it's necessary, we'll kill you all." Yet her husband worked as a chauffeur for a wealthy Greek Cypriot whom she described as a good man and who sent her husband home only when he began to hear rumors that EOKA might punish him for employing a Turk.

Although they had heard the rhetoric of Greek nationalism for several decades, it was only in the 1950s, when their Greek neighbors took up arms, that local Turkish Cypriots began covertly to organize. Some Turkish Cypriots registered to become police, in some cases because they had lost their jobs with Greek Cypriot employers. But their registration in the police force created resentment, as they aided the British colonizers in attempting to quell the anticolonial struggle. Locally, Turkish Cypriots organized on their own, collecting hunting rifles and polishing guns that some had brought home from the world wars. Such local organization was going on in villages throughout the island, so that by 1958 a small group of Turkish Cypriot leaders decided that they had to get it under control. In that year, the Türk Mukavemet Teşkilatı, or Turkish Resistance Organization, also known as TMT, emerged to organize these disparate groups and bring some order to the struggle. Young Lapithiote men and women were quickly incorporated into TMT, which by the end of the decade had cells throughout the island. Leaders in the new organization began to receive training and strategic aid from the Turkish military. They also began covertly to recruit throughout the town, imitating their Greek counterparts in expecting young men to be prepared to fight while using girls to carry weapons and messages. And like EOKA, TMT began to establish its hegemony in the Turkish Cypriot community, often punishing those they branded as traitors.

"Treason" often took the form of quotidian acts of commerce. EOKA forbade Greek Cypriots to do business with Turks; TMT began a "Turk to Turk" campaign and expected Turkish Cypriots to buy only from within the community. A man who is today a village *muhtar*, or headman, and who had been part of TMT as a youth described the ways in which villagers were divided by both nationalist organizations: "*EOKA would want an accounting: 'Christo, why did you sell your donkey to a Turk?' And the same thing with the Turks: 'Hüseyin, did you sell your sheep this morning? If you sell them to Turks, that's okay.' That's how everything started. That's how the division started.*"

At least in its outlines, this much seems to be relatively well accepted by all sides, even if all the details are not entirely in the open. What is not agreed upon is what happened after the island gained independence in 1960. During the 1950s, EOKA aimed at uniting the island with Greece, while TMT called for *taksim*, or what is sometimes called "double enosis," a division of the island and union with both "motherlands," Greece and Turkey. Hence, the new independent Republic of Cyprus of 1960 was one that no one had wanted or expected, and it was burdened with a power-sharing constitution that many Greek Cypriots, especially, found problematic. In 1963, President Makarios tried to "solve" this situation by proposing a number of changes to the constitution that would effectively have limited the powers of the minority in the government. The result was that all Turkish Cypriots withdrew from the government, and the situation quickly deteriorated into intercommunal fighting.

In the way that Greek Cypriots of Lapithos remember things, in 1963 the Turkish Cypriot leadership began to foment trouble, walking out of the government and pushing their own people into enclaves. Greek paramilitary forces killed two young Turkish men from Lapithos in a village not far from the town, and according to Greek Cypriots it was not long afterwards that "foreign Turks"—that is, Turks not from the town—came and pressured "their" Turks to leave. This, they believe, was part of a plan to separate the communities, preparing the way for an ultimate division of the island.

A Greek Lapithiote friend, Nikos, was a young boy in early 1964, but he remembers that period and the Turks' departure. "*I remember that a couple of Turks were killed, but they were with TMT,*" he told me. "*They left in an orderly way, in buses,*" he said. "*There was pressure. Some foreign Turks came to the village and told them they had to leave.*" This is a common way of describing what happened, not only for Lapithos, but for many other mixed towns and villages in the island.

As a minority, Turkish Cypriots saw that period differently. They had already been frightened when, in 1956, a busload of Greek Cypriots arrived in the neighboring village of Vassilia and attacked many of the village's Turkish Cypriot women and children, wounding twenty. By some reports, the men who performed this act were from Karavas, the neighboring town to the east. Lapithos was immediately between these two villages, and this was one of the reasons for the organization of local defense in the late 1950s. And their experiences during that period also led them to expect more trouble after the island gained independence, so even in that period they continued to meet covertly. TMT had not been disbanded, and Lapithos was assigned a commander who had been trained in Turkey and arrived in the town as the village schoolmaster. Turkish Cypriots in Lapithos began to meet in the basement of the elementary school to organize, including collecting and hiding weapons.

In late 1963, violence exploded throughout the island. Turkish Cypriots heard of killings of women and children in neighboring villages, and they felt under siege. Many claimed that their neighbors whom they'd known their whole lives suddenly came and threatened them. Others described men sitting in the coffeeshops, aiming at the children with shotguns. On Christmas Day, 1963, when the two young men from Lapithos, İbrahim Nidai and Şevket Kadir, left the town never to return, Turkish Cypriots barricaded themselves in the few houses that they felt they could protect. Soon, they say, they began to run out of food and medicine and milk for the children. Some people say that the real threat was not from their neighbors but from persons outside the town; but their neighbors also said that they couldn't protect them. And so when a TMT representative arrived to tell them that they were to be loaded onto buses escorted by British soldiers, most were ready to go. For them, their departure, even if orderly, was a flight.

According to one of the "foreign Turks" who helped the Lapithos Turks evacuate, they did, indeed, leave in an orderly fashion, in three buses bound for the "foreign Turk's" own village, Temblos, and to the Turkish military encampment at Boğaz, in a mountain pass on the way to Nicosia. In Temblos, they slept in barns and pitched tents in the main square, near the mosque. This "foreign Turk" was a schoolteacher known to the Lapithos Turks, since he had friends and some relatives among them. The only way they were able to leave, he says, was in a convoy guarded by the British troops who helped them.

All the Lapithos Turks left the town in January 1964, and they would live in tents and other makeshift shelters for the next decade. About a quarter of the island's Turkish Cypriot population were displaced in this period, but almost 90 percent of the community were affected, as Turks from mixed villages moved into purely Turkish ones, occupying the squares and fields with tents and hurriedly built housing, or crowding into the houses of relatives. Turkish neighborhoods and villages became armed cantons, areas that their Greek neighbors were not able to enter and that in most cases Turks could exit only by enduring humiliating and sometimes dangerous searches.

Although there was some improvement in the situation after 1968, Turkish Cypriots remained in their enclaves, continuing to deny Greek Cypriots entry. In the meantime, tensions rose within the Greek Cypriot community, as certain disgruntled factions began to demand that President Makarios fulfill his promises to use independence as a stepping-stone to *enosis*. Turkish Cypriots remained in a state of siege for more than a decade, until the fateful summer of 1974, when the Greek junta government aided in a coup against President Makarios that was intended to unite the island with Greece. The president barely escaped assassination by the ultra-right nationalists who felt he had betrayed them in accepting the island's independence.

Within days, Turkey, as a guarantor of Cyprus's independence, militarily intervened with overwhelming force. Ostensibly, Turkey should have arrived in Cyprus to restore constitutional order, but the military plan called for the creation of a "zone of safety" that had the effect of partitioning the island. Turkey had threatened intervention on several occasions but had been held back by international pressure. Turkish Cypriots had waited for the intervention of the Turkish military since 1964, and they often said that Greeks would tease them that Turkey was about to come and didn't. Even though Greek Cypriots were aware of the possibility of Turkish intervention, they were nevertheless taken unawares when Turkish troops landed in the island's north and began to march over Greek and Greek Cypriot forces, which were in any case divided among themselves. The right-wing nationalists who had taken over the government had jailed many of the leftists and Makarios sympathizers in the army, but they released them with news of the invasion and sent them to fight. The Turkish army was aided by experienced officers who had been located in various regions of the island since the establishment of the republic in 1960, but more especially by Turkish Cypriots, who acted as scouts, guides, and translators.

The battle for Lapithos was particularly hard fought, and involved strafing and bombing the town, as well as a pincer operation to attack it from three sides that was met by Greek forces arriving from the sea. It was, by most reports, the most vicious hand-to-hand combat that the island saw, and in some, probably exaggerated, reports that I heard it was estimated that up to fifteen hundred soldiers on both sides may have died in the battle. According to one older man who had fought in TMT, the reason for the ruthlessness of the Turkish army in Lapithos lay in an incident, stories about which I would hear repeated many times. "*You know the headspring in Lapta?*" he asked me. "*There's a big plane tree there.*" He then related to me the capture of several Turkish officers and their alleged death by torture at that spot. "*Because of that a lot of Greek Cypriot soldiers died here,*" he claimed. "*After that incident.*"

While the theme of reprisal is an important one in Turkish Cypriot accounts of the war, the theme of the Turkish military's violence is an important one in Greek Cypriot accounts. In books and anecdotes of the war, as would be expected, the enemy's behavior is deplored and one's own behavior is praised. But while Turkish Cypriots have spoken often of the atrocities committed by Greek Cypriots in the period of the war, Greek Cypriots circumspectly refrain from speaking publicly about atrocities that Turkish Cypriots committed, preferring to remember acts of kindness and to attribute atrocities to the Turkish army. This despite the fact that many Greek Cypriots in fact know that many of the atrocities were committed by Turkish Cypriot fighters, who spoke in the Cypriot dialect.

In Lapithos itself, as in the rest of the north, Greek Cypriots fled their homes to safer places in the island's south, and those who remained—usually too old or too sick to flee—were enclaved in a single neighborhood. I heard of at least two persons who died of natural causes during the period of their enclavement, and there were reports of rapes, some systematic. Greek Cypriots enclaved in Lapithos were some of the last to be expelled to the south, so they also witnessed the period when their former Turkish neighbors returned to the town and settled in Greek Cypriot homes, later to be followed by Turkish Cypriot refugees from the south.

By 1976, only a few hundred Greek Cypriots were left in a small corner of the island's north, and all but a handful of Turkish Cypriots had made their way to the north from their homes in the south. When the Turks of Lapithos returned to the town after the flight of their Greek neighbors in 1974, they found their own houses ruined and so settled in those left behind by Greeks fleeing south. Soon after, Turkish Cypriot refugees from the south, especially from the Paphos area, were resettled in the town by the Turkish Cypriot administration. After that, there were the waves of settlers from Turkey, many of whom fought or lost sons in the war, and more recently, European retirees.

Significantly, the Turkish Cypriot administration resettled Turkish Cypriot refugees from the south as villages, hence as communities, and indeed appears to have taken some effort to guarantee that the villages in which they resettled in some way resembled their own. So persons from villages near the sea were resettled near the sea, while those from the foothills and plains were resettled in similar areas. In contrast, Greek Cypriots were scattered, and most people with whom I spoke saw this as an intentional plan of the Greek Cypriot leadership to prevent their resettlement and to encourage the longing for return. Greek Cypriot refugees from Lapithos are now scattered throughout the south, with large pockets in Nicosia and Larnaca, but with others living in Turkish Cypriot properties in more remote villages of Limassol and Paphos. Others, of course, left the island never to return.

Following the division, negotiations to create a federation continuously failed, and the de facto Turkish region in the north soon declared itself a state. By 1983, almost a decade later, it had become clear that the stalemate was likely to continue, and the Turkish Cypriot parliament in the north declared that region the Turkish Republic of Northern Cyprus, a "sovereign" republic still recognized by no one besides Turkey. Today, the Republic of Cyprus remains the only recognized government in the island, controlled de facto by Greek Cypriots. The result has been that Greek Cypriots, as members of the Republic of Cyprus, enjoyed the benefits of recognition and so began to prosper, once they recovered from the initial economic shocks of the war. Turkish Cypriots, on the other hand, live in an unrecognized state that has been hampered by various forms of isolation and exclusion, including restrictions on trade and travel.

Moreover, the Republic of Cyprus has claimed sovereignty over the entirety of the island and so was able, in 2004, to join the European Union despite the fact that the island is divided. The EU *acquis communautaire* is now suspended in the island's north, and the new situation only increased the inequalities that already existed between the two sides. At the time of the Republic's EU accession, the Greek Cypriot-controlled south of the island was one of the wealthiest communities in Europe, while the Turkish Cypriot north was dependent on aid from Turkey and had an economy that could only grow by fits and starts.

Older Lapithiotes describe the town before conflict as one where roots ran deep, where families and land and trees and saints were entangled over generations. Their descriptions are of an organic whole, something that many people perceive as having been ruptured by the conflict. Roots there are now shallow. The original Turkish Cypriots of Lapithos continue to be a minority in the town, now outnumbered by a combination of Turkish Cypriots from the south, settlers from Turkey, and Europeans. While Turkish Lapithiotes retain an attachment to their ancestral lands, others living there today have had to recreate community from shallower histories.

Today the town has no more ring of hammers or whine of steel than any other town of its size. The waterfalls of the past have dwindled to a trickle, and not even the older Lapithos Turks appear to know the secrets to distributing water that were once jealously guarded by their Greek neighbors. The town now has much more of an orientation to the sea than it had in the past. A cluster of hotels and bungalows now lines the main coast road, though the roads leading into the mountain and toward the town still wind past fields and citrus orchards. But those are slowly being parceled off and the citrus trees torn up to make way for vacation villas of the sort that many European buyers imagine as retirement homes. And the town now has a new character, a different character, that is etched with traces of the past even as it has become something far different from what it was.

Today there are Greek Cypriot and Turkish Cypriot Lapithiotes who are staunch nationalists, as well as those who are committed to reconciliation. There are those who insist on trying to forget the past, as well as many persons with a strong sense of historical and communal wrongs that will not be easily rectified. It is a town that has been shaken and changed by the opening, as townspeople rethink the past and recreate visions of the future. As such, the contradictions faced by Lapithiotes, and the ways in which they have attempted to imagine a world beyond those contradictions, are typical of much of the island.

As typical as it may be, one town obviously cannot stand for the whole island, and a view from inside the town will always be a partial one. But what it can show is the ways in which people may map their local worlds and local senses of belonging onto ones that are larger and for most people harder to grasp. And what it also can show is that any conflict—no matter who caused it or who controlled it—is ultimately between people, or rather between persons, many of whom may know each other, and for whom the local histories of friendships and enmities, of loyalties and betrayals, may give shape both to the meaning of the conflict and to its futures.

In writing this book, I have attempted not only to reflect the uncertainties created for average Cypriots by the opening of the checkpoints and political developments since, but also to describe what it meant to be an anthropologist who is betwixt and between, pulled to declare loyalties and to take sides. In 1993, when I first arrived in Cyprus and began to move between the communities, the ceasefire line was still firmly closed. As I crossed that line and moved between those parallel worlds, it was easy to express sympathy without engaging in real commitment. But since the opening of the checkpoints, many people demanded more than sympathy, and the commitments that they wanted often put me in contradictory situations. I had to recognize that my role was no longer simply that of a researcher with sympathies and political loyalties, but had become that of intermediary and conduit of information for people who had not yet discovered ways to rebuild trust.

So while this chronicle of the "new Cyprus" is told through the voices and lives of the people of one town that has experienced conflict, I make my own presence known not gratuitously but in order to show the ways in which my presence both created new situations and provided a lens onto others. Where I invoke my own dilemmas as researcher, it is not merely to describe the difficulties of ethnographic work in a place that has experienced conflict, but more importantly to show how impossible a middle position remains in the island. It is that middle position that is at stake, those things that continue to be caught between, on the ground of symbolic and political struggle that continues to divide the communities. Certainly, there are important lessons to be learned from the fact that the opening of the ceasefire line that divides the island has not led to reconciliation but has instead led, in concrete and possibly lasting ways, to the discovery of new borders that may, in fact, be the real ones.

ONE

Paths of No Return

By now so many things have changed,
the optical signs are transposed,
perspectives modified.
Does the house exist or not exist,
has it withstood last winter's rain or has it yielded?
—Yiorgos Moleskis, from "The House and Time"

VASILLIS AND MAROULLA Kyriakou live today among olive groves and rolling pastures in a former Turkish village in the Paphos district in the southwest of Cyprus. In the winter, rains wash the land in a fragile verdancy; by late spring, the grass has withered, leaving only dun-colored earth and chalky rock. Thirty years ago, the couple hastily constructed a set of rooms here, a temporary place of refuge after the flight from their home in northern Cyprus and the fighting that had engulfed it. They built the compound in the old village style, not as a single house but as rooms interspersed with pens for chickens and goats. Although it has remained their home for three decades, it retains an air of the temporary, a prefabricated shelter that has lasted beyond its expected life.

The land around is filled with olive trees that Vasillis planted when they built the house. Gazing at his cracked knuckles, he tells me, "*We watered them with the water that we drank.*" The trees have matured in the period of their exile, but still, he insists, "*You don't feel like it's your land. You feel like you're in a foreign place. It's not where you have your roots.*" He tells me that as soon as they receive word that they can return, they will gather their clothes, close the house, and turn their backs on this village where they've taken refuge for so long. I ask what will become of the olive trees; he replies that it doesn't matter.

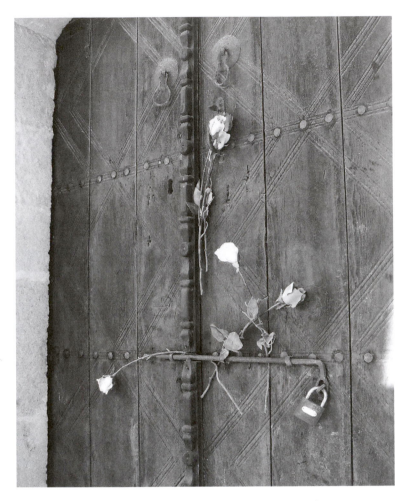

3. Locked door of a Lapithos church (May 2009).

In their natal town in northern Cyprus, Maroulla and Vasillis came from large, land-owning families, and the marriage of two children of such respectable families was considered a good one. Lapithos is lush with spring-fed fields and orchards, and many of those near the sea belonged to Vassilis's family, which also owned two large stone houses perched side by side on a wedge of mountain underneath the church of Ayia Paraskevi. Maroulla's own family was of more modest means, with houses and land above the church, where the mountain plateaus before climbing to the summit. Maroulla is open and warm, though there is also sometimes caution in her behavior, as well as something taciturn and resentful. When she appears outside the home, she dresses in black, still in mourning for a son lost to cancer before the war. Vasillis still maintains the self-assured bearing of a man who knows his place in the world, though it is also possible to glimpse in the deliberateness of his movement and in sudden flares of temper a man who has fought hard in the struggle for dignity.

When the checkpoints opened on April 23, 2003, Vasillis listened dumb-founded to reports of the first trickle of those who wandered across the divide in a daze of disbelief. Within hours, as news spread that it was not a trap, that people were actually able to cross and go freely to see their homes, the trickle became a flood. By the following day, when Vasillis made the trip from Paphos to Nicosia, he waited in line all day before finally being permitted across.

The next time he went he took Maroulla, who is much more eager to talk about what it meant. "*Put yourself in our place and imagine what it would be to go back to your home after thirty years. The home that you left without even a handkerchief. Once we crossed the checkpoint, I cried and cried all the way there.*"

Maroulla tells me this as I drive the two of them across the mountains to Lapithos. I am still in the initial phases of my research and have not yet gone to live in the town, and Vasillis has agreed to show it to me as they remember it. He has already given me a set of maps, which I discuss in a later chapter. The maps themselves are an anthropological treasure and an incredible mne-monic feat: Long before the checkpoints opened, he had sketched and labeled all the houses and all the workshops of all the households for a town that in 1960 had a population of thirty-five hundred. The maps would later become an important guide for me as I tried to understand what had happened to the town since 1974.

As we drive through the narrow lanes, they point out homes of brothers, sisters, cousins, uncles. As they comment on changes in the houses—an addi-tional room, the loss of a tree, a different color of paint for the balcony—I am made viscerally aware that these homes are not only houses but stories, and that these stories wind their way through a past that takes its shape through family and networks and relationships. It appears to me then that their sullen outrage at the changes in these houses is partly a cry against violation, partly a simple helplessness in the face of those dissolving ties.

Following this chain of relatives, we wind up the mountain through the town, finally arriving at the house that Vasillis says was Maroulla's birthplace; Maroulla remains silent. It turns out that over the past months, despite their repeated visits, she hasn't ever dared to enter the house, because a peasant family from Turkey lives there, and they speak no Greek, unlike many of the Turkish Cypriots. When I offer to go with her and translate, she grabs the opportunity. We leave Vasillis in the car as we approach the door.

A Turkish woman of indefinable age answers it. Maroulla immediately takes her by the arms and kisses her on both cheeks, and the woman understands what the visit is about. She tells me later that she's had many such visits, and I learn that they were the children and grandchildren of Maroulla's sister, who had inherited the house. Later, the Turkish woman tells me that her name is Düriye and that she raised seven children in the house herself. They came to the island not long after 1974, at the insistence of their son, who had been wounded during the invasion. They immigrated from Kayseri, in central Anatolia, later selling their land there to marry off their children. The reward for the wounded son had been land in north Cyprus, and he had arranged for a house to be given to his parents, as well.

We enter through a kitchen that has new cabinets, installed slightly askew. In a gesture of habit, I remove my shoes outside the door, in Turkish fashion, and am immediately confused by the fact that Maroulla has barged through the house, as it seems to me, wearing her low black pumps. The Turkish woman will be offended, I think. But what if Maroulla is offended that I've removed my shoes, as though the house belongs to the Turkish woman and not to her? As we walk through the house, I hang slightly behind Maroulla, hoping that she will not notice my stockinged feet.

But Maroulla is far ahead of us, hurrying through the parlor and into the living room. I engage the Turkish woman in conversation in order to leave Maroulla to herself, and when we catch up with her, she is standing on a balcony that overlooks the village and the church of Ayia Paraskevi, and which has a clear view of the coastline. "*It's a nice view,*" says the Turkish woman, but she seems unimpressed. Instead, she talks to me about all the improvements her family had made to the house, about how the house had been looted by the Turkish army, and there was almost nothing left of it. We make our way to the adjoining room, and Maroulla comments that it was not a separate room before. She points to an area under an open window; that was where she slept, she says.

As we leave, I ask permission to take a photograph, and the Turkish woman asks me if I want them together. So the two women stand uncomfortably side by side, facing the camera. On our way down the steps, I tell Maroulla that I will photograph her alone in front of the house. She tells me to be sure to get the balconies in the photo. After I put down the camera, she says to me, "*When I die, I want this photograph on my grave.*"

In the car, she tells Vasillis that it was a mistake, that she should have had me photograph her while she stood on the balcony. Instead, we have a photograph of her dressed in black on the stone steps of the house, and another of the two women together in the doorway. One woman fled the house, and the other received it as a trophy. And now, in my photograph, they stand uncomfortably side by side, a fragment of the new Cyprus.

A decade earlier, the thought that Greek Cypriots would ever return to their homes had been unfathomable to me, an unrealizable dream. After all, I crossed often to the north, I spoke to Turkish Cypriots, and I saw how different their world was from the one that Greek Cypriots imagined. In the Greek Cypriot imagination, their Turkish compatriots were hostages to Turkey, kept in an open-air prison. According to this version of Cyprus' history, Greek and Turkish Cypriots had always been like brothers until Turkey invaded and divided the island. As a consequence, it was a common belief that Turkish Cypriots also wanted to live together with them and that the only thing separating Cypriots from their homes was the Turkish army. Neighbors who knew that I crossed often asked me, "*Do they have enough to eat? Do they miss their homes?*" I found the questions disturbing at the time, and I fumbled for answers that they would believe.

It seemed futile to try to explain that there was an entirely different world on the other side of the ceasefire line, a world with schools and supermarkets and the usual neighborly competitiveness over who had the newest car, the biggest house, or who threw the grandest wedding. It seemed even more futile to try to explain that there were Turkish Cypriot versions of the past that were very different from their own. Even though I was not allowed to name it as such, the ceasefire line was, to me, a border as much as anything could be—or so I thought then. It took the opening of the checkpoints to make me realize that borders are created not only through isolation but also through interaction, not only in their closure but also, and perhaps even more, in the act of crossing them.

One day more than a year after I made that first trip to Lapithos with Vasillis and Maroulla, I sat in my car on the Turkish side of the checkpoint and telephoned their home. One of the more irksome facets of the two states' mutual non-recognition is that phoning the other side of the island becomes an international call, circuitously routed. In the past, a call from south Nicosia to Istanbul had to be routed through an operator in Athens, and there was one UN number for calls between north and south. Most people assumed that all calls made through the UN line were tapped, probably recorded. Part of the recent thaw has been the possibility of direct dialing, but it's still expensive. And cell phones from one part of the island don't work in the other, except in areas near the ceasefire line, where they usually pick up signals from the "other side." For this reason, like most Cypriots who travel between north and south, I kept several numbers—one from the south, one from the north, and in my case also one from Turkey. That day I sat on the Turkish side of the line, hoping to pick up a signal on my SIM card from the south.

I had then been living in Lapithos for some months, and I had avoided calling Maroulla and Vasillis. I felt terrible about this, but I told myself that I had been busy, that I had been establishing myself there. I knew, though, that the real reason was fear of what would happen once I contacted them—fear of what they would think, fear of what they would want me to do. As much as they liked me, living there could only seem like a betrayal to them, even if they would never tell me that. I knew that they would want to come and visit, and I feared being seen with them, and having to explain it all to my Turkish neighbors and friends. Even though everyone knew that I talked to people on the "other side," this was different because Vasillis and Maroulla had interests in the town, and I was probing for answers to sensitive questions. And for many people I still had to circle carefully around the question of loyalties.

I dialed hurriedly and pressed the phone hard to my ear. It rang several times, and then Maroulla picked up. I thought she sounded tired, and I wondered if I'd woken her. After all, it was late afternoon, and she might still have been napping. But soon I realized that it was a deeper exhaustion. I said that I wanted to come see them, and we agreed on a day. Before we hung up, I could hear a hesitation. "*Tell me,*" she demanded softly, her voice barely audible. "*We'll never return, will we?*" Her voice was small and anguished, and I could feel something catch in my throat. "*I don't know,*" I answered. And then, more truthfully, "*I don't think so.*" It was probably the closest I came with any of the refugees to expressing what I feared.

Much had happened between my first visit with Vasillis and Maroulla to Lapithos and this phone conversation that left me shaken. Not long after that first visit Cypriots had voted on a United Nations plan to reunite the island,

something commonly known as the Annan Plan, after the former UN sec-
retary general. After three decades of diplomatic jousting, Cypriot leaders
had grown accustomed to and seemed lulled by the rhythms of the game.
Point, thrust, and withdraw. Circle and attack. Some fancy sword-play now
and then to keep the audience's attention. Staying *en garde* was the key, but
even then one could occasionally break for a cup of coffee, since, after all,
your opponent was well known to you.

Meanwhile, in the chambers of the United Nations, other cogs in other
wheels were steadily churning out page after page of what would become
the most controversial plan in the island's history. The plan took all previous
negotiations and previous concerns and produced what most observers considered to be a true compromise: a bizonal, bicommunal federal government
and a mechanism for settling property claims related to the island's division.
The plan landed on the Cypriot *piste* with all the gusto of a new referee who
actually wants to bring the match to a conclusion. The combatants were rather
surprised to find that their spectators had also grown weary and cheered the
referee's entry. But soon things were back to normal, when what seemed the
final moments of the match got underway, and the referee's decisions for one
side or the other raised catcalls and cheers. Taking the plan to referendum
was a bit like asking the spectators to vote on the referee's calls.

The plan was not a perfect plan; in fact, in many ways it was an idealistic
plan. The new state that it asked Cypriots to create would have relied a lot on
good will, and in the end no one would have come out the winner. It was one
of those darlings of neoliberal diplomacy, the "win-win" plan, which is to say
that you attempt to convince each combatant that he's won by changing the
stakes. The primary stake in this case was European Union entry, promised
to the Greek-controlled Republic, whose entry date hung over the heads of
Turkish Cypriots like a guillotine ready to drop. Greek Cypriots, on the other
hand, saw the threat of partition, made more vividly real by the checkpoints'
opening and given urgency by the possibility that they would enter the EU
without their Turkish Cypriot partners. The Annan Plan would have solved
both these problems.

But for Maroulla and many people like her it also created a potential future that was hard to imagine. Because she is more than sixty-five years old,
she would have been able to return to Lapithos, but she would have had to
leave her son and his family behind. She and Vasillis would have automati-
cally received one-third of their property, but in all likelihood that would
not have included the marital home from which they had fled. The Turkish

woman who occupies her childhood home would have remained in the town, perhaps even would have kept the house because of all the improvements that she had made to it. And so in the new, unified Cyprus envisioned by the Annan Plan, Maroulla would have lived in a new house, probably built with compensation for the house that she was unable to reclaim, in a town now occupied mostly by Turkish Cypriots, where her son and grandchildren would visit her by crossing into another state, and where she would encounter at the market the woman she considers to be illegally occupying the home of her childhood memories.

The plan raised as many questions about the future as it answered, creating new possibilities and calculations that had not been part of the contest before. Greek Cypriots had always been told by their leaders that any negotiated settlement would ensure the absolute right to return, as well as the reinstatement of their property. Turkish Cypriots had been assured by their leaders that any plan would give them a zone of safety, as well as ensure the protection of their political rights. While in the abstract both might be possible, in reality it has never been possible to satisfy both. How can one have a federal government with ethnic constituent states without artificially maintaining an ethnic balance by limiting Greek Cypriots' return? How can one meet Greek Cypriot demands for demilitarization and disengagement from the protector states of Turkey and Greece while still ensuring that the Turkish minority feel secure?

For Greek Cypriots, especially, the plan did not appear to satisfy these most basic demands, and when Cypriot leaders negotiated the plan's final version Greek Cypriot president Tassos Papadopoulos returned to the island to vilify it. By that time, the Republic's EU entry was only a few weeks away, scheduled for May 1, 2004, and most Greek Cypriots were certain of their own future as the wealthiest of the new EU member states. Papadopoulos made a now infamous televised speech, filmed in front of the window in the presidential palace from which former president Makarios had escaped with his life during the coup attempt of 1974. He tearfully asked the Greek Cypriot public to reject the plan in favor of the advantages of unilateral EU entry, which they could use to pressure a Turkey that was still struggling to get its own EU bid accepted. In the weeks leading up to the referendum, the plan was presented to the public in bits of propaganda and in the diatribes of the church, many of whose leaders condemned the plan as "satanic" and threatened their flocks with damnation if they voted in favor.

Turkish Cypriots, on the other hand, were eager to have the plan, or almost any plan, because the Republic's imminent EU entry meant that their own dreams of European citizenship and its advantages seemed to be fading. They had been hard hit by Turkey's 2001 economic catastrophe, and they were also troubled by a change of government in Turkey and the fear that the new government might "sell out" Cyprus for its own EU membership. Turkey had always been the big brother waiting in the wings and prepared to make an appearance when things got tough. And its thirty thousand troops stationed in the island were always Turkish Cypriots' trump card. Partly from hope, partly from fear, Turkish Cypriots began, in late 2002, a rebellion against the regime led by long-time president Rauf Denktaş, who, like Papadopoulos, rejected the plan on principle rather than on its particulars.

It was this rebellion that had led to the opening of the checkpoints in April 2003, a moment of euphoria followed by its own disillusionments. And so, when a year later the moment of reckoning came, the results of the referendum were lopsided: 65 percent of Turkish Cypriots voted in favor of the plan, and 76 percent of Greek Cypriots rejected it. Greek Cypriots felt bullied, Turkish Cypriots felt betrayed, and the initial euphoria that followed the checkpoints' opening was dispelled. In the days immediately after the referendum, traffic across the Green Line almost ceased. Resentment was palpable in the air, and perhaps for the first time in Cyprus's recent history, people began simply to ignore each other, as though they couldn't be bothered anymore.

And this I could hear in Maroulla's voice. Vasillis had always been more eager to talk politics with me and always wanted to discuss with me possible legal solutions to his own bind. He voted for the Annan Plan, and he forced Maroulla to do so, as well. In fact, I saw him twice sitting with village men at his kitchen table, arguing with them in his deliberate, forceful way about the plan and the president's assessment of it. Vasillis follows DISY, a neoliberal party with a nationalist past that was the only one to come out in support of the plan. He also reads their newspaper, *Alitheia* (*The Truth*), which gave a much more comprehensive analysis of the plan than any of the other papers dared.

I would often hear Vasillis and Maroulla arguing in whispers about Vasillis's unwavering conviction that they had to return to Lapithos. They both wanted it more than anything, but they didn't want it in the same way. Vasillis was willing to make political sacrifices, even to go against many of his former principles, for the sake of a plan that sketched for him a vision of return and allowed him to plan for what he would do with the one-third of his property that it gave him the right to use. If he couldn't get back his own house, he would build a small house there, and he would return as soon as it was complete. Perhaps he would even return before; he had a couple of schemes to rent an apartment from a Turkish Cypriot he knew in the town.

I could see that Maroulla wasn't so sure. She was eager to visit their old homes, but I could see that she was uncomfortable. Unlike Vasillis, who spoke to every Greek-speaking Turk he could find, Maroulla was more withdrawn. She would kiss the women, calling them *yitonissa*, or neighbor, but she would never enter into Vasillis's eager discussion of his schemes. Vasillis would tell them openly that he planned to return, perhaps testing the waters, perhaps assuming that they would welcome him. Maroulla often seemed embarrassed by his eagerness, as though sensing that their former neighbors' silent acquiescence did not mean acceptance.

When she asked me the question that disturbed me so, I knew that it was not in Vasillis's hearing. When she asked me that question, I envisioned her on the steps of her childhood home, and the way that she stood next to but not near the Turkish woman as I photographed them. She may not have believed in Vasillis's dreams, but she would let him have them. After all, for many of the refugees, only dreams were left.

Vasillis returns often to Lapithos, though he doesn't take Maroulla with him every time. Maroulla's younger sister Eleni, the educated one in the family, doesn't approve of Maroulla's visits. It was Eleni I had met first, going to visit her in her Nicosia home. The two women are a contrast. Eleni is a retired schoolteacher, and she presents a neat, professional demeanor. Her husband Kostakis was also a teacher, and that's how they met in the 1950s. Even before the division of the island, they were living and working in Nicosia. They built the house where they now live in the early 1970s, in what was then a Nicosia suburb, though the city has now grown to engulf it. The house is also neat, carefully dusted and swept, decorated only with family photos and Eleni's paintings of Lapithos, which fill the dining room walls. There is something that seems to me prim and polished about Eleni, in contrast to the harried air that Maroulla often carries. And while Maroulla expresses her own longing for return in terms of hopes and fears, Eleni expresses it in terms of principles and rights.

The Greek Cypriot mayor of Lapithos had introduced me to Eleni. The mayor, a trade unionist, is a quiet man of conviction who, like many in his position, has his life circumscribed by state fantasy. He is, in official terminology, the "mayor in exile," making him the "real" or "official" mayor for a town to which he has no access. As a result, instead of the usual duties of mayor, he can do little besides organize policy meetings and social events for elderly refugees. Some Greek Cypriot mayors have returned to their villages and towns and even sought cooperation with their Turkish Cypriot counterparts since the checkpoints' opening. The mayors of Famagusta, for instance, have begun work on environment and cultural preservation, while the Greek Cypriot Kontea refugee association applied with the Turkish Cypriot Kontea village council to USAID for funds to restore the village's cultural heritage sites. But most mayors found their constituencies resistant to such cooperation, and in the case of Lapithos, it was explicitly rejected.

This quiet man of conviction, then, is the "real" mayor for a town over which he has no control and that he can't even visit, because to do so would be a violation of the very principles that put him into office. Like other mayors, the mayor of Lapithos also works closely with the town's refugee organization, which sponsors cultural events aimed at memorializing the town and maintaining social ties. It also organizes protests at the checkpoints, the planting of forests in memory of the town's missing, and youth events whose goal is to tie the next generation to a town they've never seen. Eleni is a volunteer of the Lapithos refugee association, so the mayor knew her well.

Eleni has been to the village only once since the checkpoints opened, and she adopts the official stance of the refugee organizations, which is that visiting the north is pandering to Turkey. "*We will not be tourists in our own country*," official slogans say. In similar fashion, she and her husband were opposed to the Annan Plan on principle because of its concessions to Turkey. Like most schoolteachers of the 1950s and 1960s, Eleni and Kostakis imbibed Greek nationalism from an early age. For them, Cyprus is unquestionably a Greek island. Eleni wrote about her return to the town in the most nationalist daily newspaper, where she discussed the violation of Lapithos' Greek heritage.

Her one visit to the town is something that Eleni recounts again and again. She told me about the young woman who helped translate for them. She told me about entering the ground floor apartment, and the kilims on the floor, and the shoes outside the door. She thought that the family were from Trabzon, on the Black Sea coast, and I had some trouble explaining to her that they were from Kayseri, in the center of the country. I wasn't sure what this difference meant to her, or why she wished to insist, but I sensed that it has something to do with the now iconic status of her one visit to the home.

"I had to go just once," she told me, *"but I won't go again. Not until all the refugees return."* This has been the official stance of the refugee organizations, that no one should visit the north until a political solution is found. Many refugees believe that presenting one's identity card to cross to the north is a recognition of the authorities there. Many lawyers have assured them that it means no such thing, that there is no implied recognition. Although I originally took lightly this objection of recognition, I began more and more to see that the refugees have a point.

But there's something else in it, as well, something that became an open topic of discussion only after the referendum. The dream of return—the *right* of return—has been a central theme of Greek Cypriot politics for thirty years. Refugees have been told again and again that the only acceptable solution to the island's problems is one that will evict the Turkish army and ensure the return of everyone to his or her own home. However, the idea that all refugees would return was also a paradoxical stance, since at the same time the Republic has always paid lip service to the idea of a federal solution. With the advent of the Annan Plan, people suddenly became conscious of the fact that a federation would mean two ethnic constituent states, and two ethnic states would mean that not everyone would return.

Many people understood this paradox and saw the ways that politicians manipulated the simple desires of villagers who had been displaced from the only homes that they had known. And so it was not hard to see that the refugee organizations' stance on visiting one's home was not only a matter of principle, but also a matter of quotidian politics. Ironically, since the opening of the checkpoints, politicians and refugee organizations are struggling to keep the dream of return alive. Part of this struggle is urging them not to visit their homes. Everyone tacitly recognizes that refugees are now confronted not with a dream but with a reality: someone else living in their home, someone else working their land. Many people, when confronted with these realities, began gradually to accept that "real" return might not be possible.

Many also began to consider that perhaps in fact they had no desire to return. Some refugees told me that they were too old to work the land, so what would be the point? Others didn't want to return precisely because they *do* work—in Nicosia and other parts of the island. Others wanted to be near their children and grandchildren. But most, when they got down to it, said that they didn't want to return because they could now see that things would never be as they once were.

I see these paradoxes, too, in Eleni's position, which is both official and very personal. In the series of newspaper articles that she wrote, she often employs high-flown metaphor and snippets of poetry, intoning that the land "cries for its lost children." She adds a few references to ancient Greek poets and claims that the land calls to her in Greek. Hyperbole, I've learned, is a common rhetorical strategy and often a way of life among staunch nationalists.

If asked why she voted against the plan, Eleni would say that it rubber-stamped the violation of their human rights. The right to property, the right to freedom of movement, and the right of return are the particular rights to which she refers, and all of these center around the image of the lost village, the lost home. The Annan Plan itself focused on the house as the object of possible return or reparations, but none of its provisions satisfied someone like Eleni. The plan assumed that the main desire of individuals was to get back their property, and the writers of the plan based this assumption on the same rhetoric of human rights that Eleni employs. But ultimately, Eleni's dissatisfaction with the plan was not about the way that it dealt with a house, a piece of property, but about the way it handled what that house represented. This comes through not when talking to her about politics but when talking to her about what we might think of as the intimately personal.

When I began to ask Eleni about life in Lapithos, about Lapithos as she remembers it, her thoughts about the place were less ideological, much simpler. And what she described was not the house itself but the web of community in which the house was located. Like Maroulla, she recalled the constant coming and going to see neighbors and family. She remembered the festivals and weddings in the village, and how the village women gave their spare time to organize plays and musical events at the gymnasium. Like so many people, she remembered the social life of the village, and like so many who've returned since, she commented on how dead the village seems now. "*There's no life in the streets,*" she said. "*It isn't the same at all.*"

Eleni and Kostakis have a beach home in the Famagusta district, and she told me how, one weekend, there was a festival, and the whole village turned out. "*You have no idea how it feels,*" she said. "*You're jealous. You wonder why they have this and you don't.*" When I asked her about the kinds of celebrations that they used to have in Lapithos, she went into detail about the foods that they cooked, how they celebrated Christmas and Easter and weddings. And then she broke off at the end with a final, "*And it's all lost now.*"

The dream of return, then, may be expressed as a longing for ancestral homes, but for most it is really a longing for what those homes represent. The home was not only a place, but was the center of a social network that included both the living and the dead. Greek Cypriot refugees have believed for thirty years that any solution to the Cyprus Problem would mean their absolute return to their homes and the reestablishment of their communities. And so when someone such as Eleni says no to the plan, it is a cry against the injustice of having her community torn apart, and against the realpolitik that says that she must sacrifice the dream of recreating it one day.

In *The Poetics of Space*, Gaston Bachelard refers to the "topology of memory," or the ways in which memories are not only material but spatial, dependent on the home, the school, the village—on the place with its particular scents and seasons. As with Proust and his madeleine, the visceral evokes the vanished, and memory is sustained by the mundane. A particular taste of lemon may evoke an entire era that's passed. But this also shows that in the work of memory, the mundane is marked as a site of loss. It is precisely the process of losing what we once were that gives to the mundane a sustained melancholy.

Greek Cypriot refugees talk about their past in mundane terms. They talk about the footpaths in the village that linked relatives and neighbors; they talk about the orchards, and the trees in their gardens; they talk about the house, and the trousseau; they talk about the soil; they talk about the odors; and they talk about all the elements that made the village a place for them, *their* place. These memories are very personal, but they are also, at the same time, social memories. The footpaths are worn by social commerce. The orchards and trees are divided in a tapestry of social networks that is written in the landscape. The house is the place of one's family and one's roots. The trousseau symbolizes a struggle and an accomplishment. And the soil is not only the moist odor of home and past, but also the place where one's ancestors are buried, making the trees that grow there symbolic of one's own roots.

And so the mundane, too, is marked by life with others, while the habits that sustain memory inscribe in us the shape of the social. The routes to the orchards and the fields. The path up the mountain to the graves of one's ancestors. The channels for water, and the gnarled olive tree. The fig tree in the shade of the house. Steps that lead to an open door. All of these are places worn by habit, places so familiar as to recede into the background of daily life. But in being so, they are also the spaces of our habitual interactions, the routes by which the voices and faces of others weave into the unnoticed texture of our lives. The relationships that constitute our comings and goings, the habitual patterns of our lives, become etched into the paths whose dips and turns are inscribed in our bodies.

And in the ways that Greek Cypriots talk about their villages, there is always an interpenetration of place and person that is mediated by the quotidian ways in which they worked and strove to build there. In discussing what they "owned," villagers talked about how their parents had acquired it for them or how they had built it themselves: a piece of land bought by selling lemons; a house built over several months, in one's spare time; the years of labor invested in a trousseau. The house itself was negotiated as part of an alliance and located in relation to others. Houses, fields, and orchards have particular historicities tied to marriages, deaths, and the birth of children.

What is most apparent in such stories is the relationship between *care* and *belonging*, or between the transformation of the material world and an ethical relationship to place. And that care itself is also social: one works for one's children, for the honor of one's family, for the grandchildren yet to be born. So many descriptions of working the land express the physical interpenetration of self and soil, and thereby of community and place. Vasillis had said to me that they watered the olive trees with the water that they drank. Others described to me the ways that their fathers sweated over the land, and the way that their sweat watered the soil. Land and parents, trees and children all interweave in a tapestry that becomes the ground of one's life.

The mundane, then, is more than simply evocative; it weaves the social into the fabric of self and memory. And because the mundane is all of these things, it may be expected that the mundane would also have political potency. Indeed, precisely because the mundane takes the guise of the personal, the private, it is relegated to the realm of the uncontestable, making it ripe for political uses. The Greek Cypriot slogan "Dhen Xechno," "I Do Not Forget," is one particularly potent example of the political uses of the personal. It is a phrase that needs no referent, since one already knows that one does not forget the village, the house, the church, the trees, the graves of one's ancestors. And so because one always already remembers those things, one forgets that the slogan is not only descriptive but imperative, commanding one not to forget. Remembering is a moral, and hence a political duty.

But when remembering becomes a moral duty, the mundane is marked not as a site of loss but as a site of right. The mundane describes not a past but a truncated present, not what was lost but what was torn from one. The mundane evokes not mourning or even melancholia—not going beyond or even living with loss—but rather a denial of loss, its indefinite suspension. Unlike Proust's madeleine, which evokes a lost era, the mundane here sustains the hope of time's return.

*   *   *

It should not be surprising, then, that for many Greek Cypriots the opening
of the checkpoints became a confrontation with loss, one that had been suspended by that time for almost thirty years. The possibility of loss remains
a largely unexpressed public secret in the Greek Cypriot community. It is
acknowledged only implicitly, as when Greek Cypriot refugee organizations
discourage refugees from returning, in fact cast those who have returned as
traitors to the cause of "real" return. The slogan *We will not be tourists in our
own country*" encapsulates in one neat phrase objection both to the idea that
they must receive a "visa" at the entry point to the north and to the idea that
they will be only guests. There is, of course, an important political stake in
the matter. But there is something more: even from the first opening of the
checkpoints, these organizations saw that crossing was the potential death
of the sense of belonging that has fueled Greek Cypriot refugee politics for
thirty years.

Anna, a volunteer of the Lapithos refugee organization, expressed it most
clearly. Anna is from a wealthy family, and her father had worked hard over-
seas to bring back the capital that would allow him to succeed in the island
and educate his children. Anna had already become a teacher in Nicosia before the war, but she lived in Lapithos and commuted, as did quite a few Lapithiotes at the time. She experienced many of the horrors of the war, including
the bombardment of the village and relatives who were enclaved there by the
Turkish army after she and her family escaped.

Over the past thirty years, she has written widely and poetically about
loss, devastation, and taking back their homes. She is the author of several
children's books that have won prizes from the Ministry of Education. All
of these are set in Lapithos; one describes the horrors of the war, the other
imagines the secretive return of a child, and yet another relates Lapithiotes'
involvement in the Greek War of Independence. She told me that over the
course of thirty years as an elementary school teacher, more than three thousand children passed through her hands. "*And do you think that any of those
children will forget about our lost lands?*" she asked, her face twisted in anger.

Anna is an unapologetic Greek nationalist, and she is aware of her own
intensity. She asked me several times, "*What do you think of me? Am I too
much?*" But precisely because of both her intensity and her intelligence she
was able to express most clearly the secret reason for refusal to cross, the
reason that many people do not dare to speak. "*My memories of Lapithos are
beautiful*," she told me, leaning across the table, her eyes moist with tears. "*I

don't want to ruin those. Either we will all go back, and things will return to the way they once were, or we'll continue to live in our dreams."

The refusal to cross to the north, then, is not only a political maneuver but is a refusal to acknowledge the possibility of loss. It is a refusal to let the self become other to the very place that one has remembered, dreamt about, and refused to mourn for thirty years.

I think often of the two women in the doorway. Everything about the encounter is freighted with a single question: To whom does the house belong? This question is visible in our palpable discomfort. The uncertainty with which Maroulla knocks on the door; Düriye's anxious dismissal of the view from the window; my own tentativeness as I walk through the house in stockinged feet—all of these bespeak uncertainty, even anxiety, in the face of this question. Düriye was anxious to show me that she has invested in the house, that she cares for it, that it is not simply to her the winner's spoils. My own worries about etiquette revealed my deeper anxieties about the demand that I feel placed upon me to make a judgment, to say who's right. And Maroulla was anxious to find beneath change the continuity of the familiar. For all of us, then, the question that freighted the visit to Maroulla's house was not only, *"To whom does this house belong?"* but perhaps more importantly, *"Who belongs in this house?"* Even for Maroulla, the latter question is no longer so easily answered.

Since the opening of the checkpoints, many Cypriots have been faced with a return to places that are no longer "their own," both in the sense that they are occupied by others who are now quite real to them, and also in the sense that they are not the house or village held in constant remembrance for three decades. Many Greek Cypriots told me that when they returned to their villages, everything seemed much smaller than they remembered— that the houses seemed stunted, the streets narrow. Many others told me that everything seemed too quiet and dead, that the village seemed a ghost of itself. Turkish Cypriots, on the other hand, often found literal ghosts—shells of houses, parking lots, dams where a village once stood. They have returned to a place that is no longer the place to which they belong.

The anticipation of this is visible already in Maroulla's hesitation in the doorway, and in her rush through the house, as though someone might prevent her from seeing it all. That hesitation marks the distance she must cross in order to return. Of course, this is not what Greek Cypriots mean when they talk about "return," since any Greek Cypriot would say that real return means nothing less than resettlement in their homes. But there is another, more basic sense of return as a crossing—from present to past, from here to there, from us to them, from action to memory. There is the distance not only of space but also of time, and so there is, in any return, a hesitation, a pause before the final tumbling towards a familiar that may no longer remain. A fear that the house may no longer exist, that it may have yielded to the last winter's rain.

Maroulla enacted this most literal meaning of return—a turning back, an act of crossing. And just as the memory of the mundane evokes a past that is irrecoverable, so return must surely be marked by loss. She pointed out where the stove used to be, around which the children would gather in the winter. She pointed out the window under which she once slept. And in the process that crossing also became a disruption—not only of the present by the past and the past by the present, but, more important, of the self that she had been by the self that she had become. And of the places of memory by the places of the present.

For thirty years Greek Cypriot refugees had imagined their triumphant return to their villages, a return from places that they perceived as foreign. Greek Cypriots describe themselves as *prosfiges*, or refugees, eschewing the international terminology of "internally displaced persons" in favor of a word that has an emotional content emphasizing the foreignness of the place to which they've fled. Indeed, I heard some describe the state in which they find themselves as exile, *xenitia*, a word related to *xenos*, or "stranger." *Xenitia* is to be far from one's homeland, but it is also the act and quality of being a stranger, of being estranged from one's roots. Although this is not a description that is commonly used, I often heard Greek Cypriots talk about their new neighbors in the south as *xenoi*, foreigners or strangers, people who were unknown to them after more than thirty years. The place where they had settled was a *xenos topos*, a foreign place, making it clear that one's homeland, the place to which one belongs, is the place where one is known, the place where one has ties, the place where one is not a stranger.

Greek Cypriots had dreamed of a return from foreign lands, a return to the place where they are known, and instead have been confronted with houses and streets and orchards and mountains that are not the ones of their memories, and with a place that is no longer their own. This sense of not belonging has produced contradictory reactions among those returning. Those who return often show either a defiant anger or a timidity and uncertainty in their approach. Sometimes it is both.

Only a few months after the opening of the checkpoints, I sat with friends in a restaurant that was at Lapithos's headspring—Kefalovriso in Greek and Başpınar in Turkish—at the point at which the paved mountain road fails and turns to a gravel path. It was early evening, and our group spoke Turkish. At a table not far from ours, two Greek men stared out at the panoramic view as the village tumbled down the mountain to the sea. Dusk was approaching, and lights flickered on below. The men were at a border age—perhaps born before the war, perhaps after. The one facing me clenched his fists and banged one down on the table: "*En' kleftes,*" "*They're thieves,*" he said loudly, repeating the phrase several times. Given that many Greek Cypriots expect their Turkish compatriots to speak Greek, it was difficult to know if he intended to make himself heard. But when the Greek-speaking Turk who owned the restaurant brought them beers and came to sit with them, they joked and laughed together for more than an hour as we ate our dinner.

"*We are guests in our own home,*" "*Eimaste xenoi sto dhiko mas spiti,*" Greek Cypriots often complain, using the word *xenoi* to signify both those who are guests and those who are strangers. At the same time, they reinforce this sense of guest and host through gestures of reciprocal hospitality, or by bringing gifts. Vasillis, for instance, stocked up on boxes of sticky loukoumi—what we call Turkish delight—to distribute on his rounds in the village. They are unused to this sense of entering places where the networks and relationships are unknown to them. Not knowing those fine threads of relationship is what makes a place foreign, a place where one does not belong.

There is, then, a social discomfort that can be eased either by seeking a common ground or by defiance. Maroulla, on entering her childhood home, kissed the Turkish woman in a gesture that linked them in a belonging to that place. It expressed both a forgiveness and a fundamental sameness. Defiance, though, is also a common theme. My landlord in Lapithos, a man of my own age originally from a small, mixed village in the Paphos area, exploded one day in frustration and anger at the Greek owners of the house where his parents now live. "*They come unannounced, in the middle of the day!*" he exclaimed. "*My mother's watching my sister's baby, and the baby's sleeping, and they want to barge in! They don't like it when my mother doesn't want to let them in. They keep saying, 'We're coming back. We're coming back, and we're going to take this house, so pack your bags.'*" After the referendum, especially, this defiance, even threat, became by report common among refugees returning to visit their homes.

Some of this defiance appears to be provoked by the appearance of prosperity in the town. For three decades, Greek Cypriots had heard tales of the impoverishment of their Turkish Cypriot neighbors, of their oppression by the Turkish army and settlers from Turkey. What they found instead was a certain modest prosperity, if at a slower pace than in the south. This was the point of the young man's remark that the Turks are "thieves": that they have taken Greek property by force and profited from it.

But there is clearly something even more here. For it is not only the general modest prosperity—decent cars, well-kept homes, the ability to travel—but also, and more importantly, the sense of *life*, a life that has gone on unbeknownst to them and does not include them. It is the sense not only that what belongs to them has been taken and that others have profited, but that that to which they belong now rejects them at its surface: they can see the houses, walk the streets, and drink from the springs, but they can no longer penetrate the life there. They are now strangers.

If we think of Maroulla pausing on the threshold of her childhood home, it is not hard to see why many refugees, in returning to their homes, feel a sense of distance, of estrangement. And the estrangement that many refugees find in returning to their homes is more than a remembered place transformed, and even more than a past brought into question. It is a confrontation with the ways in which, on both sides of the island, violations against the other have been inscribed in visible and tangible features of daily life in such a way that they exclude the other even at the surface. And so, experientially, one crosses a border to visit the past, then recrosses that border to return to what now seems even more than ever one's "own" world, the world and ethos that are now familiar to one, and with a new sense of its familiarity. And so in a paradoxical way, the very institutions and structures that create those worlds have been reinforced by the very act that everyone hoped would help bring them down.

In the story of Genesis, the fall from grace is conceived as an exile. Innocence is lost, we discover shame, and all human striving becomes a struggle to return to the place from which we began. The loss of innocence is accomplished through exile, and that exile is one from a garden of ease and repose, the site of birth and belonging, into an unknown world where we must scratch out a living from the soil. That exile is also marked by the impossibility of return. We know that we will never again find that garden, because the garden itself is now a past that is lost to us.

I went one day to see the parents of a friend, a relative of Maroulla by marriage. I wanted to speak to his mother, Meropi, an elderly woman with a smooth face and quick hands and the blank gaze of Alzheimer's. A few years before showing the signs of the disease, she wrote a memoir that she called *The Story of Three Generations*. My friend was at first a bit embarrassed to give it to me, because, as he put it, "*she's just a village woman.*" She had received very little education, but in her simple language she traced the relationship of her family and the land in Lapithos over several decades. In it, she poignantly described the ways in which her family had struggled and worked to acquire the land, to make it fruitful.

When I entered their building, I made my way up a dirty staircase and into a dim hallway. A weak bulb cast a yellow light, and I had to squint to make out the number on the door. The apartment I sought was at the end of the hallway, in a shadowy corner near the top of the stairs. As I raised my hand to knock at the door, I thought of the photograph on the cover of Meropi's book—a faded snapshot of Ayia Paraskevi, swathed in a haze of sea-blue and sage green. The light is clear, the photograph taken from the mountains above. It resembles many such photographs that adorn refugees' walls, illustrate their memoirs, and are turned by them into impressionistic paintings. "*Their so-called refugees aren't poor,*" many Turkish Cypriots would say to me. "*They shouldn't call them refugees, because it's misleading. They're not living in tents.*" And yet that dark hallway, it seemed to me, could only be a place of refuge, a place where one could pass a life but not fully live it.

On the day that I visited, I would have liked to talk to Meropi about her memoir, but she didn't remember writing it. Instead, I talked to Yiorgos, her husband, who told me about the coffeeshop he had in the village, and discussed with me his thoughts about the Annan Plan. But Meropi interrupted, anxious to ask if they were going to return to Lapithos.

"*You can go and come back,*" Yiorgos told her. "*Boreis na paeis kai va epistrepseis.*"

The blank look. "*But who's there?*" she asked innocently.

His answer was curt: "*The Turks.*"

But what are they doing there, she wanted to know. "*O babas mu edhrose yia tin periousia mas. Edhrose. My father sweated for our inheritance. He sweated. He worked day and night. All night he would water the orchards. And now there are Turks there?*"

Yiorgos turned in her direction but didn't look her in the eye. "*The Turks don't care that your father worked so hard,*" he replied. "*It doesn't matter to them.*"

I sat in silence. Yiorgos's answer was freighted with an entire history of community and sorrow, of violence and violation, of people who come and go across a land that remains. His answer was framed by a village and imbued with a sense of the history necessary to give care meaning. That world, because it is no longer one that belongs to them, is one to which they no longer belong. It is framed by a door, and by a threshold, across which one peers without quite daring to cross.

Cypriots' hesitation as they stand on that threshold, or anger as they barge into the garden, a protest against their exile, reveals a knowledge that they no longer belong. But unlike the story of the garden, there is a sense among many Cypriots that they are the ones who have waited, that they are the ones who have remained unchanged, while the place to which they once belonged has become something that is no longer their own. The garden remains elusive, at the end of a path that they no longer know.

TWO

The Anxieties of an Opening

MANY OF THE older houses in the town that today is known as Lapta appear to their Greek owners as shabby and untended. This worries quite a few of the refugees, who puzzle over it. "*Why is everything so dirty?*" many people asked me. "*Why have they not cared for things?*"

Maroulla also asked me this question during our first trip there, as we stood by the spring known as Koufi Petra, today only a trickle, and gazed out over the neighborhood below, now occupied by settlers from Turkey. "*Why have they not cared for things?*" she asked. As though in explanation of her question, Maroulla described to me how she and Vasillis had built their house, as so many villagers do, first as one floor but with the possibility of adding a second. Like many villagers, they had built the original house with a flat roof that sprouted supports for what would later be an apartment on the floor above, and the possibility of building stairs to one side. According to Maroulla, it had taken them many years to put aside the money to build the upper floor, and they had completed it only a short time before the war that forced them to flee. "*We had a renter,*" she told me. "*He was going to move in on that same day, the day of the invasion. Everything was there. It had new furniture, new curtains. It had everything, right down to dishrags and tablecloths. Right down to the sponge for washing dishes.*"

Today their house is "owned" by a Turkish Cypriot originally from Lapithos whom Vasillis knows. On that first day when we visited the town together, Vasillis had muttered under his breath, "*I'm going to talk to him. He should go back to his own property and let me have mine.*" But the current owner has already made changes and given part of the house to his children, who use the ground floor as a kindergarten. The house is now surrounded

4. House in the Ayia Paraskevi neighborhood today.

by a stone fence held together by splotches of concrete that are cracking, and a large, colorful sign announcing the kindergarten's name hangs above the front door. Even as Vasillis muttered this, I knew that he was not hopeful, since he was already talking about other plans, about the possibility of building a small house on some of his land.

We left the spring that day and made our way to the top of the town, in the mountains, to survey some land that used to belong to Maroulla's family. We ascended along roads so steep that I shifted into first gear, stopping and starting to maneuver the hairpin turns. We climbed to the point where the paved road turns to a rutted dirt path, and where the mountain plateaus in an open stretch of field, that day covered in white and yellow spring daffodils that undulated in the breeze like a sheet being unfurled. The field is not large, ending in a series of impassable cliffs wrought from the mountainside. A portion of the field had been inherited by Maroulla, and today it stands empty apart from a small shelter which was once probably a shepherd's hut and is today half-destroyed, covered with fading graffiti in Greek and Turkish.

We stood at the town's highest point, looking out over the neighborhoods tumbling down the mountain below us, and Maroulla took me by the arm and pointed out to me that her childhood home was visible off to our right. "*From here it looks the same,*" she remarked. "*The same as it used to.*" From that height, from that distance, it was possible to forget the new construction, to forget the signs in Turkish, to forget the unfamiliar faces and children in the streets, and to dream oneself into a younger time, a time when all was right and everyone was in her place. I found myself falling into such a reverie, as well, imagining the town thirty, forty, fifty years before. And yet even as I tried to imagine, I found myself spiraling back farther and farther in time, to a time when Maroulla was just a child, even to a point before Maroulla's birth, in order to find a moment about which I would not feel guilty imagining that it was a time of peace.

As we stood gazing down at the white house of Maroulla's memories, a police car unexpectedly bounced down the mountain path and slowed to a stop near us. Vasillis approached the car and leaned in to talk to the driver, immediately understanding from the thick accent with which he spoke Greek that he was from Paphos. Vasillis soon learned that this Turkish Cypriot policeman was originally from Kouklia, near where they now live. When Maroulla heard that he spoke Greek, she also leaned into the car, and they began asking him what Greeks he remembered from Kouklia, trying to establish some link with him.

The policeman was polite but reticent. Finally, Vasillis straightened up and asked with a sigh the inevitable question: "*Wouldn't it be better if we could just go back to the way things once were?*" I had heard this question many times, an expression of a core axiom of Greek Cypriot politics, namely that the Cyprus Problem is not one between Cypriots but a problem of invasion and occupation by Turkey. I had come to see, though, that this is also a core belief for many Greek Cypriots regarding their own pasts. The policeman, in response, bent toward the steering wheel and gave a slight, reluctant nod of the head. He couldn't acquiesce, but he also didn't want to offend.

When the car drove on, Vasillis watched it disappear down the dirt path. He was silent, his face frozen, and I wanted to probe him, "*Why do you ask that question?"* I wanted to say to him, "*You already know the answer to that question,"* but I held myself back. Vasillis continued to watch after the car, and I turned to the white houses below, which reflected the sharp light of early spring.

I still don't know what prevented me from asking the question, except that I felt embarrassed for him, embarrassed for myself. I was embarrassed by the way that he fumbled for a familiar foothold, someplace to begin in building relationships. I was embarrassed by the sullen resistance that he received, and the way that silence often masked anger. I was embarrassed that when Vasillis asked the question to the policeman, I wanted to intervene, to tell the policeman in Turkish that Vasillis was a good man, that he had lost a lot. I was embarrassed by an insistence on returning to a past that few Turkish Cypriots desired, and a refusal to see why they might not desire it. I was embarrassed that even though Vasillis knew that past, even though he had spoken with me about it, he still felt a need to ask a question that was destined to remain unanswered.

I realized in that moment that even though the checkpoints had opened, so little had really changed. Even at the level of simple, interpersonal interaction, Vasillis's insistence and the policeman's resistance maintained two parallel worlds. Vasillis might see the Paphian policeman as acquiescing, admitting that they should return to the past. The policeman, in turn, might see Vasillis as trying to impose a Greek version of history upon him. As far as I could tell, each turned away from the encounter with the sense of his own world reinforced. And those worlds were reinforced just at the moment when they should have been open to disruption.

The problem was not only that the policeman refused to accept Vasillis's version of the past, but that in keeping silent, he also refused to accept that Vasillis might understand his own. It was an encounter I would see repeated often, as Cypriots discovered not only that the other might see the past differently, but also that seeing it differently had shaped their lives in the present and given them different hopes for the future. For if the past is, as one historian called it, a foreign country, then it is also surely a land with its own borders. Like the impassive soldiers at checkpoints throughout the island, the policeman stubbornly guarded those borders with his silence. And I was embarrassed, and frustrated, that Vasillis stood at the border of a land he once knew, presenting the passport of his past without being permitted to cross.

At the time of this encounter, I was staying in south Nicosia, the island's divided capital where a large community of Lapithos refugees still lives. The referendum on the Annan Plan was only a month away, and there was much bustle, as well as palpable anxiety. There were meetings and conferences and discussions on television, though much of the real debate of the plan took place in homes and coffeeshops. In the south, a tangible consensus was building that the plan was wrong, that it was a concession to Turkey. It would not allow everyone to return, and it would not give them the return to the past that their leaders had promised for so long. There was a visible indifference to other possibilities that felt strongly like denial, as those in support of the plan feverishly tried to explain its positive sides to an audience that wasn't listening.

During this period, I would often cross the checkpoints to Nicosia's north. Unlike in the south, where there was a sense of anxious expectation as Greek Cypriots awaited their political parties' pronouncements on the plan, there was a palpable hope and excitement in the north that had been generated by tens of thousands of Turkish Cypriots joining together over a period of months to oppose their leadership's intransigent resistance to the UN compromise. There were meetings; there were demonstrations. There were meetings that turned into demonstrations as they grew larger. In contrast to the south, where the main slogan visible everywhere was "*Oxi*," or a simple "no," the main slogan in the north became "*yes, be annem*," an affirmation in a Cypriot idiom. In the north the words for "peace" in Turkish and Greek, *barış* and *irini*, were ubiquitous—on signs and posters, T-shirts and caps, even newly incorporated into the names of shops and cafes. It was a time of high spirits, when it seemed that anything was possible, and that the isolation under which Turkish Cypriots had lived for so long would finally come to an end.

Their movement had begun before the checkpoints opened, a revolt against an old, nationalist regime that seemed out of step with the times. They called it the Jasmine Revolution, a nostalgic reference to a time of perceived purity, a time before Turkey and Turkish immigrants had, as they put it, "taken our political will." Peasants and farmers from Turkey had begun to arrive just after 1974, part of a plan between the Turkish Cypriot leadership and Turkey to repopulate the island's north and prevent Greek Cypriots from returning. In those early years, about 25,000 were given citizenship and Greek Cypriot houses, and by the time of the referendum, they had children and grandchildren born in the island who saw themselves as Turkish Cypriot.

These settlers had been an issue for Greek Cypriots since their arrival, because they created a new demographic situation that would clearly be hard to change. And they created a problem for Turkish Cypriots because they were poorer and less educated than Cypriots themselves were, bringing habits from their homelands that many Cypriots cast as uncivilized. By the time of the referendum, settlers and their children constituted only about 25 percent of the citizen population in the unrecognized state, but the island had, in the previous decade, been flooded with economic migrants and students from the "motherland," causing Turkish Cypriots to complain that they were becoming a minority in their own country. So when Turkish Cypriots said in their protests that "*we'll become masters in our own country,*" they meant that they would take it back from the hands of others.

Of course, as with so many things, the issue of immigration was subject to manipulation and much speculation. The press inflated the numbers of immigrants and blamed crime on them. Immigrants became an other in contrast to which many Turkish Cypriots began to feel more and more Cypriot, even to revive small differences that they shared in common with their Greek neighbors. *Kıbrıslılık*, or Cypriotism, gained momentum as a way of emphasizing their ties to the island. Before the checkpoints opened, there was a rise in sales of everything "local," everything "traditional," at the expense of things Turkish. Before the opening, many Turkish Cypriots began to think of themselves simply as Cypriot, as islanders divided by minor differences.

Perhaps expectably, it was the opening of the checkpoints that began to change that. For many people, it was the act of crossing to the south that brought it home to them. One woman who enjoyed crossing often to the south to shop told me, "*Well, it's like when we were in the enclaves. We'd go over to their side to shop and work, but we were glad to get back to someplace safe at night.*" Although about three thousand Turkish Cypriots began to work in the south, only a handful went to live there. Instead, Turkish Cypriots seemed to rediscover an attachment to what one friend called the "made-up state" that they had founded. As one writer told me not long before the referendum, "*Before the border opened, because of the* Türkiyeliler, *the immigrants from Turkey, I began to feel more Cypriot. But now, because of the Greeks, I've started to feel more Turkish again.*"

In the period before the island's division, Turkish and Greek nationalisms had been dominant, and Cypriots tended to call themselves Turks and Greeks. After 1974, on both sides of the island, a Cypriotism began to develop that was primarily in contrast to what they saw as the betrayal or oppression of their "motherlands." For Greek Cypriots, they had been betrayed by Greece's sponsorship of the 1974 coup that led to the island's division. Turkish Cypriots, on the other hand, were tired of living in an isolated state that had become a de facto province of Turkey. But what both sides seemed to discover in the opening of the checkpoints were local nationalisms, of the Turkish Cypriot and Greek Cypriot variety. They discovered that their own interests and identities were tied up with the states that had come to represent them.

During the time of the referendum, it also became clear that they were divided not only by interests and the states that might protect them, but also by very different understandings of what had happened in the past to get them to this point. Numerous Turkish Cypriots had told me, "*France and Germany fought wars and managed to put all that behind them. So can we.*" But wars with frontlines are different from intimate conflicts fought in the neighborhood and the village, where friendships and loyalties are often at stake. At a bicommunal meeting on the process of reunification held in the buffer zone, an elderly Turkish Cypriot man stood up at the end and took the microphone. Stooped and clearly shaken, he claimed that there could be no reunification on the basis of the Annan Plan, that there had been no preparation of Greek Cypriots, who still hated Turks and Turkey. "*All right,*" he insisted, "*you can come to my side, and we'll eat and drink, and I can come to the south and we'll eat and drink, but that's not real friendship. I knew real friendship before, but then everything fell apart.*"

The elderly man's statement was met with an embarrassed silence by those at the meeting, as at the time the public expression of such a view seemed to signal resistance to reconciliation. After the results of the referendum, however, I began to hear such statements more and more. Like this elderly man, many people found that even though they crossed the checkpoints, even though they spoke to their former neighbors, there remained a rupture between them, a rupture of experience, and one that had been reflected in the referendum's lopsided results. One older Turkish Cypriot, a retired policeman who now works in construction in the south, told me, "*We eat and drink together, but there's a vacuum between us. Things can't be the way they once were.*" I would hear this again and again: "*We used to have neighbors, and they even looked after my mother when she was sick,*" one Turkish Cypriot woman originally from Paphos told me, "*but you don't know what they're thinking. Eskisi gibi olamaz. Things can't be the way they once were.*

After the checkpoints opened, then, the buffer zone that divides the island came to stand for more than a political division and began also to symbolize a rupture. On either side of the ceasefire line, new worlds had been created, and at the juncture where these worlds now meet, silences have arisen. These are sometimes silences that express a lack of words, and they are often silences that express that the words at one's own disposal no longer fit, no longer allow one to grasp the thing at hand. Sometimes these are silences that hide open secrets. More often, though, like the policeman's bowed head, they are silences that express that the other simply cannot understand.

Not long after my first trip to Lapithos with Vasillis and Maroulla, I decided to go there with a Turkish Cypriot friend who had once taught in the town's Turkish high school. I was curious about something that one older Lapithos Turk had told me several months before, namely that the Turks of the town had lost twenty-one şehits, or martyrs, in the hotly contested period between 1963 and 1974. When I mentioned this to a Greek Cypriot friend, he replied, "*But I don't see how that could be. We knew about two young men who were killed, but I never heard of any others.*"

I went with my Turkish Cypriot friend to one of the town squares, where a monument had been erected in the center of a roundabout on the main road between Lapithos and the neighboring village of Karavas. The prevalence of such monuments throughout north Cyprus—along with the books, photographs, and museums that document their suffering—might be seen as a stubborn resistance to what they view as the world's refusal to acknowledge that suffering. The problem with such monuments is that in a persistent attempt to maintain the memory of their suffering the monuments often emphasize the grotesque, the extremes of violence. As in the south of the island for missing persons, these monuments to the dead tend to emphasize both their individuality and their numbers, giving details of their deaths even as they fix on numbers of deaths.

In this instance, we indeed found twenty-one names, but the places of their births and deaths were elsewhere in the island. My friend suggested that we ask the mayor, a former student of hers, so we made our way up the street to the municipal offices. The mayor, in common Greek Cypriot parlance, is the "pseudo-mayor," the one whose existence cannot be recognized and who is illegally occupying the municipality. He is also a refugee from the Paphos district and had followed his family to Lapithos when they fled their own village in the south.

When we arrived, the mayor offered us coffee, while his assistant Hasan, also a former student of my friend, hovered about. Hasan, it turned out, was the nephew of one of the two young men whose murder on Christmas Day in 1963 sparked the Turks' exodus from the town. They explained to us that the monument honored not only Turks originally from the town who had been killed, but the relatives of all those now living there.

"*We erected it a couple of years ago because of pressure from the Cypriot martyrs' families,*" the mayor explained. "*Afterward, the Turks from Turkey who had lost relatives wanted their own memorial, but we decided to wait to see what's going to happen.*" The Türkiyeliler, or Turks from Turkey, to whom he referred were all those families who had lost sons during the Turkish military intervention of 1974 and who had been given property in the town.

This led us to a discussion of the upcoming referendum, scheduled for only a couple of weeks later. Both were wary, Hasan saying that he expected his family would lose quite a bit of property if the plan passed. The mayor, in turn, said that they had owned a lot of land in Paphos and had never been fully compensated. "*I went to England to work when I was eighteen,*" the mayor told me, "*and I wrote to my father often. You know, I used to see how well the English would treat their dogs, and I thought about the kind of life my family was living in Cyprus. And I'll never forget, I wrote to my father saying, 'If only I'd been born in England, and I'd been born a dog.' Can you imagine writing that? 'If only I'd been born in England, and I'd been born a dog.'*"

Hasan turned to me then. "*So what do you think is going to happen in the referendum?*"

I told them what they already knew, which was that the prospects for the plan passing looked pretty bleak.

And then the mayor faced me with the inevitable question, the one that everyone invariably asked: "*So what do they say? Do they want to come back?*"

By this time I had discerned that the mayor was fairly nationalistic, following a party that preferred a permanent partition, and so I hesitated in my reply. "*Almost all the ones I've talked to want to come back,*" I finally answered. "*Not all the refugees want to come back, but the ones from Lapta do. I've tried to ask them why that is, but they can't really explain it to me. They're very attached to the place.*"

The mayor and his assistant exchanged glances, and then the mayor leaned forward, his face dark. "*Do you want to know why they're so insistent about coming back?*" he asked rhetorically. "*It's because they worked so hard to rid the town of the Turks, and now they can't stand to see it in Turkish hands.*"

The mayor's reply startled me, not because I hadn't heard it before, but because I had heard it from a close friend only the previous day. She had told me, "*Do you know why Lapta is a symbolic village for the Greeks? Because in 1964, when all of the Turkish Cypriots left the village, it was seen as a big vic-*"

tory. And after that, when that victory was taken from them in 1974, they were devastated." Indeed, this same answer was one that I would later hear again and again. I would hear it from an old mason as we sat in the garden of his home. I would hear it from a younger friend, a graphic artist, as we had lunch. I would hear it from another schoolteacher about ten years my senior as she described the enclave period of her youth. In reply to the question, "*Why do they want to come back?*" then, this was the answer that so many people gave. Like Vasillis's question, it was a sentence that encapsulated a particular version of the past and projected it onto an uncertain future.

Both Vasillis's wistful question and the mayor's harsh explanation would recur like refrains throughout my research, staccato responses to complex melodies. These phrases seemed a type of shorthand that encoded complicated histories of friendships and betrayals, of fear, and of loss, in ways that those who had shared these histories would immediately understand. And it was also a way of excluding other histories, of shutting them off. It was a way of wrapping up history into a neatly sealed phrase and trimming off anything that seemed to dangle at the edges.

But unlike Vasillis's question, the mayor's answer required no affirmation. And that, too, made me uncomfortable—this too-neat statement that sealed off all possibilities for loss, for longing, for dreams damaged or deferred. This summation also embarrassed me, and again I did not know how to reply. Because encoded in the mayor's neat summary was not only a refusal to see the other's suffering, but also an explanation for why they refused to see. The mayor, and the mason, and all the other people who summed up Greek Cypriots' longing in this neat phrase knew very well what their former neighbors had lost, and how they had lost it. They knew very well about all those who had died in the war, and all those who had never been found. They knew very well about damaged churches, gutted cemeteries. They knew about communities scattered.

They knew about all those things, and yet the mayor's remark still circulated as an explanation for Greek Cypriot longing. And while it acknowledged their longing, it also undermined it, denying their right to *be*long. It imbued that longing with misplaced pride and thwarted ambition, as well as a fair share of frustrated enmity. And that formulaic sentence stumped me in its decisiveness, because even as it raised other questions, it simultaneously sealed the passage to the past, leaving the questions on my lips with no way to ask.

While living in Nicosia, I went often to see Eleni, who was usually home in the late morning, waiting for her grandchildren to return from school. Often,

Kostakis was there as well, waiting for the grandchildren to arrive. One day when I went to visit they had a guest, an elderly neighbor named Tassos, and the men were discussing the Annan Plan. "*We've already lost everything*," Tassos said, turning to me, "*so why should we accept a plan that gives us none of our rights?*"

He told me that in his own village there had been Turks, and they always got along well. There were never any problems, he said, until the Turkish Cypriot leadership stirred up trouble. "*They wanted to give Turkey an excuse to invade.*" He insisted that Cyprus is a Greek island, comparing Turkey's actions of the past century with Nazi Germany. Kostakis, on the other hand, compared the plan to the 1923 Greco-Turkish population exchange, which uprooted more than a million people through a treaty decision in which those same people had no voice. "*I won't sign my death warrant with my own hand*," he told me.

This was a slogan that I would hear again and again, a reference to the fact that the 1960 treaty constituting the Republic of Cyprus had been, in the opinion of many Greek Cypriots, imposed on them by foreign powers. I had heard various versions of this slogan a week earlier, when I had gone to a large meeting of Kyrenia refugees in a conference center on the outskirts of Nicosia. They had gathered to hear about the plan and its effects on them, and I had arrived to find the parking lots full and a surprisingly large crowd drifting in and out of a packed hall that held, by my estimate, around two thousand.

The mayors of the Kyrenia district had sat on the stage below banners that read, "*A just European solution*," and "*A just solution for Greek Cypriots and Turkish Cypriots.*" These "mayors-in-exile" took turns rising to address the audience, each one of them in his own way vilifying the plan. The plan was a concession to Turkey. The plan did not guarantee that Turkish troops would leave. The plan gave legitimacy to the illegal regime in the north. Most importantly, the plan violated their human rights. As a result, the referendum was their chance to say "*oxi*," "no," a reference to Greek resistance against the Italian invasion during World War II. In this case, it was resistance against what was often called an "Anglo-American plan" that foreign powers wanted to impose on them.

And only a few days after that event, Eleni had invited me to attend a meeting of the Lapithos refugee association, held in the new Karavas municipal building, a modern structure with its own conference salon and gallery. There were only about twenty people in attendance, and the mayor told them that the committee would come up with a common stance on the plan and that they would then hold a meeting to announce and discuss it. When everyone rose to go, Eleni turned to introduce me to some other people, telling them that I was writing a book about Lapithos. One older man in a suit and wavy gray hair grabbed my arm. "*When we were fifteen, sixteen years old, we got along with the Turkish Cypriots like brothers,*" he insisted. I did a quick calculation based on what I guessed to be his age and assumed that he was talking about fifty years earlier. "*But the problem was Turkey's interests and the role of your country, the U.S.*"

The roles of Greece, Turkey, the UK, and the U.S. were in any case common subjects of discussion among refugees, who sought to make sense of the catastrophe that had befallen them, to frame it within some larger plan. In this vision, everything was perfectly fine between Cypriots until they became the victims of an expansionist Turkey, a fascist Greece, and the machinations of imperial powers. The Annan Plan was substantive proof of the continuation of these machinations.

"*We had Turks in our village, too,*" Kostakis told me. "*They were a minority and so they were poorer. They mostly worked other people's land.*" He is originally from the Famagusta district, an area that contained several mixed villages before 1963. Everything was fine, he insisted to me, until some *xenoi Tourkoi*, some foreign Turks, came and told their fellow villagers that they had to leave. The Turks of his own village left for the neighboring village of Maratha, Turkish Murataǧa, but according to Kostakis, they would come back during the days to work the land, to trade. "*I went sometimes to the village where they stayed and had coffee with them. And I had a friend who always came to the village, and even to my house, to eat. Yes,* even to my house." Most of the time, though, they met in the coffeeshop.

"*There's no such thing as Turkish blood, just like there's no such thing as Greek blood,*" Kostakis insisted. "*We've had fifteen different conquerors in this island. It's all a matter of what you believe.*" Nationalism, he told me, is *fanatismos*, fanaticism, something that one gets caught up in. Yet he also insisted that the island's division was the work of Greece, Turkey, and the U.S. When I asked him if Cypriots played no role, he affirmed that they did, but only because they were supported. Regarding his fellow villagers, he asserted that Turkish Cypriots were pawns of their leaders, who pushed them into the enclaves in order to prepare the groundwork for the division of the island.

Kostakis has refused to visit his village, saying that in any case he has no plans to go back there. "*I just want to get my property back and rent it out,*" he told me. Nothing could be more different from Eleni, who wants to take back the house she inherited and at least use it as a summer home. But she also repeatedly emphasized that she will not visit again, refusing to accept the changes that she saw there. "*It was all so strange*," she told me. "*There was something freaky about it.*" There was something strange, she said, about returning to the square that she had last seen in her youth and finding Turkish settlers there. There was something freaky about the signs in Turkish, about the Turkish music playing on radios. There was something freaky about the people who stared at her, as though she did not belong.

Eleni has invested tremendous effort in the Lapithos refugee association, whose primary aim has been to promote remembrance of the town and continuation of its community. The association organizes excursions and plays, folklore dances and festivals, and the planting of trees in honor of the town's missing. As with many other refugee associations, much of the focus has been on the youth, and on conveying to them a sense of attachment to their lost lands. Refugees describe to their children the details of their homes, asking them to memorize the places visible in blurred snapshots. Through the associations, they attempt to recreate their village's festivals, asking their children to perform the traditional dances of the village. They write poetry that their children and grandchildren recite, or songs that they sing. They have kept alive their own hopes for return by reproducing its desire in their children.

And what they conveyed to their children and grandchildren in exile was not simply a sense of ownership over land but a sense of belonging in place. It's not simply that they owned homes there that can be compensated, but that the place itself evoked a sense of life so intimate as to be only theirs. But like Eleni, what many people found instead in their return was an unfamiliarity, a sense that the places they visited both were and were not their homes. And in this sense of returning to places that both were and weren't theirs, all those things in the past that had been pared away, made to fit much neater histories, returned to fragment the neat formulas of the past, formulas that worked best in the absence of the other.

This strangeness, this unfamiliarity of what should have been familiar, defied expectations and brought many people into visceral contact with another world, another narrative of the past that differed from the one they knew. Kostakis, in refusing to visit his village, also insisted on maintaining in place a version of history that many others who returned found was challenged. Like Vasillis, many people were faced with other accounts of history, either told to them by former neighbors that they encountered or visible to them in the changed landscape of a world that had once been familiar. Many Turkish Cypriots reported to me, *I told them what we suffered. I told them how we fled with only the clothes on our backs.* Others encountered a distance circumscribed by silence. And yet even in the face of silence, the strangeness of the world they had once known now pressed insistently on their memories, calling up other versions of the past. Other histories erupted into the present to challenge the narratives that they thought they knew.

By the time of my visit with Maroulla and Vasillis to Lapithos, the ceasefire line had been open almost a year, and most of the townspeople had received visits from the owners of the homes where they now live. I had already discerned from my own visits to the town that people were beginning to resent what they had started to consider intrusions, and this only worsened after Greek Cypriots defeated the reunification plan at referendum. *One visit is fine,* I heard many Turkish Cypriots say. *"Of course you want to go and look. But why do they keep coming back?"* People struggled to give these visits form and meaning, to piece them together with their own understandings of the past.

Many Turkish Cypriots visited their former homes in the south and found Greek Cypriot refugees living in them. Others found their homes in ruin, or were unable to find them at all. The husband of one Lapithiote woman returned to his Paphos village to find it underwater, flooded long ago to create a dam. A close friend returned to a relative's village to find the houses and mosque in ruins, only a few telltale stones left. A bulldozer was tearing up the mountainside for building stone and moving toward the village, while only a pristine chapel stood above a well that had also been preserved. *"When the checkpoints opened,"* a friend told me, *"I locked myself in my house and cried for days."* And yet this same friend had been involved for years in bicommunal projects that were intended to lead to precisely such an opening.

In the first months after the opening, newspapers in the south reported that visits to psychiatrists had skyrocketed, as many people who returned to their homes experienced crises. One young Greek Cypriot woman told me, *"I know my mother wants to go, but I haven't taken her. She has a heart condition, and I just don't think she can handle it."* The media in the south responded to the open checkpoints by printing accounts of returns and airing radio talk shows in which Greek Cypriots phoned in to describe their visits to their villages. Many people phoned to describe welcome encounters, but just as many described anger at what they found, or simply a sense of strangeness—that everything had changed, that nothing was as they remembered it. That Turkish Cypriots hadn't cared for things, had let them fall into ruin.

In his well-known work on the Uncanny, Freud derives part of his analysis from the etymology of the German word *unheimlich*. *Unheimlich* is the opposite of *heimlich*, which has the double meaning of that which is homely and familiar, and that which is concealed or secret. The *Heim* is the home, the familiar of the world in which we feel safe. It is the intimate world from which we can issue forth, but to which we always want to return.

However, it becomes clear from the further sense of *heimlich* that the home is not only a space of longing, or even a space of nostalgia, but is a place to which we believe that we belong, a place where we are welcome. Freud lingers on the duality of the notion of *heimlich*, as that which is familiar and that which is secret. He emphasizes that what gives a place the feeling of being a home to us is an intimacy defined by what we conceal from others. In Turkish, this is known as *mahrem*, something that is confidential and intimate, a word whose noun is *harem*, the space where unrelated men are not permitted. For the home to acquire its sense of homeliness or familiarity, then, it must also be the space that entitles us to an intimacy that excludes others from its scope. All others become guests, those who are not privy to the secrets of the home. In this view, the home and those who belong in it come to be defined by its secrets which are denied to others.

To belong in a place, to feel its "homeliness," then, is not only to "feel at home" there, but to have a history there, to be recognized by others as belonging. It is to be included, to become part of the intimacy and secrets of the home. To "be at home," then, is not only to know the familiarity of a welcome, but to assume that welcome as one's right.

On that first trip to Lapithos with Vasillis and Maroulla, we descended from the fields at the top of the town and made our way to the church of Ayia Paraskevi. The neighborhood surrounding the church bears its name, and it was in that neighborhood that Maroulla and Vasillis and Eleni and Meropi had spent their childhoods and youth. It is a neighborhood of stone houses perched on the mountain, and the church is at its center, its heart. Today the children of Turkish settlers play football in the shadow of the church, now a mosque, and the names of the streets on which they play have been changed to reflect the current residents' places of origin. There's an Aşık Veysel Sokak, named after a famous Turkish folk singer, and an Üsküdar Sokak, after a neighborhood in Istanbul. One Turkish Cypriot refugee from Paphos told me that a number of the refugees had originally been given Greek Cypriot houses in that quarter, but they decided instead to claim property in one of the lower neighborhoods. *"It was too far away from the fields,"* she told me. *"And the army was always doing exercises up there, and we were frightened."*

Most Turkish Cypriot refugees joined the Lapithiote Turks in the lower quarters, leaving the upper neighborhoods to Turkish settlers, and eventually to foreigners who would renovate the village houses to enjoy the view. The Turkish settlers in Lapithos are primarily from the Black Sea area, and many came to Cyprus in 1976 as one of several options offered to them by the Turkish government, which planned to submerge their villages under the waters of a hydroelectric dam. Uncertain of their ultimate fate in the event of reunification, many have made only the most basic attempts to restore the village houses where they have lived for thirty years.

They live side by side with English and Germans who have undertaken immaculate restorations of the larger village houses. Many foreigners acquired their houses after a 1995 law gave title deeds for Greek homes to their Turkish and Turkish Cypriot occupants. Some Turkish settlers sold those homes and returned to Turkey. Others sold the old village houses and used the money to buy apartments in the cities or newer houses closer to work or children. Some Turkish Cypriots sold the houses to buy property with a "clean," Turkish title. As a result, the upper quarters of the town are now a patchwork of holidaymakers, foreign retirees, and Turkish settlers who live in the town but usually work elsewhere.

Ayia Paraskevi, once the largest church in the town, is now its largest mosque, and Turkish rugs cover the floor. One Lapithiote refugee asked me, *"Why did they do this? Why did they need another mosque? They already had two mosques of their own!"* The conversion of churches to mosques had happened before in Cyprus's history, when the Catholic masters were succeeded by Muslim Ottoman ones. But one implication of the question was that, unlike in that period, when there was little possibility of the Catholics' return, Greek Cypriots were certain that they would one day come back, and their churches should have been safely kept for them.

I approached the mosque with Maroulla and Vasillis just before the midday call to prayer. The door was locked, but soon the imam came scurrying from a nearby building, pressing his skullcap to his head. I asked if we could enter the mosque, and he said we could, leaving the door open as he ascended the minaret. I removed my shoes, preparing to enter, but I saw that Maroulla and Vasillis held back, staring through the door. As the imam's voice flowed mournfully through the speakers above us, Maroulla asked, "*What have they done with all the icons?*" The walls were completely bare, only whitewash where icons should have been.

They turned away, going to sit on a wall beside the church. I hurriedly put on my shoes and followed them, and Vasillis pointed out to me that the house behind that wall had been his childhood home. I took a photo of them sitting on the wall, the upper floor of the house visible behind them, and although Vasillis tried to smile, Maroulla stared dolefully into the camera.

It was only later in the day, when I decided to take them on a touristic excursion to the village of Bellapais, that something came to life in Maroulla. Bellapais is home to a famous old Catholic abbey that the Ottomans had given to the Orthodox church and whose chapel has survived intact. When Maroulla looked inside and saw the icons, she hurried towards them, crossing herself and kissing them. It was something that was familiar to her, something into which she could retreat and feel safe.

The analogy that came to my mind when I saw Maroulla's reaction to the church where she had once worshipped was the corpse of a loved one. I wrote later in my journal that the Ayia Paraskevi mosque must have seemed to her like a corpse, stripped of the icons that gave it life. It was only later that I read Freud's meditation on the uncanny reaction that we have to corpses. The uncanny is not the entirely unknown; it is something familiar enough that it causes us to retreat into the cocoon of homeliness in which we feel safe. Something appears uncanny not because it is unfamiliar, and not because it is frightening, but because it "goes back to what was once well known and had long been familiar." The corpse of a loved one is uncanny both because the loved one should respond to you and doesn't, and also because the lack of response reminds you of the closeness of your own impending death.

Freud calls the *unheimlich*, or the uncanny, an irruption onto the scene of the repressed. He quotes Schelling in describing the uncanny: "*Unheimlich* is what one calls everything that was meant to remain secret and hidden and has come into the open." Freud was thinking especially of those things to which we have a fascinated aversion, such as moving dolls, or unexpectedly seeing our own reflection. The *unheimlich*, though, may be most strongly felt in relation to the *heimlich*, the familiarity of home. The *unheimlich*, it seems, is *that which should welcome but does not*. And the lack of a welcome both raises questions about the past (*How did this happen? How has time passed?*) and creates a new sense of home into which one retreats.

The uncanny, then, disturbs us because it is made up of undigested fragments of the past and of questions to which we know we have no answers. And so the most common response to the uncanny, Freud says, is revulsion, a rejection of it, and a retreat into what is now familiar. Many Cypriots visited their homes after the opening just once, refusing to go again. Others found their villages too changed, too dirty, in their words, "like they were dead."

"*There's no life in the village now,*" Nikos, a friend who was a university student in 1974, told me. "*In the old times, there were always plays, meetings, music, festivals. Now it seems like there's nothing. Everything seems dead, no life in the streets. And I was also surprised that the paths had been cut off by fences. All the paths we had used to go up and down the mountain to relatives and our fields—they'd all been cut off.*"

Nikos was especially disturbed by the destruction of Greek Cypriot cemeteries. "*We don't want to believe that Turkish Cypriots did it,*" he remarked. "*It's easier to believe that it was the settlers.*"

In the initial opening, many people clung to these easier answers, even as they found them more and more shaken. Especially among Greek Cypriots, many people with whom I spoke in the first months thought that they would return to their villages, find their former neighbors, and that the division of so many decades would magically dissolve. Many people believed that things would "go back to the way they once were." But what they found instead were unanswered questions, and fragments of the past that intruded on the neat stories that they had chosen to believe for so long. Instead of a return to an idealized past, what many people found instead were holes in that past, moments of silence and denial, and important events of the past that were destined to remain open secrets. What they found was not the return to wholeness of which they had dreamt for so long but a past that was now in pieces.

In the story of the Garden, exile is preceded by sin and marked by shame. It is in the discovery of shame, many have argued, that we learn to become other to ourselves, that we learn to look back on the self and see it as fundamentally determined by others' evaluations of its worth. And sin, in this tale, becomes the motor of history: the loss of innocence is the moment when time begins. It becomes the moment when we learn of death, and also when we learn that history cannot be turned back.

None of the original Lapta Turks now live in their own houses, most of which they have given to their children. Like Vasillis, many Greek Cypriots returning ask, *Why don't they just go back to their homes, and let me go back to mine?* Even more, looted churches and vandalized cemeteries are gashes through villages that otherwise boast well-tended gardens and decent roads. In Lapithos, the tombstones of a cemetery had been gathered and thrown, broken, into a small chapel whose roof is collapsing. Today, it is often possible to see fresh flowers beside fragments of tombstone, as Greek villagers return to pay their respects to the dead. And the question that everyone asks is, "*Who did this? And why have they left it this way?*" The unspoken question asks why these sights do not cause shame.

Since the beginning of the conflict, violation of the other has been inscribed in lasting ways in the landscape of daily life: a house destroyed; furniture that is not one's own; the well that one knows is a grave. Mosques with the minarets broken; churches stripped of icons and turned to mosques or used as stables; cemeteries in which every headstone has been broken. Such violations are especially visible in the north, where the normalization of plunder after the war meant that there has been little attempt to erase them. In the south, such violations have often been bulldozed, erased, or lost under the waters of a dam. And when people returned to visit their villages, these sights appeared as a dark hole in the past that calls for explanation, but what they found instead was a silence surrounding such destruction.

The past is plugged with open secrets, known and possibly condemned within the community but denied or defended without. The uncanny encounter with fragments of the past was not simply an encounter with unnarrated histories but was an encounter with histories that had been denied, that had been concealed. Kostakis had told me about his good relationships with the Turkish Cypriots from his village, about how those relationships had continued even after his Turkish neighbors had departed. But what Kostakis failed to tell me, and what I would discover only later, is that in 1974 some of his fellow villagers rounded up the Turkish Cypriot men who had taken refuge in Murataǧa and the neighboring village of Sandallar and sent them to a camp in Famagusta. The women and children were then collected and held in a school, where they were systematically raped over a period of two weeks. When the second phase of the Turkish invasion began, the men who held them captive killed all of them, more than a hundred, and buried them in mass graves in the village's garbage pit. Now, on the road to Kostakis's village, there is a large monument memorializing those killed by his fellow villagers.

In Kostakis's own narrative, a large cloud of silence surrounds the fate of his former co-villagers, a silence procured and papered over by a history that insists that all was fine between Cypriots until the moment of their division. Such open secrets are a form of what anthropologist Michael Herzfeld calls "cultural intimacy," or those representations of the cultural self that may produce both embarrassment and a sense of belonging. The jokes at which one laughs when "one of us" tells them are the same jokes at which one takes offense if told by someone else. Open secrets may be vehemently denied to outsiders but acknowledged within the group. Where one draws that line between acceptance and anger is also the line that one draws around the cultural self.

True cultural intimacy, then, is an inability to extricate oneself from cultural shame. Like the policeman's silence, the silences that surround the fate of co-villagers, or Lapithos's gutted churches, are also a way of guarding the borders of the past, of protecting the boundaries of the community. Silence indicates the necessity of taking up the burden of a shameful intimacy with one's cultural self. Cultural intimacy is the inescapable necessity of bearing the burden of a shameful history, as well as the collusions and public secrets that occlude or deny that cultural shame. The refusal to admit to others a guilt that is known to all is like the story of the emperor's new clothes: it does not hide one's nakedness but rather requires collusion to pretend that it doesn't exist. Cultural intimacy is that internal voice that commands one to pretend that the emperor is clothed.

THREE

A Needle and a Handkerchief

"IN CACOYIANNIS'S RENDERING, the women are hunched, wailing. Dressed in black, the folds of their scarves harboring the dim light, they appear as poised vultures. Zorba keeps watch at the bedside of Madame Hortense, the frivolous foreigner who has long led a life of which the villagers disapprove. She paints herself and dresses in clothes that at one time were fashionable, living in fantasy the world of the famous courtesan that she claims once to have been. At her bedside, the village women wait, but as soon as she expires her last breath the women chanting prayers in her room attack the house, stripping it of curtains and tablecloths, ransacking the wardrobes, carrying away paintings and icons. The tenuous thread of shame that had tied them together is broken."

Vasillis has given me a notebook, all loose pages in plastic pockets. It's a map that he's drawn, and a list, but at the back of the notebook are a few pages in his awkward hand where he has recorded events and bits of life from the town that he thought needed to be written down. Between descriptions of festivals and the workings of the irrigation system, he recorded the frenzy following the departure of the four hundred Turkish Cypriots of Lapithos on January 17, 1964. Their houses, he writes, were ransacked, looted. "In three or four days," he wrote, "the looters had left nothing of what the Turks had left behind in their houses, if it had value they took it, and if they didn't want it they destroyed it and threw it in the streets, and foreign spies photographed this."

When this event took place, Vasillis was already in his mid-twenties, a married man with fields of his own near the Turkish quarter. He was hunting that day, he writes, and his uncle Charalambos walked off toward the Turk-

5. Archival photograph of looted
Turkish Cypriot home with roof
missing (early 1964).

ish quarter, where he had a pen and where he wanted to check his animals.
He describes how when his uncle "saw the streets full of clothing and broken
glass he returned to me and said ironically that we should congratulate our
government, and afterward he said to me more angrily, 'You should be prepared to pay for what you see here, because I won't live.' And truly, it wasn't
long before it was paid with our eradication."

When I first read this account, I had to read it again to be certain that I
hadn't misunderstood. I had been doing research in Cyprus by then for more
than a decade, and I had heard that in the first periods of intercommunal
fighting, some Turkish homes in some villages had been destroyed. But it
was a history that had not been written, on either side of the island, and the
cases where homes were destroyed were largely undocumented. There was
denial in the south, where emphasis was put instead on Greek Cypriot losses
in the 1974 war. And in the north, there was detailed documentation of the
martyrs, the *şehitler*, those who had been killed by Greeks or fighting against
them, but almost nothing about this destruction. After all, in official Turkish
Cypriot accounts of Cyprus history, the property problem had been "solved"

after 1974, when Turkish Cypriots settled in Greek Cypriot property, so there was no reason to bother with it, while the *şehitler* would never return and had to be memorialized. But opening the checkpoints brought back the property issue in new ways, as refugees returned and wanted to claim their houses. And so it also brought back the histories of how those properties had been lost.

Vasillis's story is full of predictable elements: faceless looters, a prescient prediction, foreign spies. These were all the familiar elements of certain Greek Cypriot constructions of the past that also tend toward conspiracy. The faceless looters were scapegoats; the prediction refers to Turkey's alleged history of expansionism; and foreign spies explain alternative histories. But I also recognized that there was something else he wished to convey in the telling of the story, some reason for its telling, if I could only tease it from all the contradictions and evasions.

The next time I saw Vasillis, I tried to ask him about the incident, but he avoided my questions. He wanted to talk instead about the Turks who had tried to stay in the town, another incident recorded in his notebook. We sat at the long table in the center of the one room that serves as kitchen, living room, and, for one of them at least, a bedroom. He fiddled with a piece of discarded paper, folding it, crumpling it. I had noticed it's a habit he has when he's disturbed by something, sitting hunched over the table, staring at his busy hands. A study in determined control.

As I watched him twisting the paper, crumpling it, I thought of what he told me that first day. When he gave me the notebook, he explained that a former mayor of Lapithos had asked him to work on the project, to write it all down. Then, I had asked him if he had shown it to the current mayor, a man some twenty years younger than himself. He had smiled wryly, commenting, "*I never finished my education, because why should I? We had land, and I wanted to work the land. But people like the mayor don't want to read something I might write, because they think I'm not educated.*" The unstated irony of his remark is that the former mayor, the one who had befriended him, was a wealthy doctor known for promoting education and cultural activities in the town. But that was at a time when Vasillis still owned land, when it was still clear who he was and what he knew.

He gave me no more details about the Turks' departure but instead wanted to tell me about the Turkish delegation that went to the mayor, seeking protection. He gave me a couple of names, which I duly noted down. As we talked, Maroulla bustled in the kitchen area, ignoring us. And that was when I thought of the scene from Cacoyiannis's famous film, and the frenzied women in black who tear down the curtains and rip open a wardrobe to fight for Madame Hortense's clothes. She had been an interloper there, someone without roots, and in her death the quotidian ties of village life were broken. She did not belong to the village, and the village had no obligations to her.

Maroulla's bustling and Vasillis's busy hands revealed a discomfort that reflected my own. It was a discomfort with the dirtiness of the thing, the sense of forbidden familiarity. The act of entering a house, of fingering another's belongings; of taking the sheets from the bed and the silver from its tray; of littering the streets with the most intimate of garments—these are all acts of violation, acts that use the intimacy of home to destroy intimacy. These acts of plunging one's hands into drawers and dark spaces, of ripping open closets and boxes with old letters, are all ones that we recognize as a kind of violation akin to the violation of rape. And just as rape may be directed not at the woman who is the victim but at the men to whom she supposedly "belongs," so the violation of plunder in a small town is not only an act of greedily absconding with another's property but an act of power. It is an act directed not at the objects but at their owners. It is both a denial and a severing of ties of belonging.

Maroulla's bustling produced roast lamb with potatoes, accompanied by salad and fresh cheese from their goats. As we sat to eat, I faced a wall covered with photographs, some of Lapithos, some of old friends or relatives now gone. Immediately behind Vasillis hung a photo of him as a young man with three of his childhood friends. The photo was taken not long before Vasillis and one of those friends, a gunsmith, were arrested in the late 1950s by the British on charges of involvement with EOKA. The friend, he told me, was repairing guns for EOKA. Vasillis was held for six months before being released for lack of evidence.

When I broke apart the lamb, it released a hint of wild thyme, and I suddenly realized that I was very hungry. But I had barely begun to eat when Maroulla turned to me across the table and exclaimed how terrible it was suddenly to lose everything in a day. I put down my fork as she began to describe to me all that they had lost, and what it was like to leave without knowing where they were going. She had turned to the theme of the apartment that they had just finished building when Vasillis interrupted her. Although he faced her, I felt that he was speaking to me when he remarked, "*Turkish*

Cypriots had a terrible life for ten years, until 1974, and their lives haven't been much better since." His voice was full of reprimand, and I was torn between dismay that he silenced her lament and astonishment at what he had said. Although I had heard intellectuals speak of Turkish Cypriot losses, I had rarely heard anyone so clearly compare their losses to his own.

When I looked down at my plate, I found my appetite diminished. And I felt a sense of embarrassment, as I watched Vasillis groping toward something, toward some new understanding of how things had happened, of how things might be. I could see him rearranging the pieces of the past, trying to give them some coherent form that made sense in the present. But watching him in that moment, I also thought that there are surely certain pasts that can never be finished. The archaeologist of his own past digs through the shards of a life, but the fragments appear different as one picks them up in a different light, holds them from a different angle. And so while some such puzzles one finishes to one's satisfaction, others one abandons. And still others one continues to arrange and rearrange, even knowing that they are destined to remain in pieces.

A few months later, I decided that it was finally time to move to Lapithos. I had been postponing going to live there, because I knew that living there would curtail the possibility of continuing research with the refugees, quite a few of whom would object to my or anyone's living in a town "under occupation." This would continue to be a problem for me in my work, but in the meantime I felt that it was time to understand something more about how the town had come to take its current form.

Once I settled in, I began to make my way through contacts I had in the town. Within a few days, those contacts led me to an old mason, whom I found in one of the village coffeeshops. He invited me to the house that today is his home, a house that he would tell me later once belonged to a known Greek Cypriot leftist. The mason's own home, I discover, is in the Turkish quarter, and he's given it to his son.

We sat in a room below the main part of the house that appeared once to have been a workshop and which has a large arch opening onto the garden. Osman was interested to learn that I speak to their former neighbors, and he asked me what they say. *"What do they want?"* he wanted to know, the question that all the Turks in Lapithos ask. It had become a refrain that repeated and circulated through the community like blood through the heart. *"What will become of us?"* he asked. *"It's not about us, it's about our children and grandchildren."* His wife is a relative of one of the first two Turks from the town to be killed, but she holds no grudges. There are good ones and bad ones, she admitted. But her aunt, who was visiting, chuckled. *"It's a shame the bad ones were in power,"* she remarked.

I asked what she meant, and she told me the story of her house, and of the house where she now lives. When the Turks fled the town in January 1964, their houses were looted and destroyed. Several years later, she discovered who had been responsible.

"How did you find out?" I asked her.

"Around 1970 we came to visit," she told me. *"Our Greek neighbors across the street told me. They said that [---] came with some men and knocked the wall down."*

Although I was very curious about the story that she was about to tell me, I interrupted long enough to ask, *"The Greek neighbors told you?"*

"Oh, yes," she said, *"a mother and daughter across the street. We used to talk to them sometimes."*

This is the moment where the story that she is about to tell me already unwinds, I thought. This was where the moral of the story, that all Greeks are bad and have genocidal intentions toward their Turkish neighbors, breaks down in narrations of experiences. When I would ask them about the Greek neighbors of whom they were fond, they would invariably say, *"Oh, there were one or two good ones (tek tük vardı)."*

"So I went to him," she continued, referring to the man who held an official post in the town, *"and I told him to repair the wall because we wanted to come back."*

"So you would've come back?" I asked. Not many of the Lapithos Turks had talked about that possibility. Most said that in the period after 1968, when the conflict eased, they would visit their homes and pick fruit from the orchards but return to the enclaves by nightfall. Most indicated that they were afraid and were certain to be back in the enclaves before dark. In her case, I was especially puzzled, because of the way that her brother had been killed.

"I would've come back," she told me. *"It was my home. But anyway, he said that he wouldn't repair the wall. So you know what I did?"*

Here she paused and chuckled. *"After the war I came straight back, and I went right to his house."* She pointed out the window and up the street to a decaying mansion that stands prominently at a crossroads. *"That's where we live now."*

She was a good-humored old woman with a kind face, but she grinned, pleased with herself, when she related her own cleverness. "*I told him what I'd done when he came to see the house,*" she continued. "*He was a number one EOKA member.*" She also said that she asked him what had happened to her brother, whose body had never been found. "*He came, he stepped out onto the balcony. It has a really beautiful view. His eyes filled and emptied, filled and emptied. Let them empty!*" she exclaimed.

What is telling about her story is the way transgression redefines the boundaries of shame. Clearly, there is a strong element of vengeance, but even stronger than that is a way of making sense of events, of explaining Greek losses through their own. The old woman's story, then, is not only a tale of revenge, and it is not only a way of mapping memory onto "the past." Rather, it is a "just-so" story, one that tells us how things have become what they are now. It is one that tells of the destruction of community, and in the process the destruction of the intimacy that makes community possible.

Indeed, in the way that many of the Lapta Turks describe the period of their flight from the town, what was even more shocking to them than being forced at that moment from their homes was the way that after they left, neighbors they had known their whole lives looted and plundered their houses. They heard about it even while they lived in the enclaves, but a few years later they would return and see the devastation. One old woman told me, in a theme I heard repeated often, "*when we returned to our homes, not even a needle was left. . . . When we returned, we didn't find anything—they took the roof, the windows, the doors.*" While they knew that militants had frightened many otherwise peaceful people into silence, they also knew that the looting of their homes was not only the work of militant nationalists.

After their departure from the town, the Turks of Lapithos lived in crowded, squalid conditions for a decade, in enclaves from which they could exit only by passing through the Greek Cypriot checkpoints where so many had gone missing. All ablebodied men became *mücahitler*, or fighters, including the young boys, and all were responsible for guarding outposts, often in the mountains. In the Turkish sections of Nicosia and in some other enclaves schools were kept open, and boys of fourteen and fifteen would spend their days at school and their nights in the mountain, cradling a rifle. Teachers complained of their inability to discipline them: how could you claim authority over boys who had suddenly been thrust into the most brutal sort of manhood? Many families chose to send their children away when Turkey offered them university scholarships, even though it often meant that they had no news for months. Other children stayed and grew up in the enclaves, weaned on gunpowder and a melancholy bitterness. The women were confined to the enclaves, where they cared for the children and engaged in the daily struggle for existence.

As Turkish Cypriots languished in the enclaves, they had little access to their lands or to any form of livelihood. They received rations from Turkey, and the men fighting in the mountains received a salary from Turkey of about ten Cyprus pounds a month. After 1968, when a ceasefire agreement was signed, many began to return for the day, to water their trees, pick their fruit, and just see their villages. But a Turkish Cypriot teacher, Hatice, who had been a girl at the time, told me, "*Korkarak giderdik. We were frightened when we went. We didn't want to speak for fear they'd recognize us. We wouldn't say anything. We'd have a picnic on our own land and then return.*"

Hatice's husband, also from Lapithos, said, "*We were afraid to go to our own land, to our land that we owned with Ottoman title deeds. We were afraid even to cut our own fruit. We were afraid to eat the fruit from our own trees!*"

Greek Cypriots remember the decade after the Turks' departure from the town as one of a prosperity cut short by their own ideological disputes. By the early 1970s, a group dissatisfied with Makarios's failure to unite the island with Greece formed a new incarnation of EOKA, EOKA B', with the support of the Greek junta government and military. Those same Greek nationalists led a coup in the summer of 1974 that attempted to overthrow Makarios; instead, it provoked the Turkish military intervention that ultimately divided the island.

The Turkish army advanced through the north, marching into the town in early August. Lapithos was at the center of one wing of the Turkish offensive, and the struggle for the town raged for days. Those trapped in the town describe hiding in the orchards and fields, not daring to go to their houses. It was summer, and Anna, who normally taught in Nicosia, was spending those months at home. She was trapped there with her family when the offensive began, and their house near the top of the village was especially vulnerable to the aerial bombardment aimed at rooting out remaining Greek forces. Anna described the boulders that were shaken loose and rolled down the mountainside. "*They attacked us with boats, they attacked us with planes, and they attacked us with our own mountains!*" she cried.

By the time the town fell, most Greeks had already fled, and those remaining—too old or sick to leave—clung to each other and to their homes until the Turkish army herded them into the Ayios Theodoros quarter in preparation for expelling them to the south. What followed the Greeks' departure was another period of plunder, as Turkish Cypriots returning to their villages and others fleeing from the south wrangled for abandoned Greek homes and looted other homes for refrigerators and furniture. Some returned early, taking the first empty house they liked. They were the ones who saw the Turkish army sweep through, cleaning away remaining bodies and gathering the spoils of war: furniture, tractors, entire factories made their way to the Famagusta harbor and onto ships bound for the Turkish coast.

"You arrived in a house and half the things were missing," one older woman told me. *"So you'd go to some neighbor's house and take what you needed."* And despite the army's looting, they still found in the homes traces of a prosperity that had excluded them. Many marveled at the refrigerators that they carried off or remarked that they had not seen telephones in houses before their departure from the town a decade earlier. There is the occasional shudder over a body found in a field, and there is mostly silence about the town's few remaining Greeks. But in stories of that period, everything has an air of surprising normalcy: shops began to bring in goods, workshops pulled up their shutters, and schools opened that fall.

In a description of the conflict that sees it from inside the village, then, we see that the problem was not only one of violence committed by a few fanatics but the violation of a moral order, a violation that encompassed the community. In this sense, the problem of property and its plunder is not incidental to the Cyprus conflict but constitutes its very substance. Plunder is the intimate side of the Cyprus conflict, the part of its history that describes friendships betrayed, social ties broken, and communities uprooted. In severing the bond of people and things, it unravels the bonds of community.

I had been living in Lapta for only a few days when a neighbor suggested that I go to see Fadime Teyze, a tiny, feisty woman in her seventies with thick glasses and an infectious laugh. She lives today with her two sons in facing houses on a street that runs to the sea, paralleling the road on which Maroulla and Vasillis had built their home. On the first of many visits that I made to her, I went to the wrong house, where I met her daughter-in-law, who showed me the way. We found Fadime in her kitchen, cooking dolma in a large pot.

When I explained who I was, she immediately patted my hand and pulled me into the kitchen and through a narrow hallway. She seated me in her neat parlor, where she had thrown open the windows. Sunlight streamed in on the white embroidery, the wedding photographs on the walls. Her small apartment is part of her younger son's house, set among citrus orchards and within walking distance of their properties by the seashore. While she returned to the kitchen to make coffee, I gazed out the open window, through which I could see the minaret of the lower mosque and a slice of sea. Below the window, her brood of chickens squawked. When she returned with the coffee, she perched across from me on the edge of a sofa covered in handwoven cloth that she had embroidered.

"*Çırılçıplak kaçtık. We fled* completely *naked,*" Fadime immediately began, her crooked finger jabbing the air. They fled with only the clothes on their backs, the few things that they could carry, she says.

She had clearly taken a liking to me as soon as her daughter-in-law introduced us. The neighbor who sent me to her had heard that she had written her life story and thought that I would be interested. As soon as we finished our coffee, she went to find her "book," as she calls it, a document that is all of thirty-five pages. Almost all of these, I soon learned, concern the years of her family's exile from Lapithos and their struggle to survive. In 1964, she and her husband, now deceased, boarded a bus out of Lapithos with three small children and a goat, and they spent more than a decade in a camp on the other side of the mountain. Her book describes what became of them there, and their triumphal return to the town in 1974.

In our later conversations, she would always refer back to the book. "*It's all in the book!*" she would exclaim, going on to tell a story that she had not mentioned in writing. Although the book documented their suffering, she had also worked to couch the story in the language of nationalism, mentioning at the beginning her father's love of Atatürk and concluding the book with a nationalist poem learned in her youth. Nationalist language also let her cast their neighbors as Greeks, *Rum,* or more often simply "infidels," *gavur.* Although in our later conversations she would mention names and talk resentfully of betrayals, the language of nationalism allowed her to classify former neighbors simply as enemies, as a group that was better off forgotten.

But no sooner had we sat down on that first day than Fadime began to talk about what had happened to their homes. She told me that they fled them naked, meaning with nothing. And when they visited the town in the early 1970s, she said, they found only the skeleton of a house: *Bir iğne bile kalmadı, Not even a needle was left.* "*Beds, quilts, we didn't take anything,*" she told me. "*They tore down our homes, starting from the roof. They took everything, to a needle. To a needle! I had four chairs, and glass from Turkey. It was made in some city in Turkey. Nothing was left! . . . When we returned, we didn't find anything—they took the roof, the windows, the doors.*"

Not even a needle was left: I would hear the expression often. Once I became aware of it, I began to notice that everywhere I went, women used it to indicate the thoroughness of the pillage, that not even the smallest object had escaped the plunder. *"They took our dowries,"* many women told me. *"They took them and used them to marry off their daughters."* Dowry chests filled with painstaking embroidery, handmade silks, intricate laces.

Not even a needle was left. There is also something in the phrase that pricks of betrayal. In the way that people speak of the town in the past, relationships were defined by obligations. People depended on each other. Men worked together; women visited their neighbors, taking them eggs or jam they had made. Many Lapithiotes described to me how they would help each other in different seasons. There were small acts of giving and taking—a basket of eggs, preserves one had made, favors and exchanges of labor. What one gave today one might receive tomorrow.

Reciprocity in villages was a motor of village economy and a fundament of the moral order. What was shocking to many people was that the plunder of neighbors' property attacked this foundation of the community. It attacked it because plunder is, in its most basic sense, a destruction of exchange relations, by taking with no obligation to give back. Plunder is an act that says "*I owe you nothing.*"

And soon when I heard the phrase, it also began to mean to me something else. A needle was not only something small, it was something that for women was one of the most intimate of objects, one associated with family, work, creativity, fantasy, and hope. When I heard the phrase, I would think of women in their doorways with needles in hand, greeting neighbors as they pass. Or of young women gathered in the afternoon shade, weaving bedcovers and tablecloths for their dowries. Or of mature women gathered around coffee cups, mending dresses and knitting sweaters for their children. Soon, whenever I would hear the expression, I would think not only of the shattered glass, the littered streets, some fevered frenzy, but also of women sitting in the protection of their homes, busy needles in their hands. Needles that wove together homes, that stitched inheritances, that designed futures. The looting of their houses plundered not only property and objects but also the most intimate structure of the lives that they had known.

"You can't imagine what it is to return to the home that you left without even a handkerchief." This is what Maroulla said to me as we drove through the mountains the first time, a phrase that I would often hear from Greek Cypriot

women. "*We fled,*" they would say. "*We left without even a handkerchief.*" The phrase describes the urgency of their flight, the fact that they fled so suddenly that they couldn't even take something as simple and necessary as a handkerchief.

Maroulla's sister Eleni paints naïve landscapes of the town. Each time I visited her house, she would show me new ones: fields in spring, the church of Ayia Paraskevi, their house above the church. She occasionally displays them, at the exhibits for other refugees from Kyrenia and elsewhere who have taken up similar ways of making tangible that which is lost. A sliver of cypress tree beside a steeple. A path between houses that she once knew. In all of her renderings, the town is bathed in a clear light, ideal. It is a portrait of innocence, a portrait that she retains. It describes all that was left.

Maroulla and Vasillis fled in the first days of the war. They fled from the home that they had built together, and what Maroulla has told me about the new apartment that they had just built is also a common theme in so many stories: the new home with fresh paint, never lived in, the product of labor and dreams left unfulfilled. Their home is now a daycare center, with swings in the yard and a large sign in bright colors near the road. On that first trip Vasillis assured me that he would be able to take the house back, that he knew the Turk there and that he would just talk to him and explain that he should go live on his land. But by our second trip a year later Vasillis mentioned nothing about going to live in the house, or the Turk and his land. "*Think about what it would be like to go back to your home after thirty years, the home that you left without even a handkerchief.*" There is something unfinished in these words. They express the suddenness of flight, but also a life in abeyance.

And the phrase "*We left without even a handkerchief*" begins to mean something more. There is something solemn in Maroulla, a steady resentment that has worn away at her. There are moments of lightness and warmth, but then something in her seems to collapse back into a hopeless waiting. Their loss remains an open wound, like the one in Christ's side that was unhealed even in the Resurrection. The wound itself remains a witness, so that the Thomases among us need only probe the gash to know the reality of their suffering. There is nothing that will staunch the bleeding, and no cloth that will bind it.

"*We left without even a handkerchief.*" It is the act of leaving that is important, of looking back over one's shoulder in flight. The phrase itself is a perpetual looking back at all that remains. And it says: We left without even a piece of cloth to bind our wounds, or to dry our tears. It is a statement that is inconsolable.

*   *   *

A needle and a handkerchief. The first is a statement of finality: *Not even a needle remained.* The second is a statement without closure: *Everything remained.* The first asks for forgetfulness, erasure. The second for remembrance, even memorial. The first is a rupture, the second a wound.

The grocer from whom I would buy newspapers every day told me that he spent his teenage years in a camp in Boğaz, on the other side of the mountains, and that he missed the town the entire time. He missed the fig tree under which he used to play, and the view of the sea from his bedroom window. "*We couldn't forget, and they can't forget. We don't want them to forget.*"

But he also told me that after 1967 the Greeks painted the fronts of the houses in the main street running through the Turkish quarter. The houses were almost four years ruined, four years empty. They painted only the façades, he says, in a tidying effort to show to the world that the Turks could return. Yet behind the paint there was nothing: everything had been taken, down to the doors, window frames, and roof tiles. Plunder as politics, and intimacy inverted.

In my first days in Lapta, I set out to orient myself, driving and walking through the narrow streets, using Vasillis's map as my guide. Just as a basic exercise, I wanted to work out who now lived where, in whose houses, and how they had come to be there. I soon mapped out the basic contours of the town, with Cypriots, both those originally from Lapta and refugees from the south, living in the lower quarters, near the orchards and fertile land, and settlers from Turkey in the upper neighborhoods. I also noticed then that although there were some areas where the houses were well kept, freshly painted, many of the houses that seemed shoddy were occupied by Turkish settlers, who had not received title deeds for the houses until 1995 and who, even then, often couldn't find the money to invest in the properties. The most immaculate homes of the town were owned, it seemed, by foreigners, who had restored ruins and renovated former mansions.

I had gone once again to the neighborhood where Maroulla had spent her childhood, looking at it through new eyes, trying to see it as a place with another life, one only visible now in its traces—the familiar columns of neohellenic architecture, store signs in Greek that had barely been whitewashed over, graffiti in Greek left for nature to erase. There were a number of renovated Greek houses occupied by foreigners in that area, and I noticed that most bore the plaque of one restoration company, whose sign I had seen at the main junction leading into the town.

As I was returning that day, I saw the same restoration company's wooden sign on the turning into a narrow, winding road that I soon discovered leads from the Ayia Paraskevi quarter down to the upper mosque. To my surprise, I found the same sign outside a small chapel, and around the chapel were piled wooden beams and blocks of old stone. The chapel itself was neat and freshly painted, in contrast to the other churches in the town. It also had a picnic table in its courtyard, and large Turkish and Turkish Cypriot flags flapped and swayed on the roof, out of all proportion to the building's size. As I slowed the car to get a better look, a man in his sixties wearing the cam-ouflage pants preferred by hunters rose from the picnic table and waved for me to stop.

"*Are you looking for a house?*" he asked me in English, leaning into the car. I was driving a rental car with the telltale red license plates, and I real-ized then that this was why he had pulled me over. With the boom in home sales to foreigners, anyone who seemed to be one had become a potential customer.

"*Maybe,*" I replied in Turkish, interested to see what he had to say.

I parked the car and followed him into the chapel, where he offered me coffee. I soon learned that his name was Kamran, and his intensity and en-ergy belied his age. As I explained to him what I was doing in the town, I got a closer look at his red military beret, which I now saw sported a small pin of the Turkish and Turkish Cypriot flags intertwined. The chapel-cum-real estate office was a tiny, one-room affair, with just enough space for a couple of tables and a computer. They had whitewashed it and put icons on the walls, part of the circulation of antiquities so common in the north. Their main clientele were foreigners looking to buy village houses and who presumably enjoyed the "authenticity" of the renovated chapel.

Kamran set the book that he was reading on the table while he turned to make coffee, and I noticed then that it was a copy of *Giriti Mu*, a popular Turkish novel about a love story between a Muslim boy and a Christian girl in Crete. The affair takes place on the eve of the 1923 Greek-Turkish popula-tion exchange, another wrenching of people from land. Kamran explained to me that his family is from a small Paphos village, and he boasted of speaking excellent Greek. I would learn later that in fact he and his wife speak Greek at home, as their first language—as did, coincidentally, many of the Muslims from Crete. As we sipped our coffee, I began to ask him about the property that they sell, which I knew from Vasillis's map was mostly Greek. Isn't that a problem for them? I wanted to know.

His answer seemed at first to be a diversion. "*The first time I fled my village,*" he began, "*was in 1958. I came back in 1960, but we became refugees again in 1963. When I was fifteen, they sent me into the mountains. We used to take our lessons in a small room about this size, and we'd put the automatic rifles on our desks for protection.*" But then his story continued with the claim that at least one-third of the land in the north was Turkish, and that much of what wasn't in Turkish hands in 1974 had been Turkish earlier and had been stolen by the Greeks by various means. He insisted that almost all of the villages in Paphos were Turkish, that 80 percent of the land was Turkish.

He pointed up the road to the house where he lives now. The Greek owner of the house came to visit, he said, and kept talking about coming back. But she also told him something that he thought was revealing. "*Do you know what she said to me?*" he asked rhetorically, leaning forward and watching me with his intense gaze. "*She stood right there,*" he said, pointing at the gate to the garden of her childhood home. "*She told me that when she was a child, their neighbor was the Turkish muhtar.*"

When I was just a child, our neighbor was the Turkish muhtar, she told him. *The Turks were leaving the village*, the woman continued, *and my mother insisted that we go to say goodbye. The muhtar's wife told us, 'We're fleeing here now. But some day you'll flee this village barefoot.' And that's really how it happened.*

Kamran repeated to me, "*That's how it really happened. That's what they know now.*" And as he related this story to me, he appeared to savor its prophetic quality. It seemed to him to prove something, to conclude something, as though justice had been done, history had been brought full circle, and even the Greek Cypriot woman standing in the garden of her childhood home, in the shade of the trees her father had planted, had to acknowledge this. The story does not end with Turkish Cypriot flight from the town but begins there. As with Vasillis's way of telling the story, it seeks to explain what happened afterward.

But the story also has a vengeful element, which is also its moral. In Kamran's retelling, what is important is not only that the Greeks were chased from their homes, but that they left them barefoot. To leave one's home barefoot is to leave without dignity, to leave destitute. But even more than that, in both the Christian and Muslim traditions, to walk barefoot is a sign both of penitence and of mourning. So in the inflection that Kamran gives to the story, it is not only that their Greek neighbors endured what the Turks had endured a decade before. Rather, it is that the muhtar's wife predicted a moment when their neighbors would be forced from the village in shame, barefoot and in ashes. If they returned at all, it would have to be in repentance, to a place that they had not lost but had, in this interpretation, forfeited. For in this telling, to leave barefoot is also to leave without hope of return.

It has been surprising to many Greek Cypriots that their Turkish compatriots speak little about their villages, or that when they do speak of them it is not with the same longing and nostalgia. Indeed, one of the most shocking discoveries for many Greek Cypriots after the checkpoints opened was finding not only that Turkish Cypriots lived in their homes and had made them their own, but also that they had no desire to return to "the way things once were." As in Vasillis's encounter with the policeman, there is a persistence in asking that becomes almost ritualized, as though its repetition will bring it about. What Vasillis asked the man in a concealed way was, *"Don't you miss your village? Don't you want to return?"* And the man, in reply, bowed his head. It was a hesitation, an inability to acquiesce. But it was also a silent assertion that said that Vassilis just could not understand.

A year or so after the border opened, Cypriots had become jaded. Some still refused to cross; others would cross to shop or work. But when it came to the visits to their homes, Turkish Cypriots were more wary. And they had become tired. *"Why do they come so often?"* many people would ask me. *"Coming once to see is one thing, but they keep coming back. It's been thirty years! Why can't they put it behind them?"* People complained to me that they had visits at all times of day, without warning. While they were working, while they were sleeping. While a child was sick. Even more important, they said to me repeatedly, *"We can't go back to the past. We don't* want *to go back to the past."*

Several months after our first trip together to Lapithos, I met Vasillis and Maroulla once again at the Nicosia checkpoint to take them to Lapithos. They knew that I was staying in the town and had begun interviews with the Turks living there. On that day, Maroulla wanted to visit the home where Vasillis had spent his childhood. They were relatives, after all, and had grown up together in those houses. Two magnificent houses side by side had belonged to Vassilis's family, while one next to them had been sold in the 1950s to the British consul. Glowing stone and whitewashed houses, nestled just underneath the church of Ayia Paraskevi, now a mosque.

Maroulla and I climbed the steep steps up to a walkway that led through a garden. All the wooden shutters of the house had been thrown open, and the Cypriot cotton mattresses were hanging on the windowsills to air. We stood at the threshold gazing into a wide hallway that opened onto rooms at the sides and was covered in a dark red kilim. The rooms that we saw through the open windows were pleasantly furnished in a sparse Orientalism. I sensed that the "owners" probably rented the house to tourists, some of whom, it seemed, had recently left.

All the doors to the house were open, and yet we stood on the threshold peering in. When the British "owners" finally appeared from upstairs, I explained to them that it had been Greek property, that Maroulla had a claim on it. But the man protested, insisting, "*This was all foreign land.*" I explained to him that there had been a large, wealthy Greek family in those houses, and that only the one next door had British owners. But I was also by this time aware of the various deceptions and self-deceptions, including titles in Turkish that the foreigners cannot read. A fountain stands at the bottom of his drive, installed by the British administration in 1950, like fountains throughout the island. He took the English writing as a sign that the house was not Greek. And he insisted.

We gained their permission to enter, and Maroulla immediately took me to the kitchen, with its large stone oven. They would bake bread there, she said, and the children would gather there in the winter. This was the room that she had wanted to see, and she wiped her eyes as she gazed at the oven. It was this room that welcomed her, with its memories of warm childhood winters. It had not been her home but the home of her husband. Yet this room was infused with a welcome, the welcome of the place of belonging that it had once been.

Although it was his childhood home, Vasillis had not come with us; he didn't like the sentimentality. Instead, he wandered to the house next door, where a Turkish Cypriot family from Kouklia, the policeman's village, was making halloumi. Maroulla and I joined him, and I commented to the mother that her neighbors refused to believe that their house was Greek prior to 1974. "*They don't want to believe,*" she remarked. She brought us coffee, and her husband with handlebar mustaches stomped about in high boots. Vasillis talked about ingredients for halloumi, trying to trade secrets with him. The husband was taciturn, grumbling, and his wife turned her back to them and asked me in Turkish, "*What do they want? Why do they always talk about coming back? We don't want to go back. I don't want to go back, even though I miss the sound of the sea from my window, and the odor of seaweed. We're far*

away from the sea here." Her house in Kouklia was new, she said, even though
the other houses in the village were old. "*They suffered, but we suffered more,*"
she insisted. "*They never had two men leave home one evening and never come
back.*"

And so in response to Vassilis's question, "*Wouldn't it be better if we could
just go back to the way things once were?*" the persistent reply is, "*There is no
going back.*"

A threshold in tatters and the shade of a fig tree stand as silent markers
of a past that is gone but not forgotten. It was an intimacy destroyed, and a
violation guarded now by reticence and silence. And while the insistence on
not going back often takes the guise of forgetfulness, what it really indicates
is a very present remembrance. It is a refusal to return to a past that they have
mourned and memorialized for thirty years.

In the moment of the checkpoints' opening, particular scenes were captured
on camera and replayed again and again. Even before the opening, stories had
circulated of those who had kept things that they found in the houses they
occupied—family albums spared and returned, pieces of a trousseau carefully guarded. Many people who found photographs and other mementoes
in the homes that they occupied had kept those, thinking that the owners
might want them one day. And so the days after the opening of the border
were filled with such tearful exchanges. It's humanity, *insanlık*, many Turkish
Cypriots would say, and indeed, it was exactly this evidence of humanity that
created a euphoric moment of hope.

Not long after the referendum, Fadime Teyze told me such a story, one
from before the checkpoints had opened. In fact, although she insisted that
the house where she now lives was "*completely empty*" when they found it,
there was apparently one exception: wedding photographs. She told me about
the photographs only because I asked, Was there really *nothing* left, not even
photographs? When she told me that there were three or four wedding photographs, and that she had kept them, I asked what she was thinking in keeping them.

"*They'll want them one day, I thought. It would be a hostile act for me to
throw them out, I mean. I kept them in a cabinet. And some English came, and
they said, if there are photographs or anything, we'll take them. There are photographs, I said.*"

The owners sent those English people?

"*My daughter-in-law has a hotel down by the sea. One of their workers came and said, a client's asking. Ask your mother-in-law if she saved anything from the Greeks, the English will come and take it to them."*

You mean, the owners of the house knew the English, they sent them.

"That's it, they sent the English. I said to my daughter-in-law, 'They should definitely come. We built three rooms, we built a veranda. There was just one room here, we built all of it. They came and took the photos, the wedding photos. There were three or four, I forgot about it."

When did this happen?

She considered. *"I don't know. Before the roads opened, long before. More than that I can't remember. I wrapped them, put them in a bag, and sent them. They also had another house in the upper part of the village, and those people also gave something to the English, and they took it all. The people took the photos out, and when they saw them, they supposedly said, 'My God, the people living in our house are this good that they sent us these photographs.' They went and asked the English, 'Who are these people who were good enough to send these photographs?'"*

She told me of how years passed, but then one evening after the border opening a neighbor knocked at the door. *"'Fadime, look,' the neighbor said, 'Auntie,' she said, 'the owners of your house are here. They say you sent them photos. They want to see you and thank you.'"*

They were the children of the woman in the wedding photographs, and they brought their mother's greetings. *"They were very pleased,"* she said. *"In fact, I wouldn't do anything to a guest who comes to my home."* They came, and they looked, she said. Later, the mother and father came. *"We sat and talked, found people we knew in common. They came quite a few times. Then after the referendum they stopped coming. And then one day unexpectedly they came."*

"I felt sorry for her," she insisted. *"It could be Greek or Turk, she was also a bride. They kept coming and coming. Come see us, come see us, they would say, but we still haven't been able to go. What can I do? I haven't gone. They came, if I want I'll go. But we can't live mixed anymore."*

The contradictions of Fadime's description run through all such encounters. There are the photos: *"I felt sorry for her. Greek or Turk, she was also a bride."* There is the approval: *"Who were these good people who kept the photos?"* There is the encounter: *"They were very pleased. In fact, I wouldn't do anything to anyone who is a guest in my house."* And there is the commentary: *"But we can't live mixed anymore."*

Photographs, wedding flowers, and other such mementoes have an intimacy attached to them that makes them difficult to destroy and impossible to claim. Some people from the town told me that they burned photographs and clothes that they found in an anger or shame that still implied a sense of intimacy. To save photographs may be humanity, *insanlık*, but it is humanity of the sort that partakes of what Georg Simmel calls the simultaneous closeness and distance that defines a relationship with the stranger: "The stranger is close to us, insofar as we feel between him and ourselves common features of a national, social, occupational, or generally human, nature. He is far from us, insofar as these common features extend beyond him or us, and connect us only because they connect a great many people."

One sees this in Fadime's remark, "*I felt sorry for her. Greek or Turk, she was also a bride.*" The element of strangeness was evident, as well, in the ways that people chose to draw lines around that property that was intimate and that property that was useable. One woman who told me that she burned the photos she found at the same time kept the furniture that was in the house, and now she fumes that the owner returns and points out to her grandchild which pieces of furniture had been theirs. And so a general humanity may grant one hospitality—"*In fact, I would never do anything to someone who's a guest in my house*"—but at the same time it already marks one as an other, a stranger who is near enough to be known but distant enough to lack intimacy. It draws a line between those about whom one asks, *What does she want?* and those whose motives are assumed, anticipated. It already draws the line, then, between those who are guests and those who belong.

On their visits, many Greek Cypriots would bring sweets, or gifts, and the hosts would offer coffee. They would chat about how the town had been, about people they knew in common. The Turkish hosts would offer sweets of orange or walnut dripping in a sticky syrup, and if time wore on, they might bring lemonade. But ultimately everyone would feel that it was time for the guests to leave. Because to belong in a place is not only to "feel at home" there, but to have a history there, to be recognized by others as belonging.

And so while Vasillis and many others sought the welcome of someone who belongs to the place, someone who is part of the community, they instead were given the welcome of guests. One implies a door that is always open, the other a door that ultimately will close.

FOUR

Geographies of Loss

E LENI WAS THE one who told me that I should go to Paphos to see her
brother-in-law, Vasillis. *"He's writing something about Lapithos,"* she
explained to me. *"I don't know what it is. He's not very educated, but
he's a smart man."*

When Vasillis first presented me with his notebook, I imagined that it
would be memoirs, or another attempt at a "history" of the town, perhaps
in the form of a memory book. I have a collection of such books, which are
often compiled with the assistance of the refugee organizations and aim to
record everything worth recording about lost villages. The arc of the memory
book invariably moves from the farthest reaches of antiquity to the truncated
present, from the ancient Greek past to a chronicle of the missing: their faces,
the last places they were seen. But when I cracked open the binder, I was
confronted not with words but with lines, not with a cry of longing but with
its most intimate geographies. Much to my surprise, I was confronted with
a map.

The map was in a deliberate hand. It meandered through the village, following the curve of each street and the dip of each lane. In places where the
paths descend the mountain, he had sketched steps. And each house was
there, an uneven square, and most of the workshops, all labeled with owners' names. I turned the page; the map continued. Indeed, the map continued for twenty-four pages, sketching the churches, the graveyards, and all the
houses of a town that in 1960 had a population of about three thousand five
hundred.

I stared at the map in confusion, unable to piece together the pages. We
sat at their long kitchen table with the waxed tablecloth, on the plastic chairs

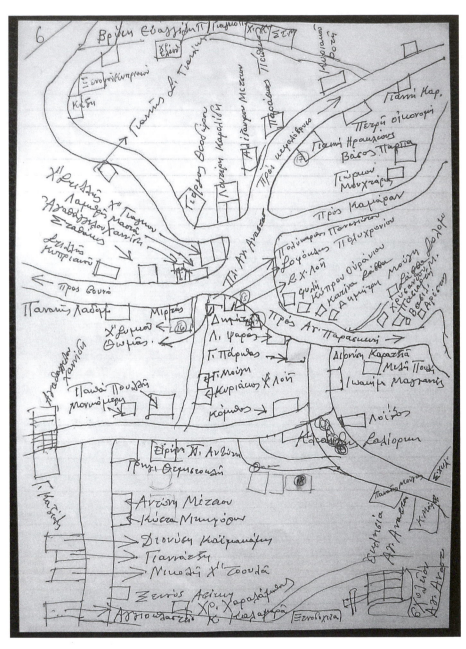

6. Page from Vasillis's map, with notes by author.

that they use year-round, dragging them between an open space in the car-port where they sit in warmer weather to the kitchen where they sit on cool days, or in the heat of the summer sun. Although I would visit them quite a few times, this single room and the tidy outhouse were the only spaces that I would have an opportunity to examine. This simple, single room appeared to serve all their purposes: kitchen, dining area, sitting area. There was even a single bed which was clearly not large enough for the two of them, though I never found another place where they might sleep. Such one-room arrange-ments were quite familiar to me from the homes of other older people in other villages. I would learn only later the contrast with the homes where they had lived, and with the home that they had built.

I stared at the map, and roads trickled off into corners and forked from the page. Vasillis took the binder from me, bending the sheets back and forth, showing me how they connected together. There were of course no exact matches: some roads bulged on one page and narrowed on another; where there were duplications of a street, houses might appear on it on one page and vanish on another. And as a template there was something at once full and empty about it, as all of the life of the village was extracted in black ink on lined paper. Even with the lists of names, there was something too still about it all, a quality that I recognized only when I noticed my own relief at seeing the arrows he had drawn indicating "to the school," "to the municipal offices," "to the mountain." I felt the motion in those arrows, and it made me realize how unnervingly fixed the rest of the map seemed. This map, drawn from a vision inside the village, was literally disorienting to me.

"*It was Paraskevaidhis who encouraged me to do it*," he told me. "*He knew my memory was very good.*" Former mayor Paraskevaidhis had remembered that Vasillis was one of the few Lapithiotes with a tractor, and that he had at some point worked for pay almost every parcel in the village. And so, some-time in the early 1990s, Paraskevaidhis apparently encouraged Vasillis to put his memory to use and draw a map. What he wanted from the map is not clear, but what Vasillis produced was a record of belonging: most specifically, of what belonged to whom in the village, but also of how people belonged in it—of the clusters of neighbors, the distance between family members, the routes between house and field. It became clear to me as his thick, cracked finger traced the winding streets that my disorientation in staring at the map could not be righted by knowing north from south, east from west. What I needed to orient myself in this map was not a compass but a genealogy. The orientation of the map was not spatial but historical.

What Vasillis had produced was a map of belonging. And in that map, the most fundamental dimension of that belonging was the house, but the map was not limited to that. Vasillis's squares might be houses, might be fields. They were defined not by a structure but by a name, and consequently by a relationship. In cases where the owner was a woman, he was certain to list her maiden name. And unlike a street map, or a topographical map, or even a land registry map, both the labeled land and the arrows indicating direction told of life in the town. A street map might indicate places of historical importance, but not local sites of importance, such as Koufi Petra, the rock at the top of the mountain that gushes a stream of cold water. A topographical map would give some indication of the relationship between plain and mountain, but not of the paths one took to traverse the two. And a land registry map might tell the exact shapes and sizes of plots, but it would not tell us of those plots' histories. In Vasillis's map, the shapes and sizes of those plots were imprecise, but he was precise and careful in delineating where they fell in relationship to each other, or rather how the squares of property tell us of the relationships between the names that represent them.

In some way, Vasillis's map should not have surprised me so, since maps are a common, and commonly available, element of the conflict in Cyprus. For thirty years, most maps of Cyprus have been sliced by a line through the middle. In some Greek depictions, the line appears as a wound dripping blood, like a swordcut through the island's belly. And as in many conflict areas, maps in Cyprus take on a contentious air, making claims for oneself and denying those claims to others. The "other side" as represented in official maps becomes both a space for making claims and a form of fantasy about the other. In southern Cyprus, maps of the island portrayed the north as a blank, unknown zone, written over with the words "*inaccessible because of Turkish occupation.*" In the north, maps simply dismissed the south as "*the Greek part,*" "*Rum kesimi,*" acquiring their punch from labeling their own half the Turkish Republic of Northern Cyprus. But maps are certainly much more than coarse tools of ideology. Even maps that appear blatantly and superficially ideological write a certain history of the land that, for those using them, has its own intimate geographies. As I think Vasillis's map shows, maps may also become spaces of longing, ways of representing not only claims on the land but also relationships to it.

As I looked at the map, I was visually struck by the preponderance of Greek names. I had heard conflicting reports about the relative numbers of Greeks and Turks in the town, with Turkish estimates usually inflating their own numbers and Greek estimates decreasing them. But here was another kind of evidence: their names on small, irregular boxes that represented houses. If the map is accurate, I thought then, there would really have been very few Turks in the town, far fewer than some Lapithos Turks had told me. And while the Greek names tended to be written in full, with their surnames—Sofoklis Ignatiou, Kostas Orfanidhis, Kostas Christofidhis—the Turkish names tended to be truncated—Rifat, Şevket, or Cemal. Of course, most Turkish Cypriots in the time before they left the village still had not acquired surnames, but there are some who appear to have had nicknames, and some of them also appear on the map: Hüseyin Hasan Lordou, Halil İbrahim, and Mustafa Lokmacı, for instance. But the very fact of their truncated presence makes these names stand out, along with the houses that are simply labeled "Tourkiko," "Turkish," or those few with women's names—Anastasia Tsimouris Theodorou (a relative of Vasillis), or Emine, from the Turkish quarter. There is something in the map that makes the very presence of these differently labeled boxes a form of alterity.

And yet there was something else in the map. In the absence of any way to recreate village life before 1964, the map gives some concrete form to the talk of neighbors, or of working together in the fields. Even though there was a well-bounded Turkish quarter, there were also Greek houses and fields in that quarter, as well as Turkish houses and fields beyond its bounds. One could see, for instance, that Halil Onbaşı's and Christoforos Kaimakamis's fields abutted, and that the house of Rifat was situated between a parcel belonging to Vasillis and the lands of Hüseyin Hasan Lordou. Hüseyin Nizam had several parcels that were located in a wedge between Christodhoulos Tsimouris's house and Leonidas Paraskevaidhis's and Kostas Allamenou's lands. The lower lands, where the Turks had their homes, were particularly mixed, divided into small parcels of fields and orchards.

And yet the feeling of increasing clarity dissolves in the sense that there is yet another ambiguous history here, one bundled into parcels of land and written into the margins of title deeds. There is something in the fact that the lower mosque is labeled Ayios Ioannis. There is something in the fact that the small square before the municipal office is labeled Plateia ton Hroon, or Square of the Heroes. There is something about the way that some coffeeshops are labeled and others are not. There is something about the way that this very intimate history of the village is written over in a cramped Greek hand.

Vasillis's map is a geography in its original, etymological sense, from γη and γραφη in Greek, a writing of the land. In this case, the map is not only a way of writing the land, but also a way of writing its loss. And if Vasillis's map could only be decoded with a genealogy, is there not something in the map that tells us whose genealogy it must be?

When I moved to Lapithos, for the first month I rented a small apartment in what was historically a British house and that appeared on Vasillis's map in Latin script with the name "Jeffrey." A disagreement with my landlord would soon provoke me to move, but in those first weeks I took advantage of the apartment's central location in the Ayios Theodoros quarter, one of the more modest neighborhoods of the town and one that blended at its edges with the old Turkish quarter. The road above the house ran straight into the Turkish quarter and was only a couple of hundred meters from the upper mosque. A small turn in the road led me to the Ayios Theodoros church and in its shadow, the coffeeshop of Old Christodoulos, now a grocery store owned by a Paphos refugee. I had interviewed Christodoulos once in his small apartment in the Lakatameia refugee housing outside Nicosia, and he had regaled me with amusing tales of characters from his café. Another short walk and another turning would take me to Yiorgos's coffeeshop, with its own stories. Suddenly, these places seemed to take other form, the form of a past inseparable from the place that to so many of the refugees seemed inaccessible now.

I had spent a couple of weeks just walking about the surrounding neighborhoods, trying to get a sense of how things had changed. I would examine Vasillis's map and then set off, trying to make mental notes of the state of the houses that appeared on the map, as well as who seemed to be living there now. Although the street on which I lived and the area immediately above it were occupied mostly by Turkish Cypriot refugees from the south, especially from Paphos, a steep incline that was the beginning of the mountainous part of the town divided that neighborhood from the one in which Turks from Turkey had settled. Along with the new Turkish street names and the conversion of church to mosque, the coffeeshop in the square is now a café that caters to tourists, while a grocery that had once belonged to one of Vasillis's relatives is now run by a Black Sea immigrant. But the erasure of former owners is only partial: hellenized motifs remain in stone on the houses, while attempts to paint over older signs in Greek are gradually fading, allowing the Greek letters to seep through.

Meropi's book had been sitting untouched for some weeks on my desk, and its faded cover photograph of the church of Ayia Paraskevi had become even more bleached by the sun. I had begun reading it several months earlier but had felt that the details were meaningless until I could actually see and touch the places she described. Having spent some weeks in the town, I wanted to give faces to some of the names on Vasillis's map, to give substance to the routes that he traced there, and so one day I opened the memoir again. As soon as I cracked the cover, I was affected once again by the opening paragraphs, both justification and lament:

> I thought it my duty to write the history of my ancestors, of my parents, and of myself. I'll write, of course, of their manners, customs and occupations, and of those of all the people of that period. The pain that torments me is so deep, that I cannot not describe it to you.
>
> I cannot bear any more the injustice of the world. When I think constantly, day and night, of the house where I was born and grew up, the desire that I feel to run in the footpaths and sloping hills, to stop at the springs and drink of the cold water, it lights a fire in my chest, and I'm seized by such despair that I overflow with tears. I want to cry hard, to cry out, so that the mountains and plains will hear. And I stop when I can stand it no more.

Each time I read these paragraphs, I felt a burning in my own chest, as I witnessed the way her attempt to write an "objective" history ("their manners, customs, and occupations") immediately broke down in a confession of pain.

I read the memoir slowly, trying to piece together events with other histories, sites that Meropi describes with other places. In the book, she spends almost two hundred pages describing her family's struggles and trials, the way that her father sweated over the land, a brother's emigration to America, her marriage and children. And it describes in detail their flight from this place whose paths and lanes, whose scents and soil, she knew so intimately: what she cooked that day, how her daughter persuaded her to leave, where they stayed when they fled, and what happened to them afterward. I was struck when reading it by the richness of a life lived within the confines of one square kilometer.

But I was also struck, when reading the book, by the fact that there was not a single mention of the town's Turks. I had noticed this when I first looked through the book and had asked Meropi's son about it, who remarked that she lived in an area of the town that was entirely Greek. "*As a woman, I don't*

think she left the neighborhood at all. She probably never saw the Turks," he
tried to explain. I hadn't questioned this answer before going to live in the
town, but after settling there it began to disturb me. The upper mosque was a
short walk from my own house, across the street from which was the building
that had once been the Turkish primary school. Around the corner was what
had been the main Turkish coffeeshop, a place Vasillis remembered well. If I
began from the road that ran beside the upper mosque, I could walk up the
winding path past the Ottoman konak, or village mansion, of the muhtar
Halil Ibrahim, now owned by a British couple who have renovated it, and
follow a footpath up a steep incline to arrive at the church of Ayia Paraskevi
in about five minutes.

It was very difficult for me to see how Meropi had never encountered
Turks in the town, especially when she had relatives and friends who lived
next door to them. Rather, in all her descriptions of families and churches,
of weddings and festivals, what she described was a place and a people that
were Greek and that in being so were familiar to her. She described the way
that things, for her, simply were: Lapithos was a place where people spoke
Greek, a place blessed by certain saints, a place where their ancestors were
buried, where she expected to be buried herself, and where she hoped that
her children and grandchildren would continue to live. What she described
is a very intimate geography, a place familiar to her, *her* place. The land takes
on a character that is Greek, because that is how she saw it, and that is what
she knew. And it is in this intimate sense, I suddenly realized, that one's natal
land, the *natio*, may also become the nation.

When I first arrived in Cyprus in the early 1990s, I had been unsurprised by
Cypriots' strong attachments to the land, since my own grandparents and
their grandparents had been farmers, and I had grown up in the sort of small
rural town where rootedness remains important. Even if I had been spared
the labors of rural life, I was used to many of its rituals. Women sitting in the
shade of trees shelling beans, or stirring a pot to make preserves, were for me
nostalgic reminders of lost childhood summers.

Perhaps it was this seeming familiarity that made it hard for me, at the
time, to see the specific ways Cypriots imagine land and rootedness. I was
also concerned then with the more abstract workings of nationalist ideology
and how they had taken hold in the island, and my one attempt to write about
relationships to the land was in that context. In my first book, I produced an
argument in which I linked nationalist imaginings of the relationship of land

and people to the logic of history in each community. Blood shed in conquest, I argued, was what metaphorically linked Turkish Cypriots to the land
of Cyprus, while Greek Cypriots, I claimed, imagined that they were linked
through a historical Greek spirit.

When I presented a first draft of that chapter at a conference in England,
a Greek Cypriot academic in the audience rose to make a comment. "You've
presented a convincing argument," he said. "But I think about my parents,
who don't even read and write very well. I don't think that they would recognize themselves in this."

I realized at the time that he probably was right. Such abstractions would
have had little meaning to my own grandparents, as well. But in speaking to
Lapithiotes, it was not hard to see that the land itself, the place where they
worked and lived, was a substance laden with symbolism. *The land where
I was born. I ghi pou ghennithika. Doğduğum toprak.* This is a powerful, an
emotional, phrase that expresses all the semantic fullness of metaphors of
land and rootedness. In all these languages, land—*ghi, toprak*—is both a real
place and a space of imagination.

The land is in the first instance the soil, the place where one's ancestors are
buried, becoming part of its substance. One waters the land with one's sweat;
one drinks the same water that runs through it. It has an odor as familiar as
the scent of one's own child. At the same time, it is a space where metaphors
of rootedness point to the intermingling of land, person, and community. At
the most basic level, one dwells in places that have a historicity that is already
given. Houses were part of marriage alliances. Fields and orchards were interspersed in patchworks that could be understood only through the history
of their exchange. Trees are understood through what they produced or failed
to produce for one's family.

One may trace one's history, then, in the soil itself. At the same time,
the land acquires a character in interaction with those who live there. There
are weddings, there are holidays, and these are all celebrated in the "local"
way, with the red figs that grow there and nowhere else, or a special bread
that uses herbs found in the mountains. The land has its saints, the ones
who sanctify it. It has its special caves and grottoes and wells with names
and stories behind the names that come from one's grandfather's grandfather. The land has a language, one's own language, the language spoken by
one's ancestors who always lived there. And the land has a God, the God of
the saints who protect it. And as one looks up the mountain at the form of
houses, at their clusters and their colors, the landscape itself has a language,

which is the language of form. The familiar forms of human life in the land also make it one's own.

At the same time, it becomes clear in Vasillis's map, or in Meropi's autobiography, that such imaginations of belonging always include by excluding others. During a lull at one point in my research, I decided to go to the library of the archbishopric in Nicosia, a place where many years before I used to go to escape the summer heat and to read their collection of old newspapers in Greek. While looking for articles or older books that related to Lapithos and the Kyrenia area, I stumbled across a collection that I had not noticed before. It was a collection of folktales, gathered by students of the Pancyprian Gymnasium in the 1960s and published by the gymnasium's headmaster. Students had been asked to talk to their parents and grandparents and to collect folktales from their villages, part of the *laografia*, or folklore, movement that was common in Greece at the time and that aimed to link contemporary Greeks to their ancient ancestors by way of legend.

The two collections contained transcriptions of folksongs, local sayings, and explanations of local ritual practice. But what was most striking was that almost every village seemed to have folktales explaining the presence or absence of Turks there. So, many Greek Cypriot legends tell of villages whose saints were strong, who protected them from the Turks who would have come to settle there. The bloodiness of the Ottoman conquest and Greek resistance to it is a theme that runs through these legends, especially ones that explain place names and village histories. There are places whose names mean "the pool of the black one," or "disgusted by blood," indicating where a Turk was drowned, or where there was so much blood shed that the land itself became ill with it.

In the village of Yialousa in the Karpassia, for instance, the Archangel Michael turned the Turks who came there to stones and cast them into the sea. Others were not so lucky: Ayios Sozomenos, for example, was supposedly razed by a pasha who was insulted by the villagers. In other villages, saints gave a clever man or woman supernatural powers to outwit the Turks. "In the period of Turkish rule," one such story goes, "the leaders and pashas used to come to Aglantzia to entertain themselves." Wild and drunk, the story continues, they would roam the village, annoying the inhabitants. One day the villagers could stand it no more and killed four of them, and the whole village fled in the night. "The Turks reached the village and prowled the streets like rabid wolves." They found only one man, still asleep in bed, who through a ruse tricked the Turks and led them away from where his co-villagers were hiding. The Turks killed him to slake their blood thirst, and the story remarks that "Agathoklis died like a true Greek, in the service of his village."

The tale speaks of the village as world and ethnos, a patriotism for the *patridha*. And only a short time later I would hear a similar story from Eleni. Eleni, of course, eulogizes the pure Greek nature of Lapithos. It was famed in legend, the Greek Kingdom of Lambousa, she emphasizes. When I went to visit her in her home, she pointed to a photo of one of the schools perched on a clifftop, and its neoclassical façade. "*It looks just like the Parthenon, doesn't it?*" she asked. And she continued, "*The Turks were marauders. They seized the land.*"

Eleni told me about the Turks who came to a place near Lapithos. "*Do you know what they did? In the time of the Turks, the pasha in Nicosia used to demand every girl who was to get married. There was a girl who was to marry, and he sent his men to fetch her. But everyone knew that they were coming, and as they descended the mountain through the pass, the men of the village attacked them, chopped up their bodies, and threw them in a well. Ever after that, the water of that well is bitter.*"

These are, one might say, "only" legends, and it's difficult to assess what they really mean to people, or even what people think when they invoke them. But they take on the quality of "just-so" stories, ones that tell us how things came to be the way they are today. And there is an interesting consonance between the sensibility expressed in such legends—the relationship of land and people, a land that's Greek and saints that protect it—and ways that many people talk about the land today. Many people asked me, *When you see Lapithos, isn't it just obvious that it's a Greek village?* Like Eleni's invocation of the Parthenon, what is important is a particular sensibility, a way of perceiving the place as something that is particularly one's own.

Not long after the checkpoints opened, Mustafa Kemal Sayın, a Turkish Cypriot whose ancestors are from Kyrenia and who still has much land in the town today, published a book he called *Lands of Legend* (*Efsane Toprakları*). In it, he tells of a man who came to his neighborhood in the early 1980s looking for property to build a house. The man, whom we understand to be a foreigner, drove up in front of Mustafa's house and asked about land for sale. His reply was that there were one or two parcels for sale at the time, but that they had Greek titles. "No, I want land with a Turkish title," the visitor answered. "You never know what might happen. Land with Turkish titles is guaranteed." The visitor asked about Mustafa's own land, assuming that it also had a Greek title.

"It is one hundred percent Turkish title," I said. Then he wanted to learn the price. This really upset me. I came up with some unbelievable price. The man didn't know what to say. Greek land was being sold for nothing, and I multiplied the price in such a way that he exclaimed, "Hii!" Now it was my turn to talk.

"Sir, this is the land of our forefathers (*ata topraklarıdır*). I gave you a price accordingly. As you can see, it's not for sale," I said. He left without saying a word; I never saw him again.

In the land where one is born, the land of one's forefathers, territory and property elide, cannot be easily disentangled. The issue of selling Turkish land was one about which all the Lapta Turks were sensitive, and all of the older Turkish Cypriots originally from the town repeated their own legends about the land of their forefathers. "*In the old times we were rich,*" they would say. In our grandfathers' times there were no Greeks here, that is until one who was expelled from his village came here and began to make shoes. Then others came. We had all the land, but our men were fond of the Greek women. They had children with them and began to parcel up the land among them. Before long, almost nothing was left to us.

Or, they would say, it was because the Turks were too used to being rich and had grown lazy. The Greeks, who had to struggle, were more industrious, and they began to buy up the land. In their stories, their own plight begins to elide with the past of legends. "*In our ancestors' times,*" Fadime Teyze told me, "*all this land belonged to the Turks. All of it! There wasn't a single Greek here. Then one day a Greek was thrown out of Lefke [a town to the west], and he came here and started making shoes. Then more came.*"

"*But what about the land?*" I asked.

"*They sold it!*" Fadime Teyze insisted. "*The Turks sold their land! There were Greek grocers, and the Turks would go, and they would shop, but they couldn't pay. They got into debt, and in the end they'd pay with a piece of land. For instance, my mother-in-law had some gardens, and in the middle of those a* gavur *had a garden. My mother-in-law would say to us, that garden had belonged to one of her relatives. That relative bought two mules from a Greek, and one of those mules fell and broke its leg. After that, that relative couldn't pay the debt. Buying and buying, they got into debt, and they weren't doing any work. They sold everything.*"

At the time, I was still trying to understand the demographics of the town, the ways fields had been bought and sold. According to many people, it had been because of Turks selling in this way that the patchwork of fields was created in the lower quarters. "*I had an Uncle Halil, he also got into debt, he couldn't pay, and he had fields down below that he sold to a* gavur *named Haralambi. He took everything, that* gavur. *My mother's aunt was the same. She had fields in the lower quarters.*"

In the tales I heard, then, histories of land sales were not only tales of commerce but stories of trickery and deceit, of persons who took what belongs to one "by right." These are more than simple stories of possession but are tales of belonging: "to possess" is to master something, to be master of it, as in "to possess a woman." In contrast, the word *belonging* appears to come from the old English *long*, which has the sense of being appropriate to, referring or relating to, being a part or dependency of. In both Turkish and Greek, one may use a phrase that would translate roughly as "those of ours" (Turkish *bizimkiler*, Greek *oi dikoi mas*) to refer to persons who "belong" to one's group. One may use the same construction to refer to objects that "belong" to one, things with which one is interdependent. The lands of legends, then, are those places of rightful belonging, where one belongs because one knows what is one's own.

Salih Usta remembered Vasillis, or at least knew his family. In fact, the two men bore a surprising resemblance to each other—round face, thick, sturdy body, and a rolling walk. But unlike Vasillis, who appeared to have had only tangential political links, Salih said that he worked in TMT from the early 1960s, though from the neighborhood where he then lived in Nicosia. He called himself an *eski teşkilatçı*, literally an old organization man, with many of the same connotations of secrecy and unquestioning devotion as in English. At the time, I had reasons to trust him: I had met him several months earlier, and he had spoken with me twice for several hours. When I moved to the Ayios Theodoros neighborhood, he also became my muhtar, and I saw that everyone viewed him with a guarded respect.

But one day, several months after Vasillis had given them to me, I made a mistake in showing Salih Usta the maps. I had been trying to update them, to work out patterns of settlement after 1974. Just walking around the town, it was not hard for me to see which houses belonged to Turkish Cypriots, which to Turks from Turkey. But I was having more difficulty locating Turkish Cypriots' original homes on the map, and I also wanted to understand the trajectory of their return. Who had gone to live where? In whose house? And why? I was beginning to piece it all together, but it was slow going, and so I decided to turn to Salih Usta, thinking that he would be interested in helping.

We sat at my kitchen table, and Salih Usta took his thick glasses from their case. I asked him if he remembered Vasillis, and he nodded reluctantly. I opened the notebook before him, and he began to twist its pages, repositioning them as I had done. Immediately he drew back and glanced at the pages of the map and then at me with suspicion. *"You'd better not show these to anyone else,"* he warned. *"People will think you're a spy."*

Of course, I realized then that I had made a tactical error, and I had made the error even though I understood the problem well. Indeed, I had considered for some weeks before approaching Salih Usta with the maps, but his seeming understanding of my project when I had spoken to him before had led me to think that he would understand why I wanted the information that I did. But that information was, I knew, too useful to others. Knowing the names and origins of the person now living in the house that one had abandoned would have been a great tool for Greek Cypriots seeking reparations, and it was understandable that Salih might put up his guard and wonder if this American who spoke Turkish like a Turk might be hiding some other purpose.

Instead of helping me with the maps, Salih Usta told me a story. By the time I showed the maps to him, I had already begun to understand that for Salih and others the whole question of title deeds, land distribution, and land rights in the town was one complicated by folktales, legends, and other unofficial histories in which belief and self-justification were impossible to disentangle. These were tales that they had heard from their parents and grandparents: tales of buying, selling, and cheating; of marriages, children, and fortunes; and of inequalities written in the land but passed in the blood. But while the stories that many people told me were of events that had happened in the time of "our grandfather's grandfather," Salih's story was somewhat different, one less shrouded in the mists of history and more discovered in the margins of documents. The story gave a particular spin to the history that I knew, localizing in a striking way the methods of rule and control that had changed the structures of power in the island under British rule: *"In 1914 when the Ottomans went to war against the English,"* he began, *"all the Turks [in Cyprus] in official positions started to be harassed and thrown into prison. When the rich Turks in Cyprus saw what was happening, they started fleeing to Anatolia. All the rich Turks fled to Anatolia. The ones who stayed were the poor ones, or the ones of more modest means. If you think, you take the doctors, the judge, the police, the officers, the landowners, if they all leave, what's going to happen?"*

Over twenty or thirty years, he told me, many Turkish Cypriots left for Anatolia. This I know to be true, reflected both in the island's census records and in those of the town. First it was the world war, when many Muslim Cypriots didn't wish to surrender their Ottoman passports, and then it was the establishment of the Republic of Turkey, when some of the Cypriots who had been newly christened Turkish chose to join the nation-building project. *"They were all landowners, professionals, rich people,"* Salih Usta told me, *"and they all took off. It was the ones without the means to leave who stayed."* After the departure of the wealthy Turks, he told me, the British administration passed new property laws that benefited the Greeks. *"And of course a lot of the property of these rich people who left was being looked after and worked by Greek servants or workers. So they went and said, 'I've been taking care of this part of this property.' The owner isn't anywhere to be seen, and so that's how title deeds were distributed. In other words, the title deed is the most important thing that determined the way that the Greeks got hold of Turkish property."*

One of the great complaints of Muslim Cypriots at the beginning of the century was the way the Evkaf Dairesi, the office of Muslim religious foundations, then run by the British, had broken up large tracts of land belonging to Muslims. Salih mentioned two such foundations in Lapta, both associated with the town's two mosques. One of these had been established by one of the pashas of Cyprus, who Salih claimed had been ancestor to many of the Lapithos Turks. *"A lot of pashas came here,"* he continued, *"and they had homes and property here, because it's a beautiful place, with water, lots of fruit, lots of trees. And the pashas who came to Cyprus always married off a child and left it here with the land. Because it's a beautiful place. Of course none of these pashas' families are left. That is, not the direct descendants. They all left for Anatolia, for Turkey."* He then described the way in which, in 1917, the English *kaymakam*, or judge, of Kyrenia bought both these endowments for three Cyprus pounds each and split them up into parcels of land, distributing them to poor villagers. *"He bought them for three Cyprus pounds each, can you imagine? Because at that time the Evkaf Dairesi was under British control. That is, the director, the accountant, the surveyor, the advisors were all English."*

In Salih's tale, then, the pashas settled their children in Lapithos because of the town's beauty, and they built lasting monuments there and left their wealth there. But their descendants "returned" to Turkey, leaving the poorer Turks without protection, without their powerful patrons. And so gradually, at the hands of a British administration seeking to destroy the old Ottoman privileges, the lands of the town passed into Greek hands.

Thus the title deed, that symbol of ownership, becomes a form of dispossession, a way in which, in Salih's perception and that of many other people I encountered, the law may be used against justice. Of course, in Greek Cypriot legends that land had already been acquired by force during the Ottoman conquest and was then "returned" to its "real" owners through the distribution of title deeds that had not existed before the end of the nineteenth century. In both forms of legend, however, there is an explicit contrast of a sense of belonging based on love to acquisitiveness based on law. And in Salih's telling, a title deed may become not only a form of belonging but also a form of disinheritance. The lands passed, in other words, from the hands of those who truly loved them into the hands of those who only wanted to possess them.

It took some searching to find the apartment where I eventually came to live in Lapithos, half of an old stone house that had belonged to one of the town's Greek millers. I had tried very hard to avoid staying in what had been Greek property, but after my disagreement with my first landlord, I had been unable to find anything with a "clean" title that wasn't far from the center of the town. In any case, I reasoned to myself, the current owners were Turkish Cypriots, and they lived in the house, too. They were refugees, as well. But it was harder to justify the fact that my new landlord was Kamran's son, in other words the owner of the restoration company that bought up and rebuilt so many of the old Greek houses.

An old friend introduced me to my new landlord, who lived in the larger wing of the miller's house. I recognized Ozan's surname immediately and soon discovered that he was the real owner of the restoration company that used the small chapel as its office. When I asked him about his business, he insisted, *"The main thing is to save the village houses. To save the character of the village. Of course somebody has to live in the house! The Greeks want to come back so badly, but what do they think they'll come back to after thirty years?"*

Since he always heard Greek spoken at home, he also spoke the language, even though he is my age and so was born at a time when the conflict had already torn apart his Paphos village. Because we were the same age, and because he was educated and understood more than most about the research I was doing, I grew quite close to him and his wife Hayriye, who came to Cyprus from Turkey and met Ozan when she was a student in one of the universities in the north. They make a smart couple, attractive and ambitious. But at the same time he clearly represented everything that Greek Cypriots resented after the checkpoints opened, and my relationship with him was a condensation of all the contradictions of my position.

About ten years before the checkpoints opened, Ozan had begun his business of restoring old village houses, primarily with Greek titles, and selling them to foreigners. Until the Annan Plan period, such sales were a gamble, since foreigners were taking a chance that the Greek owners of the houses would never return. Many didn't understand the legal ramifications; I met several who believed that the land was Turkish when they bought it. But on both sides of the island I heard little sympathy for the foreigners who bought Greek land. "*They took a risk,*" one Greek Lapithiote told me. "*If there's a settlement, they'll just all have to go.*" Turkish Cypriots were hardly more sympathetic.

Ozan expressed real anger at the destruction of the town's character as a result of a building boom, but at the same time his own house, as well as the apartment where I stayed, were packed with antiques such as tables and dowry chests that most likely came, at some point in the relatively distant past, from Greek houses. The materials he used for his renovations were often cannibalized from other Greek houses that had been left to ruin. And Ozan rented the chapel that was his "office" from the Ministry of Property, which allows the use of such properties for commercial enterprises. "*It wasn't a church,*" he insisted, "*just a place for making wishes.*" How he knew this was not clear to me, nor was the provenance of the icons that decorate the cleanly painted chapel walls.

Several people remarked to me on the irony of Ozan being opposed to reunification even though he still has relatives living in the south. Indeed, Ozan might be considered in some technical sense a nationalist, evident in his desire for partition, his opposition to the Annan Plan, and his support of a party that has supported a separate state. But many of his family members, including his mother, aunt, and uncle, all of whom also live now in Lapithos, spoke Greek as their first language, and he enjoyed showing Greek Cypriots who were visiting that he could communicate with them. He has at least two relatives who still live in the south, married to Greek Cypriot women, and after the checkpoints opened, Ozan and his parents would go often to visit them there. He talked in relatively pragmatic terms about the young nephew who was teased in the schools of the south for being a Muslim.

Ozan told me that what he remembered most from his childhood was being always on the move, and always without his father. His father was gone for months at a time in the mountains, and he would return with a long beard and rags for clothes. He described to me their trek over the mountains in 1974, when they fled on foot. "*We came here with nothing,*" he told me. "*Just the clothes on our backs.*" When I arrived in his house, he had a relatively new SUV, and his own house was an immaculate restoration that he showed to foreigners thinking of buying village property.

Much of the time he was all nervous energy, and I would see him rushing about, trying to cut deals with foreigners anxious about the tenuous property situation. His nationalism seemed to me to have very little ideology in it and a lot of fear, sliced with pragmatism. Like so many people, Ozan asked me, "*Do they really want to come back?*" He had his own theories. "*It's the politicians,*" he asserted. "*They lie to them all the time. I feel sorry for people who lost their houses, but thirty years have passed! You can't expect us just to leave. And you notice, you won't find a single Turk who wants to go back.*"

He was especially angry about the Greek owners of his parents' house, who would show up at the door and say that they planned to take the house back. But he saw this as standing for Greek greed. "*Thirty years have passed,*" he repeated. "*What do they expect? It's just because they want it all! They've got everything in the south, but they want to come back and take this house, as well.*"

One day Ozan arrived home quite worked up, and I learned that the own- ers of his parents' house had visited once again. "*They tell me 'Papadopoulos is number one,'*" he complained. "*They say Papadopoulos is going to protect their rights against the people who want to take them. So I guess they mean me.*" His anger echoed the fear of other Turkish Cypriots, who had begun to recognize the possibility of Greek Cypriots' return. "*You know what he said to me?*" Ozan continued. "*He said, 'Einai to spiti mu,' 'It's my house.' And you know what I said to him? I said, 'Itan to spiti su.' It was your house.*"

For someone like Ozan, it has become impossible to disentangle the psy- chological from the historical, the personal from the social. One might argue that he has profited from Greek Cypriot property and so has a vested interest in preventing Greek Cypriots from returning. But at the same time, Ozan was not only making a statement about property but one about politics and history. Ozan's defiance was one that I encountered often, across the political spectrum. "*Sure they left their homes, but I was a refugee three times*," many people told me. "*I've been here thirty years*," the speaker would invariably continue, "*and now they expect me to pick up and move again?*"

In making such a bald statement, Ozan was not only denying the Greek owner's right to return to his house; he was denying his right to return to a place. He was making not only a statement about property, but one about a territory. For someone like Ozan, it was impossible to disentangle the house from its destruction, or the town where they live now from the village from which they fled. Certainly, by the time I moved to the town, the subject of property was on everyone's lips, but in a way that made it clear that it was inseparable from other histories.

Indeed, in the dispute over the territory that is Cyprus, it is clear that property has always played a central role. In particular, Turkish Cypriots aver that at least since the 1950s nationalist claims of territory were acted out as matters of property. Turkish Cypriots claimed that there was a systematic campaign to buy up their property as an incentive for them to leave the island, and many Turkish Cypriots consider it a matter of pride and of "nationalist" loyalty that they didn't sell. One older man, Hüseyin, told me that at the height of the EOKA rebellion, he was sixteen and was apprenticed to a Greek carpenter whose shop was in the center of the village, between the municipal offices and the Turkish school. He got along well with the master, but one day a group of seven or eight Greek youths attacked the shop and him. The reason, he asserted, was that his family had a parcel of land in the upper quarters, and a Greek woman had wanted his father to sell it to her. "*They were pressuring him. They wanted us to sell and leave.*" His father refused, and he claimed that the attack was at her bidding. "*The rich people would make an investment in EOKA*," he insisted, "*and after that they'd use EOKA to get Turkish property for cheap.*"

Most said that these attempts only intensified after independence, and many claimed that after 1960 the Cyprus government offered rewards to Greek Cypriots who managed to buy Turkish land. One woman who was a young elementary school teacher in the 1960s was adamant about it: "*If the Greeks had just been more patient and followed Makarios*," she insisted, "*all the Turks would have sold their land and left the island.*" Many had started to leave, and even though she and her husband, as a teacher and a policeman, had reliable, civil servants' salaries, they had still gotten their tickets to Australia and were just waiting for their visas when the coup and invasion happened. "*The Greeks offered every kind of help for the Turks wanting to leave*," she said, even finding countries for them to go to. And they were offering large sums of money for Turkish property, she claimed. They offered her father quite a lot of money, and the children wanted him to sell so that they could leave the island. But he refused, saying that Turkish property would one day be worth even more.

According to Fadime Teyze, it was İbrahim Hakkı Bey, a school inspector who had spent much of his career outside the town and who would have been quite elderly at the time, who convinced them that they shouldn't sell. "*Ibrahim Bey, he was an inspector. They always lived in Nicosia, but their lands were always here*," she explained. "*May God bless them and their children! Everyone was saying, Let's sell. And Ibrahim Bey said, 'If we sell, the Greeks won't let us live. That land is staying in that village,' he said. May God bless his soul! What Ibrahim Bey said happened. We were refugees for ten years, and the Greeks were always offering to buy. But we didn't sell. We didn't sell!*"

The small histories of property, then, are inextricably entangled with the larger histories of territory, just as belonging in the village comes to stand for the nation. For someone like Hüseyin, life in the town changed with the transformation of exchange relations into a one-way transaction: "*They wanted us to sell and leave.*" It changed with the explicit attempt to dispossess his family of their land, to make it clear that they no longer belonged. Indeed, most understood the destruction of their property after their flight from the town as an attempt to destroy their roots there, while the few Greek Cypriots who were willing to talk about the incident confirmed that it was an attempt to prevent the Turks' return.

And so when someone like Ozan says, "Itan *to spiti sou, It* was *your house*," it is a statement that does not deny historical right but rather asserts the rights of a different history. It is a history in which the title deed is no longer a birthright but is tied to one's right to belong.

Only a few days after the checkpoints opened, Eleni went on the only visit that she would make to the town, and she wrote about it in the south's most rightwing daily. In her essay, which was printed over three days, she described, moment by moment, the experience of crossing the checkpoint, of ascending the pass through the Pentadhaktylos mountains, of descending into Kyrenia. "Yes, it welcomes us," she writes, "it waits for us. . . . The desire grows. It ascends. . . . it is never extinguished. . . . Everything speaks to you, greets you, awakes buried memories in you. And you cross yourself: Why, my Lord? Ah, Kyrenia, my mother!"

In the language that she uses to express her belonging, the land speaks to her in Greek. Even of the new houses, she says, "I don't know, but it seems to me that they speak in a Greek voice." She describes each thought, each emotion, as they drive west along the coast road toward Lapithos. Finally, they reach the village and wind through the narrow streets to the square of Ayia Paraskevi. "We arrived at Ayia Paraskevi. There's the square. The clocks had stopped at 1974. A known place (*gnorimos topos*). 'Leave, settlers, your hour has come, all of this land is ours, it wants its real owners.'"

But then, after this silent pronouncement, it all begins to appear strange to her. "The scene before me was freaky, if I may use that word. It smelled of jasmine when we left. . . . Thoughts go back three decades, and the memories come alive. It brings to life the beauty, when we lived in peace. Then, when our coffeeshops around the square would compete with each other to bring you better entertainment. Now all the laughter is gone, the joking and joshing—all broken in two. You no longer meet co-villagers, relatives, friends, all those who wove you so tightly together. We were all children of the same mother—you, my Lapithos. Now you see with your own eyes how changed is the scene."

They go to see her home, the home that I would later visit with Maroulla. The pain of this visit is captured for her by "a foreign odor, an odor of the East, and not a pleasant one." It is that most intimate of expressions, the odor of the home, that is foreign to her now. She leaves her home with a greater pain than before she saw it.

As they descend through the village, they stop to breathe the air, to survey the landscape from the village's heights. "Seen from there, it is like the places heard of in Greek legends. Seen from there, it is waiting to be roused from its sleep by a Greek hand. . . . It is our fathers. It is our ancestors. It is the rightful inheritors of this land."

Eleni often slips into poetry, into an expression of belonging in the only language that she knows. She wishes to reflect the beauty of the town in the beauty of words, to express her own pain in words that will also tear through the reader's heart. The land of one's ancestors, the Greek land, must be freed, she cries, and she quotes the poet Kostas Palamas: "Barbarian enemies envied you/they took you in your soul/you lived bound up with others/and now you are alone."

In her vision, the land itself had its children taken from it, its community, and is left in silent imprisonment. It can only cry to them mutely, in a language that only they understand. In Eleni's vision, it is the land itself that weeps.

The confusion of love and interest, of familiar form and a familiar language, all give to the uneven boxes of Vasillis's map a mute poignancy. In Eleni's depiction, the land is imprisoned, alone, denied the community to which it belongs. The land itself wants "its real owners," and it cries to them to return it to its community. The land's affinity to them, *its* love for *them*, is of course a way of expressing *their* belonging to *it*. Eleni is certainly self-consciously nationalist, something realized in her politics, both past and present. But what she expresses is not nationalism in any simple ideological sense. She expresses a nationalism that is truly natal, or a patriotism that returns to the original sense of *patridha*, or fatherland, land of one's birth.

The key term is, of course, the land—$γη$ in Greek or *toprak* in Turkish—in all its semantic flexibility. People may not live the nation in their daily lives, but they certainly live the land, in all of its layered meanings of belonging. And so it should not be surprising that in Cyprus property maps onto territory, and territory comes to stand for property. For in rather uneven and unpredictable ways, a territorializing that has often taken the form of ethno-nationalisms is understood by very many people through local geographies of their own sense of belonging.

FIVE

In the Ruins of Memory

I T WAS ON a muggy May evening while I was living in Lapithos that I
crossed to the south for a meeting of Lapithos refugees at the Kyrenia
municipality near the Ledra Palace checkpoint in Nicosia. It was "Kyrenia Week," a series of festivities in celebration of the new municipal offices
that had just opened in a stone mansion that once belonged to a Turkish Cypriot. Each night featured a different area of the Kyrenia region, and they had
included Lapithos even though it had been a separate municipality since early
in the British colonial period. In fact, before 1974 Lapithos was the primary
town in the Kyrenia region, larger than the Kyrenia municipality itself. Kyrenia had been a sleepy harbor town, known for its carob exports but dwarfed
by the larger ports of Famagusta and Limassol. Lapithos, however, had been
a center of citrus export and craftsmen, and it was the latter that the Kyrenia
municipality intended to celebrate in a crafts exhibition that they were opening that night.

The evening was clear, and rows of chairs had been set outside. The event
was more crowded than I had expected, with around three hundred refugees
and their children in attendance. I was grateful that it was already dusk when
the meeting began, since I didn't want the people at the meeting to observe
me crossing the checkpoint from the north. Those who knew me understood
what I was doing, but Lapithos was a large town and its refugees had dispersed, and I was still unacquainted with many people who would no doubt
have found it suspicious that a stranger was crossing from the north to attend
their meeting. I arrived a bit late and sat near the back, and I saw that most of
the people I knew sat toward the front. A mother and daughter squeezed into
a space next to me, and they greeted passersby. I fumbled with my program

7. Statue of the "Lady of Lapithos" at the Ledra Palace checkpoint.

and checked messages on my cell phone until the music began, when everyone's eyes turned to the stage.

The Lapithos chorus, a surprisingly large group mixed in age and appearance, gave a brief performance. They sang a couple of folk songs before concluding with the "Hymn of Lapithos," a composition that had won an island-wide competition in 1990 to become the official song of the Lapithos refugee association. The hymn begins,

I have you shut away inside me
In my soul, in my mind
You are installed in the depths
In the beat of my heart.
   My Lapithos

You are a girl who is admired
And envied throughout Cyprus
Caressed by angels
Worshipped by your children.
   My Lapithos

The song continues with angels singing hymns of praise and birds scattering flowers at the feet of the dignified lady that is their town. Not everyone in the audience knew these stanzas, but they joined in for most of the chorus:

I worship you and wonder at you
I hold you in my heart,
And I cry with a groan,
My Lapithos, I love you.

Tuneless voices cried the last lines loudly into the night.

After the brief musical performance, the mayor of Lapithos took the stage. The mayor is a soft-spoken man in his late forties who works in his ordinary life as a trade-union activist. Because he was already the so-called "real" mayor of Lapithos when the checkpoints opened, the Greek Cypriot "mayor" has not been to the town since 1974. He conducts his business from a spartan office near the presidential palace, using the help of volunteers.

That evening the mayor took the stage in what was intended as an in-nocuous introduction to the main events of the evening, namely, a talk on Lapithos's needlework by Anna, whom I had not yet met at that time, and a second lecture on its other handicrafts, especially its pottery. The mayor opened with remarks about the importance of crafts production in Lapithos, emphasizing that

As an occupied municipality, we have at the top of our priorities protecting and extending our cultural inheritance. I consider this to be an important weapon in the struggle that we are waging for the reunification of Cyprus and for return and justice. Besides, it is significant as long as the Turkish occupier is trying to erase from our enslaved lands all that represents tradition and civilization.

The mayor discussed the importance of Lapithos's crafts traditions, encouraging the audience to visit the exhibit in the adjoining hall and then introducing Anna, who would talk about needlework.

Anna, like Eleni, is a woman in her early sixties who is always very neatly dressed, her hair carefully coiffed. She has an intensity that even she realizes can be too much and that I gather derives partly from the fact that she now lives alone, having buried her husband and lost a son to emigration abroad. She is very intimately involved in the activities of the refugee organization, and her intensity gives her an icy strength. When she began to speak, there was complete silence in the darkness of the gathering. Even listening to the tape many months later, there is a sense of the audience holding its breath.

Anna was mesmerizing. And although I wasn't aware of it at the time, I realized later in listening again to her speech in daylight and many miles away that one of the ways she produced that effect was to write her talk in a type of free verse in which rhyme was not systematic but embedded into the rhythm of the text. Even in her welcome to those present she drew them into the rhythm of her talk:

Kalos irthate apopse	You are welcome this evening
entimotatai vouleftes	honorable members of Parliament
aksiotimi dimarhoi	respected mayors
kai oloi eseis	and all of you
pou eisaste apopse edho.	who are here this evening.
Sas proskalo	I invite you
Na taksidhepsoume mazi	to journey together
Stin omorfi mas Lapitho	to our beautiful Lapithos
Kai tin ghiro perioxi.	and the surrounding area.

She invited her guests to stop beneath the lemon trees, where girls have gathered, their needles busy with designs that one can glimpse—jasmine, the local flowers.

Afisan mia-mia na mazevontai.	They left [their work] one by one to gather.
Simera na kentisoun sto spiti tis Theodoras,	Today they embroider in the house of Theodora,
Avrio tis Ragoulas,	Tomorrow in that of Ragoula,
kai istera-istera tis Stelas,	And after that and after that in [the house] of Stella,
tis Stavroulas,	of Stravroulla,
tis Elenis.	of Eleni.
Etsi ghinate. . . .	That's the way it was. . . .
Etsi ghinotan panda.	That's the way it had always been.

The repetition and pause in the last lines—"Etsi ghinate. . . . Etsi ghinotan panda"—has the effect of saying not only that it had always been this way, but also that it always should be this way. It was repeated. It should always be repeated. That's the way things were, and the way they should always be.

She continues:

Tha kendoun.	They will embroider.
Tha kouventiazoun.	They will converse.
Tha traghoudhoun.	They will sing.
Kai i gheitonia tha ghimizi omorfes fones	And the neighborhood will fill with beautiful voices
kai omorfes . . . dhoulies.	And beautiful . . . work.

These next lines project into the future. They *will be* embroidering. They *will be* conversing. They *will be* singing. The tense is a continuous future that places the listener in an idealized past that is also a vivid present in which this pastoral scene becomes something that must take place because it always has. And the neighborhood will fill with beautiful voices, with an innocent joy.

Having brought the listener to the point in which she imagines a future that is also a continuous past, she then pauses to mark a shift. The pause before "dhoulies," which she rhymes with "fones," also marks a break in the focus, as she turns the listeners from the scene that is now vivid before their eyes to the reason for these girls to gather together. They have gathered, she says, to work on their dowries, for everything must be ready before the wedding day. And so she takes us from a pastoral scene of girls happily stitching under the lemon trees to show us their place in the community, the futures for which they are preparing. Even as the talk continues, describing types of lace work and their uses, display, and even sale, the listener always has before her eyes the girls who have always been under the lemon tree and who should always have their place there.

The next presentation was a talk on pottery and other handicrafts, with slides. The speaker was a stocky, masculine, middle-aged woman who spoke with enthusiasm and even with surprising cheer. This was quite a contrast to Anna's somber intensity and in general to the rest of the evening, which proceeded much like a wake. Anyone coming from outside simply to listen to the talk would have learned about Lapithos's extensive pottery trade, and the famous craftspeople who were known throughout the island. They would have learned about designs and workshops and the ancient and marvelous history of Lapithiote pottery. And all this was demonstrated by nostalgic slides projected into the night onto a screen beyond which the walls of northern, "occupied" Nicosia were visible.

In her talk, the speaker showed photographs of Lapithos pottery—pots encircled with coral and blue flowers; plates painted with medallions; wasp-waisted pitchers. She described the methods of their making, as well as the special quality of the clay that could be found nowhere else. Before their departure from the town, plates made in a pottery shop next to the chapel where Ozan had his office were sold in tourist shops and exported to Europe, where they won prizes. The master, Kostas Christodhoulakis, reportedly never revived his business in exile.

But even though the second speaker's presentation was imprinted with the banal flatness of scholarly work, this was surely not the way most of those present heard the talk. Anna's presentation had already evoked a particular scene, a particular life, one marked by what all those who lived it describe as the vibrancy of work and a thriving local economy. Even as the second speaker cheerfully discussed the virtues of Lapithos pottery in comparison to that in other parts of the island, I could imagine in the background the excited descriptions of the town by older Lapithiotes: the bustle of trade, the pounding of hammers, the whir of a potter's wheel, the whine of knives being ground. As both Greek and Turkish Lapithiotes described it, traders took Lapithos's goods throughout the island, and eventually the women's handiwork to England. Men and women were proud of their work, and of what they produced together. They exported lemons by the ton, and in the middle of the century Cyprus's silk became especially profitable. Many people had been excited to describe to me the system for distributing water, or the months of hard work spent tending silkworms.

In such descriptions, the town appears as an organic whole, one where relationships were understood through kinships and family histories but were also defined by work, while land—along with the trees that grew on it and the water that ran through it—was not simply a possession but part of the society. Work grew out of that very particular place—the clay that made the pottery, the water that caused the lemon trees to blossom, the mulberry trees that fed the silkworms, the soil that one tilled and sweated over. And work was woven into the society, both supporting and producing it. Women gathered to sew or shell peas, men and women shared harvest labor, neighborhoods rotated the duty of making halloumi cheese and distributing it to everyone in the neighborhood who had contributed milk. All that they achieved, they achieved with others, and one of those others was the land. They worked not simply *on* the land but *with* the land.

What was once a texture of clay in one's hands, the whine of a potter's wheel, and the bustle of a vibrant local economy had been reduced to grainy slides projected into the dark night, near a border that for those watching that evening hid not only a land and a dream but a whole life lost. The speaker showed slides of lace and silk creations. The busy needles were women's work, but the silk again grew from the land, from the silkworms they all nurtured, while husbands and fathers and brothers took the lace to Kyrenia, to Nicosia, even to Europe, where they sold it as a product of the town, of their work together. The slides clicked on, but they were clearly no simple ethnographic document or description of a folkloric past. Rather, they were a reminder that an exiled life could only be two-dimensional. And they were also a reminder that there had been a rich life that was now held together only by the fine thread of memory, and so they demanded that the viewer refuse to forget.

Although it may be a truism to say that we all live in the ruins of our pasts, Cypriots have been more viscerally confronted than many of us with their history's aftermath. They live in a divided island with the world's last divided capital. Familiar roads are truncated by barricades; enemy flags wave on distant hilltops; a lost home may even be visible across what until recently was an impassable line. Even more than that, though, village names evoke massacres, hilltops invoke battles. Home itself, the most intimate of spaces, may be tainted with violation. One must live with and within these places, imagining them anew.

Within only a day of my first arrival in Cyprus in the early 1990s, I found myself sitting at dusk on the terrace of a house in the hills of outer Nicosia, facing toward the Pentadhaktylos Mountains. The grandmother of the family with whom I was staying pointed across the jumble of concrete below us toward the blue streaks of mountain visible in the distance. "*You see that village there?*" she asked, indicating white specks in the foothills on the horizon. "*That was our village. On clear days, I can even see my house.*"

By that time, almost twenty years had passed since her displacement; by the time I began my second project, another decade had gone by. It remains difficult for me to understand the thoughts and feelings of someone who had settled in a house that overlooked the village from which she had fled, for so long inaccessible to her. It seems an irritant to a wound, a way of prolonging suffering.

At the same time, the many institutions that surround Greek Cypriot refugee life clearly have such an aim: maintaining an open wound, preventing its closure. Indeed, much of the literature on Greek Cypriot refugees that has proliferated over the past decade or so focuses on the tension between the political and the personal, in which refugees and their children and now grandchildren must negotiate the thin line between labels and longing, between the actual desire for return and the way that desire is reproduced. In its reproduction, much of the aim is to keep memory alive, to irritate the wound rather than allow it to heal. The symbols and institutions of refugee life emphasize keeping the wound open in the present, even as they say that the wound *will* be healed, *must* be healed, but only at a time in the future when all will return to the way it once was.

Each person's experience of displacement is surely different, but there is also the social phenomenon of displacement, both as it was lived and as it has since been socially reconstructed. Part of the tension between these is expressed in the label "refugee," which Greek Cypriots who cannot return to their homes insist on using in place of the seemingly more appropriate "internally displaced persons." The latter would seem more appropriate, in that Greek Cypriots took refuge in their own state, and using that term would also coincide with the insistence that Cyprus is a whole, that it has no border, and that the problem is only one of occupation. To use the term "refugee" appears to suggest that they were displaced from one state into another, something that they surely do not wish to imply.

But the word "refugee," Greek *prosfigas*, seems more aptly to evoke the sense of fear, of flight, of taking refuge, of helplessness. It also seems to evoke a particular experience of temporality: they have taken refuge, but refuge cannot be permanent. The present is a temporary stop in a "foreign land" (*xenos topos*) from which they will return to places that are their own. The word "refugee" also evokes a foreign power. Not only does IDP (internally displaced persons) not capture their pain, but it also does not seem to capture the experience of being "refugees in our own country," the result of invasion and occupation. It was not that they fled their country for a foreign land, but that a foreign land came to them, pushing them out even as it imbued the places that were theirs with what Eleni had called "an odor of the East."

This sense of foreign invasion and occupation, as well as its temporariness, is expressed in almost all publications that write of the taking of Lapithos. For instance, a history of Lapithos published in 1982 by a Lapithiote journalist, Fokas Fokaidhes, attempts to describe the town's fall. But the author, who was not living in the town in 1974, was confronted with the inability of people he asked to recount to him what had happened. And so he comments,

> Their silence, though, speaks loudly, as they try to hide their pain. They try to forget, without being able. It was not only that they lost all that they had toiled to create, their riches and profits, their fragrant fruit trees and lemon orchards, but that they lost the luminous, dreamlike, and ever-beautiful Lapithos, without expecting it, to the bloodthirsty and vile hands of the wild Turkish barbarians from Anatolia. The horror, the frenzy, the sadism, the mania, the shame that they felt is indelible. It is inscribed in the History of humanity, the bestial violence, the cruelty, the unprovoked and predatory attack, the appropriation and occupation, the barbarism and criminality, that characterizes a wild people who have overrun the forces of civilization of the Earth.

And in the following section, "The Little Lost Homeland," he mourns, "There is no more Lapithos. Not for its inhabitants, nor for any Greek Cypriot." It has become, he says, an area under the control of the Turkish military, "a central strategic bridgehead of Turkey."

At the same time, his depictions evoke temporariness, as he describes how "The 'pashas' from Anatolia now perch in the newly built houses, which the true inhabitants were still raising for their children until July 1974. The intruders of Attila are now enjoying the use of the rich orchards, the water and the gardens." Even the verbs used in this passage to describe the foreigners' occupation (*kourniazoun* and *nemontai*) imply a sense of temporariness. *Nemomai*, especially, implies not only enjoying the use of property but that the property belongs to another.

One way of giving meaning to the brutality Lapithiotes experienced in 1974 was to frame it in the terms that were familiar from legends. These were "a wild people who had overrun the forces of civilization," a phrase that emphasizes surprise, horror, and foreignness. Certainly for Greek Lapithiotes, the flight from their homes was especially traumatic, in that they experienced many of the most excessive cruelties of the war firsthand. Because it was close to the Turkish landing point and considered strategically important, the town was bombarded by guns from Turkish ships and planes. The town experienced fierce hand-to-hand combat, as Greek and Greek Cypriot soldiers stationed in the town faced down the advancing Turkish army. Casualties were very high on both sides, and both Greek Lapithiotes fleeing the town and Turkish Lapithiotes returning to it described streets and orchards littered with bodies.

The Lapithos refugee association gives the number of Lapithiotes killed and missing as 89, though some of those were Lapithiote soldiers fighting in other parts of the island. What that figure does not include is the number of soldiers of both sides who were lost in the town itself. In the wake of this onslaught, Lapithiotes fled with whatever transport they could find, leaving everything behind in a moment and cramming into cars to flee across the mountains. There were those who were too old or ill to leave, and others who simply refused. The refugee association counts 182 such persons in the town as of October 1974, two months after the town was taken. They were kept in the Ayios Theodoros neighborhood, which appears to be one reason that this neighborhood is now occupied primarily by Turkish Cypriot refugees from Paphos, who arrived later than the Turkish Lapithiotes and so after the expulsion of the Greek Cypriots who had been kept there.

Those who remained in the town as of August 1975 were sent to the south following the Vienna Agreement which provided for the reunification of families. Although the agreement in fact allowed Greek Cypriots who wished to remain in the north to stay, in practice only a few hundred in the northeastern Karpassia peninsula were able to do so. The agreement was interpreted by most Turkish Cypriots as a population exchange, echoing the Greco-Turkish exchange of 1923 that was also part and parcel of the establishment of the Republic of Turkey. For Greek Cypriots, of course, the agreement meant no such thing.

Lapithiote refugees, like almost all Greek Cypriot refugees, were scattered in their flight and remained scattered afterward. They fled to the nearest zone of safety, to relatives and friends who would take them in. Some found temporary places of refuge, renting rooms or small houses if they could afford to do so and waiting to see what would happen. By the time of the Vienna Agreement, the Republic of Cyprus was already beginning to implement a housing scheme to resettle the refugees, giving precedence to farmers or those who had lost small businesses and placing them primarily in hastily constructed housing projects on the outskirts of the major cities. Later, some would take advantage of self-build schemes or government loans to build their own homes, often on expropriated Turkish land. Some depended on the help of children abroad. Some others, like Vasillis, chose to take refuge in abandoned Turkish Cypriot villages to be able to continue the agricultural life that they had known.

One refugee who had been a boy of fifteen at the time of the invasion described those last days: their flight from the town, an enclaved grandfather, a sweetheart he would never see again. *"But what's most important is the loss of the community,"* he said, echoing what I would hear again and again. *"After that comes dignity."* Unlike in the north, where the administration settled Turkish Cypriot refugees from the south together, no such effort was made in the south. In fact, many refugees believe and assert that it was official government policy to separate them, to prevent their adjustment to the new situation and promote the dream of return. *"They intentionally separated us,"* Kostakis vehemently insisted, again echoing what I would hear from so many others. *"If we had been together as communities, we would've been too powerful."*

Today refugee communities are tied together by tenuous threads. There are family bonds and old friendships that people have maintained, but many ties are traced through the institutions of refugee life. There are the municipalities and refugee organizations, which try to bring an increasingly scattered population together for important events. There is the label "refugee" that still ties them together, continuing to promote an idea of difference that also manifests itself in housing and health benefits and other subsidies. Children and grandchildren born after their displacement adopt ambivalent attitudes toward a past they never knew, wanting to maintain loyalty to their families even as their own lives have taken a different, often very urban shape, in contrast to the rural life that their parents and grandparents knew.

Life was remade, then, from communities that were scattered, from pieces of the past that had to be collected and preserved. Lessons on *ta katexomena*, the occupied areas, were required in schools, and books such as those written by Anna about the war and its aftermath became standard school texts. Restaurants, coffeeshops, grocery stores, and barbershops were named after lost villages, while sports teams and other associations continued to represent those places in exile. In the worlds remade after conflict, then, local geographies of belonging were enshrined in institutions and acquired a new kind of temporality, one that emphasized not only ancestors and roots but also the temporariness of the present. Both the politics of exile and its institutional expressions aimed to create a sense of the temporary, even as the passage of time gradually began to erode that sense.

Indeed, the landscape of life after tragedy is filled with markers of the temporary, including the belief in the temporariness of the division and the future return to one's home. One way in which this has been marked has been the refusal of the government to give property titles to refugees for their housing, and the insistence by many refugees that in any case they wouldn't accept them. Much refugee housing was built on Turkish Cypriot land, so there is a widespread belief that acceptance of title deeds would constitute a de facto form of exchange. The places where they live are cast as temporary homes, places of refuge, in which the seeming permanence of the present is illusory. In its place stands the "real" house, the site of a struggle both political and temporal, that calls for "real" return.

The politics of exile, then, insists that the present is a false one, that their "real" lives will be returned to them only with a return to a past that it is their duty to preserve intact. Moreover, in Greek Cypriot depictions, wrongs are made visible as a wound that cannot heal, a wound worn on the body politic much as stigmata are born by Christian saints. In Greek a *stigma* is simply a mark or a sign, but stigmata are the wounds that appear on blessed martyrs, those who attempt to imitate Christ. The wound is a witness, but to a truth that is not visible and a future whose time is not known. Some representations evoke this directly, such as the large black cross next to the Ledra Palace checkpoint on which hangs a black map of Cyprus with three points that drip blood, representing the hand and chest wound of Christ. The wound that cannot be healed witnesses a wrong that cannot be righted, one that will disappear only at the end of time, when all will be rectified, and everything will return to its pure state, the way it once was.

There are many rituals of refugee life. There are the ordinary rituals in exile, such as marriages and funerals, which draw together a community that is dispersed. But there are also the rituals of exile itself, the rituals that signal another year in which that exile has continued—summer excursions in the mountains, plays and musical events, or the commemoration of the fall of one's village. Refugee organizations plant forests with the names of their lost villages. They hold festivals. They protest at the checkpoints and in foreign capitals. Since the opening of the checkpoints, some have organized campaigns to clean their churches and have held services there. But most of these rituals cannot take place in the village, for the rituals were shaped by the loss of the village and the struggle for its return.

My first encounter with Lapithos refugees in my capacity as researcher was an invitation to a commemoration of the fall of the town to the Turkish army, held only three short months after the checkpoints had opened. A cousin of the mayor had invited me, saying that he would introduce me to the mayor after the ceremony and assure him that I was a serious researcher. The ceremony was, as one would expect, a somber event that took place at The Tomb, a cemetery on the outskirts of Nicosia where soldiers lost in 1974 are buried. The cemetery was bedecked with Cypriot and Greek flags, and there were about one hundred fifty refugees and representatives of refugee organizations in attendance. The gaunt, grave Bishop of Kyrenia led the service, raising his arms and blessing those present, calling upon them to resist the occupier's deceptions and urging them not to cross to the north, not to be tourists in their own country. Afterward, a presenter called the names of about twenty-five representatives of various organizations, who stepped forward one by one to lay wreaths on the tomb, accompanied by a military drill.

Only a small fraction of the Lapithos refugee population living in Nicosia attended the ceremony, and many of them—like Eleni and Anna—would describe themselves as Greek nationalists. Eleni herself was there, as I discovered in conversation with her later. Indeed, in looking through old photographs of Lapithos refugee association events, Eleni's face is ubiquitous. Many of the same faces appear again and again at such core events, though the audience broadens for anything "cultural." For instance, a friend who has long been involved in bicommunal activities and who would not attend a service conducted by the Bishop of Kyrenia had brought his parents to the celebration of Kyrenia Week, which was construed as more neutral.

But clearly the Hymn of Lapithos is not "neutral," just as the mayor's remarks and Anna's eulogy were not neutral. Even the seemingly objective, scholarly work of the second, more cheerful speaker was placed within a particular context that gave that presentation a different tone, a different message. And that message was a reinforcement of the slogan around which refugee organizations have for more than two decades focused their efforts: "Dhen Xechno," "I Do Not Forget," a slogan powerful in its simplicity. It is powerful because it needs no referent: one already knows that one does not forget the home, the village, the graves of one's ancestors. And it is not only a description but a command: one *must not* forget.

The work of untiring volunteers such as Eleni and Anna has made the slogan into something both revered and maligned. When I first arrived in the island in 1993, the slogan was everywhere: in songs, in graffiti, in banners, on bumper stickers. But by the turn of the millennium, it had begun to grow old. The satirical newspaper *Enosis* did a send-up in which they replaced the slogan with "Dhen Xerno," "I Do Not Throw Up." And in summer 2006 the Cyprus Theatre Organisation premiered Aristophanes's *Ecclesiazusae* with contemporary staging. In the second act of the play, one of the actors urinates against a wall that is sprayed with the graffiti, "Dhen Xechno." The scene created a stir, leading one columnist to comment ironically that "'Den Xechno' is the vacuous message all our governments, parties, campaign groups, schools have been trying unsuccessfully to instill in people since the Turkish invasion. It is now a national cliché, which most people laugh at when they see or hear anyone mentioning it."

There is laughter, but at the same time the slogan derives power from its expression of a form of politics and way of life that is so familiar as to be unnoticed. Not only does the slogan's ubiquity create a certain way of talking about lost villages, framing talk about the future in terms of remembering and forgetting the past. Even more than that, the campaign that the slogan encapsulates is part of an institutionalized memorialization of lost villages in which their ever-present remembrance is an intrinsic, unthought, and largely unquestioned part of daily life. In the play in which the actor urinates against a wall sprayed with the words "Dhen Xechno," presumably what the director wished to point out was the sanctity attached to those words by arousing in the audience the titillation of defiling them.

This particular form of memorialization has produced institutions of memory, such as the demand that refugees vote in parliamentary elections as though they still live in their former villages, or the ubiquitous use in everyday life of the names of "occupied" lands, such as "Enslaved Kyrenia." However, most of the institutions, laws, and signs that constitute this public construction of history are not as visible as a slogan. Rather, they make up the very ground of quotidian life, the way in which one lives that life and gets things done. Those institutions of memory are so familiar as to be invisible, and in such a way they not only present a particular construction of history but create a vision of the present that makes that history seem all the more real. The effect is to produce a certain landscape, a form of everyday action and interaction, that normalizes and even naturalizes an emphasis on invasion and occupation. In this landscape, as in Fokaidis's description of the fall of Lapithos, Turkey is an ever-present force, while Turkish Cypriots seem to fade from the scene, indeed cannot have a role.

While such constructions of the past and fantasies about the present made some sense before the opening of the checkpoints, when there was virtually no knowledge about the lives or quotidian problems of those on the "other side," they have continued even in the face of increased knowledge about other versions of the past and other ways of seeing the present. Because institutions of memory, by their simple existence, allow people to live in and with a particular version of history, indeed force them to use its language in order to get things done, that version of history begins to seem like the "real," the only one. And so state fantasies and the institutions that support them have continued to produce a particular vision of reality that has been only minimally shaken even after the checkpoints opened.

Not long before the Annan Plan referendum, I met with the Greek Cypriot mayor of Lapithos and gently suggested to him that it wouldn't be a bad idea if, before voting on the plan, Greek and Turkish Lapithiotes discussed with each other what the implications of the plan would be for them. After all, most voters, in their discussions of the plan in their homes or coffeeshops, showed little interest in the complications of constructing a federal government. They were interested in more local, quotidian problems, such as the number of refugees who would return, the number who would regain their land, and how that movement and land transfer would work out at the village level.

But while Greek Cypriots worried about "rights," I wondered about reconciliation. I wondered, for instance, if Vasillis had really considered what it would mean to go back to a place that had a checkered history of intercommunal relations and where the family of a Turkish soldier now lives in Maroulla's childhood home. Under the plan, Düriye and her family would have remained and perhaps would even have kept the house. Would Maroulla ever really adjust to meeting Düriye on the streets, at the market? And how would

Vasillis respond if the Lapithos Turk who occupied Vasillis's house refused to return it, and if they met in the coffeeshop? Would they play a friendly game of backgammon?

I suggested to the Greek Cypriot mayor that it wouldn't be a bad idea if, before voting on the plan, they were to discuss its local implications with their former neighbors who still lived in the town. His reply was that while it wouldn't be a bad idea in principle, the Turkish Cypriots would have to come to them, in the "free areas." His answer was in consonance with one of the stated aims of the Lapithos refugee association, which is "cooperation with those Turkish Cypriot organizations and Turkish Cypriots who desire liberation from the Turkish army of invasion and occupation." This was also why it was possible for the Kyrenia municipalities to unite in rejecting the plan, saying that they would "negotiate a better plan for both Greek Cypriots and Turkish Cypriots."

In institutions of memory, then, the primary way in which a sense of temporariness is created is by emphasizing Turkey as an occupying invader which has unjustly seized their lands and so must leave, at the same time magically erasing the will of Turkish Cypriots with whom they have lived in the past. So, in the period before the opening of the checkpoints, Greek Cypriots would often ask foreigners who could cross to the north to take photographs of their villages, of their houses, and some of these made their way into the memory books that they published to record life before tragedy. In a memory book published for Lapithos in 2000, photographs of buildings in disrepair and broken tombstones are accompanied by a narrative that summarizes the current condition of the town. The narrative describes its current residents, the state of many of its buildings, the development of a touristic area near the sea on Turkish Cypriot land, as well as the relative abandonment of agricultural pursuits. For someone who knew Lapithos before, the narrative asserts, the state of the town is cause for both disappointment and hope:

> There is disappointment because of the general state that one sees, and hope that the temporary residents, the Turkish Cypriots and the settlers, are disinterested in the town, in its houses and its buildings, simply because they feel that they're not their own. There's a general sense of waiting and uncertainty. Neither the tourist development, especially on Turkish Cypriot land, nor the statue of Atatürk in the center of the town, across from the Mantidi house, nor the many Turkish flags change the impression gained by such a visitor.

This narrative is the first time in more than 250 pages that Turkish Cypriots had been mentioned, and although it makes mention of the "native" Turkish Cypriots, and to hotels built on Turkish Cypriot land, it also repeatedly refers to Turkish Cypriots and Turkish settlers living now in the town as its "temporary residents" (*prosorinoi katoikoi*).

This of course emphasizes a vision of the future that is consonant with a return to "the way things once were." In that vision, Turkish Cypriots must also have such a desire, must wish for "liberation from the Turkish army of invasion and occupation." Indeed, in both official and semi-official books, stories, pamphlets, and other narratives that describe lost villages, it is difficult not to be struck by the forceful, constant presence of Turkey and the peculiar absence of Turkish Cypriots. In such narratives, Turkish Cypriots become, by necessity, either oppressed by Turkey or its puppets, but in any case persons without will, ghostly figures in a landscape of memory.

In the opening of the checkpoints, one of the problems for people such as Eleni and even Vasillis was the sudden reappearance of Turkish Cypriots who did not fit the "temporary residents" of their imaginations. Indeed, Turkish Cypriots have been an absence that, in the opening of the checkpoints and the encounters that followed, has had the capacity to become an uncanny one. As one scholar writing about Israeli national histories as taught in schools observed, "Palestinians are not their significant other. . . . [T]hey are instead an uncanny other, not fully recognised, not fully known, somehow magically imagined away, and for all these reasons that much more frightening."

Indeed, in glancing through memory books of lost towns and villages, and other semi-official writings about the "occupied areas," it is hard not to be struck by the way that these books trace the permanent presence of Greek Cypriots through an emphasis on those places' historical Greekness, thus by necessity marginalizing Turkish Cypriots who may have lived in their midst. It was not only, then, an encounter with a lost wholeness but also the uncanny encounter with an absence that suddenly became a presence that threatened to change institutionalized narratives of temporariness.

A close friend who has worked for many years in the bicommunal movement told me that her six-year-old niece came to her one day in early 2005 with a drawing of Bellapais Abbey, the old crusader monastery to which I had taken Maroulla. It was in the former Greek Cypriot village where Lawrence Durrell lived and wrote his colonial diatribe, *Bitter Lemons*. It has since become a quaint, crowded tourist destination. My friend's niece had learned about Bellapais in her class at school, and she had been asked to draw it.

My friend said to her, "*I'll take you there one day soon, and you can see it for yourself.*" "*Oh, no, we can't go there!*" her niece replied, horrified. When my friend asked her why not, the little girl answered, "*Because it's occupied by the Turkish army, and they won't let us in.*"

My friend told me this story to complain about the Greek Cypriot educational system. But at the same time it expresses only one of the more egregious extremities in the spectrum of belief. Certainly, the little girl's teachers would expect her to learn relatively soon that it is, indeed, possible to go to the village, to tour the abbey, to sit with the other tourists in the coffeeshop where Durrell once sat. But her teachers want her to experience that visit in a particular way, through a framework that sees that village as "occupied," "enslaved," and unavailable to Greek Cypriots until it is fully reclaimed through its restoration to its "rightful" owners.

Slogans such as "I Do Not Forget" have not fully died, then, but have taken on new meanings with the opening of the checkpoints. Whereas before 2003 "Dhen Xechno" referred to an anticipated revival and recreation of a lost life that would take place at the moment of return, what is emphasized now is the slogan's more abstract meaning, asking refugees not to forget about the violation of their rights. Before 2003 "Dhen Xechno" had a very concrete meaning, recalling a neighbor's voice, a familiar path through the mountains, Sunday gatherings after church. For almost three decades, Greek Cypriot political parties and refugee organizations encouraged their constituents to believe that their villages remained unchanged, or that they would easily return to the way they once were. Reports circulated of violated churches, ruined cemeteries, changed roads and houses. But still, many people continued to think of their villages as they were when they left them, and those fantasies of an idyllic village life were buttressed by school assignments, television documentaries about lost villages, and memory books, which inevitably describe the ancient history of villages but focus on the village as it was on the day that it was lost.

At the same time, the slogan calls for struggle, and it is this meaning that has come to the fore since the checkpoints opened. It is not enough to say now that "*I don't forget*"; one has to say this as a denial of the present, a refusal to participate in less than full return. Its meaning is now more abstract, oriented toward a future recreated from the past. As Anna put it to me, in discussing the Annan Plan, "*The image I have of Lapithos is a beautiful one. Either everything will go back to the way it once was, or we will continue to live in our dreams.*" Not forgetting, then, means much more than simply remembering. It now means the capacity to deny the present's transformative influence on the past.

From the balcony of her Nicosia home, apart from the village that she had lost, the other thing that the grandmother I had met so many years before can see when she stares across the plain are two stars and crescents etched across a wide swath of mountainside facing the south. The flag of the Turkish Republic of Northern Cyprus painted on the mountainside is so large that it is visible from space, a red star and crescent on white, and next to it the remnants of what was once the Turkish flag and is now only another star and crescent with the inscription, *Ne Mutlu Türküm Diyene*," "How happy is he who says, "I am a Turk."" The location of these symbols is obviously not accidental, since the flag serves as both a reminder and a taunt to any Greek Cypriot who raises her eyes to look at the land that for three decades was inaccessible to them. And although the red of the Turkish flag has been allowed to fade, since the opening of the checkpoints the TRNC flag has been illuminated at night, in a shifting electrical display that outlines both the Turkish and TRNC flags and that dominates the Nicosia horizon.

As with other violent rendings, the division of Cyprus in 1974 not only tore people from land but reinvented landscapes, marking them with new signs that, whether in their pathos or their power, either excluded others or were directed at them. Greek Cypriots have called this reinvention in the north a form of Turkification, as the place names that they knew were replaced with Turkish ones, and monuments to Atatürk and Turkish Cypriot martyrs multiplied. After the opening of the checkpoints, Turkish and Turkish Cypriot flags both multiplied and increased in size, a way of stamping the landscape that was also a message to Greek Cypriots wishing to cross.

In Lapithos, this sometimes took the form of Turkish Cypriots hanging flags outside their houses in an attempt to discourage their Greek owners from visiting. One of these was Hüseyin Amca, who was already keen on displays of flags before the border opened but whose flags, like those of other people I knew, grew larger and more visible after the opening. A close friend who had known the family many years introduced me to him, confessing to me that she used to love to listen to him recite the Qur'an. He is the grandson of an imam and has long roots in the town, and I would often see him emerging from the lower mosque on Friday mornings. Even on other days, he often pressed a skullcap onto the back of his balding head, something done in Turkey but less frequently seen in Cyprus. He has also inherited the voice of a muezzin, and his voice resonates deep in his chest and bellows when excited.

Hüseyin was injured in 1974 and still has pieces of shrapnel lodged in his skull; even the army doctors in Ankara had been unable to remove them. When I first encountered him, he seemed to me severe, until he grinned at me in his boyish way. I soon discovered that despite the central importance for him of his identity as a fighter, his way of describing it is that of a boy, jumping from his chair to imitate machine-gun fire. His wife Ayşe wasn't fond of these outbursts of war-play and would shake her head, but she indulged him. Despite his gruffness, he joked with her and helped in the kitchen, and I often saw them share the same plate as they ate.

"*I know he's too much,*" his daughter told me later. "*He's pretty fanatical.*" Much of his life now centers on his work for the Şehit Aileleri ve Malül Gaziler Derneği, the Association of Martyrs' Families and Disabled Veterans. This is an organization that publishes material about atrocities committed against Turkish Cypriots and that closely allies itself to the politics of Rauf Denktaş, who remains for many such veterans a legendary hero. The far right wing of the group blends into the *ülkücüler*, or extremist nationalists of Turkey, many of whom were brought to Cyprus to intimidate voters during the Annan Plan referendum. Hüseyin's own sister whispered to me at one point that they would destabilize the new Turkish government before they would let it sell out Cyprus.

Hüseyin Amca was the regional representative of the association, and he would attend all the ceremonies and festivities, all the celebrations of victories and dates of mourning for atrocities. But his boyish grin told me something else. "*He spoke Greek like a Greek,*" his daughter whispered to me. "*All his friends were Greek.*" When her parents married, his daughter told me, "*All his Greek friends came, and they danced together for days.*" But by 1963 even those friendships had gone sour, and it was the same friends who came and threatened him. It was then that he decided to join TMT. "*They wouldn't take me at first,*" he confessed to me. "*I had too many Greek friends.*" But soon he was in training, and then they fled with the other Lapithos Turks for the enclave in Boğaz, where as a young man of about twenty he became a professional *mücahit*, or fighter. Many of his tales were ones of a young man's daring, facing down superior weaponry and living a life in constant fear of death.

The enclave period is one about which Greek Cypriots knew and continue to know very little, but knowing about it is important to understand the forms that life in the north of Cyprus has taken since. It was a militarized life that was formed by a constant sense of threat that for men like Hüseyin

shaped a decade of his youth and defined his identity. By early 1964, Turkish Cypriots had already begun to establish a state within a state, complete
with its own bureaucracy, its own police, even its own post office and post-
age stamps. This state within a state was virtually the only source of income
for the ninety percent of Turkish Cypriots who retreated to enclaves during
this period. Men received a small salary as *mücahitler*, or fighters, and many
teenage boys recruited into the struggle went to school during the day and
into the mountains at night. Many of these young men were rewarded for
their efforts with university scholarships in Turkey, where large numbers of
them were also radicalized by Turkey's growing leftist movements of the early
1970s.

Women became dependent on the men and their state in a way that they
had not been in the past. Women worked for the struggle, mostly by cooking
and sewing, but did not expect or receive a salary. Young girls were also recruited into the ranks of the *mücahitler*, and most girls learned in school how
to load and fire a gun. Many women participated in other, everyday ways.
One woman who was a child in the Limassol enclave told me that her father
would come home exhausted from his guard duties and that it was her job to
clean his rifle and bullets while he slept. Stores and businesses remained open
in the cities, such as Nicosia, Limassol, and Paphos, but these businesses, too,
were dependent upon a Turkish clientele and hence on the goodwill of the
Turkish Cypriot administration. The clientelism and dependence on the state
that emerged in this period would have repercussions later.

In 1968 leaders of both sides signed an agreement that allowed for more
freedom of movement, and Turkish Cypriots began to return during daylight
hours to their villages to water their orchards, and in some cases to take jobs
as day laborers. Again, women were often afraid to leave the enclaves, fearing
mostly the checkpoints where they might be searched. Men who went to water
their fields and orchards invariably returned the same day. The effects of this
isolation and fear were wearing, and many people reported a desire to leave but
a discouragement from doing so on the part of their own people, supported by
a Turkish government that provided subsidies to the Yavruvatan, the Babyland,
as Cyprus was often affectionately if condescendingly known.

For the ten years of their exile, Hüseyin and his family stayed with many
of the Lapithos Turks in the Boğaz enclave in the mountains between Nicosia
and Kyrenia. The enclave abutted a Turkish military camp that had only a
small force that was prevented by international treaty from intervening in the
fighting. However, Turkish Cypriot fighters received advice and training, and

Turkey used such camps to bring dried goods to the island to distribute to the enclaved Turkish Cypriots. Hüseyin fought in the outpost that the *mücahitler* had established at St. Hilarion, an old crusader castle that they had been able to claim because of its proximity to the military base.

Everyone waited for the intervention of Turkey, and there were many moments when they believed that Turkey was about to intervene. There were songs, sayings, and folk legends that reflected the desire for Turkey's military intervention. Many older women told me that their constant prayers eventually brought the Turkish army. Folktales from the period commonly describe such prophecies or prophetic signs of Turkey's arrival. Many men and women describe weeping with joy and running to greet the arriving Turkish forces when the intervention finally came. Indeed, Turkey's intervention is described in apocalyptic histories, histories that foretell its coming and mark that moment as the end of time, the closure of one history and the beginning of another. In such stories, Turkey's arrival was like the coming of the apocalypse, *kıyamet günü* or the day of judgment, when all wrongs would be righted and a new history would begin.

When that day did come, Turkish Cypriot fighters were immediately incorporated into the army, leading Turkish soldiers into the villages and helping them interrogate Greek Cypriot prisoners. As always seems to happen in war, many Greek Cypriots have tales of Turkish friends who saved them, but there are also many stories of retribution. Although for many years Greek Cypriots, both officially and privately, wished to believe that much of the violence committed against their loved ones during this period was done by the Turkish army, information that has begun to be revealed since the border opening points to many Greek Cypriot deaths at the hands of their former neighbors.

At the time of the invasion, there were very few villages in the north of the island that remained mixed. As in Lapithos, most Turks from mixed villages had fled to Turkish villages or protected areas in early 1964, and so ten years later the flight of Greek Cypriots from their homes in the north occasioned a refashioning of much of the northern part of the island. Many more homes were left empty than could be used, even by Turkish Cypriots fleeing from the south. The Turkish Cypriot administration quickly put in motion a system for distributing property by lot, returning Turkish Cypriot refugees from the north to their own villages and settling refugees from the south in villages that seemed to resemble their places of origin. Lapithos Turks like Hüseyin and his family received houses in this original distribution and moved into the homes of their former Greek neighbors, their own homes unlivable after their destruction in 1964 and ten years of neglect.

Many people, though, ignored the lottery; they simply found houses that they liked and squatted. It was in that way, it seems, that part of the current social geography of Lapithos emerged. Indeed, all the Turkish Cypriots originally from Lapithos were given or chose houses in the lower levels of the village, near their own former homes, while Turkish Cypriots coming from other parts of the island gravitated toward these same neighborhoods. Later, many Turkish Cypriots, especially refugees from the south, began to complain that the system ignored what they had left behind. In response, the administration instituted a point system, giving remaining property on the basis of "exchange points" (*eşdeğer puanları*) for those who had left property in the south and "fighter's points" (*mücahit puanları*) for those who had fought. They also distributed some property directly to the families of those who had lost loved ones. Some people were able to use these points to acquire property for their children, which is how a close friend obtained a magnificent stone house on a hillside that had once been a small hotel. And because Lapithos was an important battleground with many losses for the Turkish army, the town now has more than its fair share of martyrs' families, families from Turkey that were given property because of a son lost in the war.

And just as Turkish settlers renamed the streets in the upper quarters after folk singers and areas of Turkey, many other streets of the town were named after "martyrs"—Turkish Cypriots killed at some point between 1958 and 1974. These were either locals, original Lapithiotes, or martyrs with parents now living in the town. The two main arteries of the town, for instance, are named for İbrahim Nidai and Şevket Kadir, the two young Turkish men who by all reports were killed in an area not far from the town. The death of these two young men had been symbolic of the real beginning of the struggle and the moment when Lapithos Turks decided to flee. Some streets also bear the names of fighters from Turkey who were killed in the military intervention and whose families were given property in the town.

Lapithos had once been dominated by neohellenic architecture; streets named for legendary Greek heroes; a large monument to the EOKA struggle in the center of the town; ancient, wealthy churches; potters who made replicas of ancient Greek vases and pitchers; and a social life punctuated by festivals, plays, and musical performances celebrating "national" days and "national" themes, meaning Greek national days and themes from Greek history. After 1974, the town was divided into Turkish Cypriots in the lower quarters and

Turkish immigrants and eventually foreigners in the upper quarters. The names of Greek heroes were replaced by Turkish martyrs. A statue of Atatürk was erected at one of the main entry points to the village, and a memorial to martyrs stands in the middle of a square in the busiest road. Greek businesses were quickly occupied by Turks, and their signs in Greek replaced by ones in Turkish. The two mosques were renovated, and the largest church in the village, Ayia Paraskevi, also became a mosque, serving the Turkish settler population in the upper quarters.

At the same time, the signs of the town's former Greek occupants were only partially erased. The monument to fallen EOKA heroes that interior minister Tassos Papadopoulos dedicated in 1960 still stands in the square in front of the municipal office, but its writing has been scratched out. As in many places in the island, one may still turn a corner and find political graffiti in Greek scrawled across a wall. Some signs in Greek were never removed, and the architecture of many of the houses still reflects the neohellenic fad that hit the middle classes of the island in the mid-twentieth century. Damaged cemeteries and churches decay in the middle of neighborhoods and on the sides of major thoroughfares.

The new life in the town was erected, then, through a constant recollection of the need to forget, to put the past behind. The town's former Greek inhabitants were half-remembered, but it was a violent remembrance, the traces left of them recalling the violence with which the town was taken. The half-erased monument to EOKA heroes stands on a street that was renamed after Şevket Kadir, a young man who was loved by both Turkish and Greek Cypriots in the community and who everyone says was never part of the TMT struggle. His name becomes a constant recollection of a loss of innocence, lived today by Hüseyin Amca and inscribed in the shape the town has taken.

A stroll through the town with someone such as Hüseyin leads to stories about power struggles internal to the Greek community; a Turk who was harassed by Greeks who wanted to buy his land; and a young Turkish woman who arrived from Paphos pregnant after being repeatedly raped by her Greek neighbors. Violation is written into the landscape not only as personal memory but as institutionalized remembrance. And this institutionalized remembrance takes the form of monuments and street names but also of the distribution of houses and privileges of which everyone is aware. İbrahim Nidai's sister occupies the house of a former official in retribution for the destruction of her own. Şevket Kadir's widow received a large house in a central location in recognition of her loss, and of the importance of that loss to the community. Other former fighters such as Hüseyin, or families of martyrs or wounded soldiers, such as Düriye, often discuss their sacrifices in relation to the rewards that they received. One common complaint in the period after the establishment of the new state was the unfair distribution of property. But the discussion itself keeps those sacrifices constantly in view, as people weigh them and evaluate them against those of others.

In a similar way, young men who fought with TMT received salaries and an education, and many were given work in the new administration. The new administration gave pensions to the families of martyrs, though there was initially complaint about the form of their distribution. Not only the martyr's spouse, but also his parents and children received a small amount of money each month, though there were soon complaints about the law that required spouses to remain unmarried in order to receive that money. As one former TMT fighter put it to me, "*Now a number of the spouses stayed the course, they didn't diverge from it. But another section had partners, had friends, had children without marrying. . . . In those first days it was a really bad situation. A really bad situation. But when our administrators became aware of it, they immediately changed that law. And it was just against nature. It was against human nature.*" Soon, then, widows were able to start life anew without losing recognition of their initial sacrifice for the community.

Throughout the new society, then, Turkish Cypriots were tied to the administration, to their new homes, and to their new communities in ways that also entailed a constant remembrance of their sacrifices. Arguments about the fair distribution of resources centered on the measurement of those sacrifices, whether material or personal. Turkish Cypriots formed associations of former fighters, and associations of refugees formed not for purposes of remembrance but rather to achieve a fairer distribution of Greek property and the issuance of title deeds. Once the government began to issue title deeds in 1995, those associations disbanded. Similarly, the Turkish Cypriot equivalent of the Greek memory book describes not lost villages but the missing and the dead. These are volumes that emphasize not a wound but a rupture, not a temporary state to be healed but the permanence of death. These are compendia that argue not for recreating the past but for forgetting it.

As with the slogan "Dhen Xechno," many Turkish Cypriots may now joke that it's very difficult to find a house on a street that's not named for a martyr. Many are weary of the constant recollection of suffering, the insistent invocation of the dead. But since the checkpoints' opening, and especially in response to a Greek Cypriot emphasis on keeping wounds alive, Turkish Cy-

priots have also begun to emphasize their suffering anew. Now, though, they
have begun to emphasize their suffering not only as sacrifice but as struggle,
not as a past that was completed but as a past that must not be allowed to
return.

I had actually met my muhtar, Salih Usta, quite early in my research, long before I went to live in Lapta. I had returned to the island at the height of summer, just a handful of months after the border opening, and a friend took me
to Salih's workshop, where we swatted at stinging flies in the afternoon heat as
Salih sent one of his workmen upstairs to fetch a book. Twenty-one Turks of
Lapithos had been killed, he insisted. That was why they left. He opened the
book and quickly flipped through it, showing us the black-and-white faces
of the now dead. He pointed a thick finger at the photo of an old man with
voluminous mustaches. The caption under the picture told the reader that he
was a shepherd killed by Greek co-villagers in 1958, while herding his flocks
in the mountains. He was from the next village, Vasillia, just a short walk
away from Lapta.

"His daughter Pembe's alive, but she lost an arm," Salih told me. *"You should
go and talk to her. She'll tell you all about the Greeks."* Others would later tell
me the same thing, encouraging me to go and talk to Pembe, to learn how vicious the Greeks could be. I never did so, and without doing so it was difficult
to understand how Pembe lost her arm, given that her father was supposed to
have been killed while alone in the mountains.

Photographs circulate, stories circulate, and even the details of deaths appear infinitely malleable. Many people told me about a family of seven from
Vasillia killed by being thrown into a well. It was the first of January 1964,
when the Turks of Lapithos were huddled in several protected houses, waiting to see what their fate would be. I had heard by then that intercommunal
relations in Vasillia were poor, and I had no reason to doubt that the family had been killed somewhere outside the village, not such a distance from
where the Lapithos Turks hid. It also explained much of their fear.

It was only much later, when I acquired my own copy of the muhtar's book
and began to peruse it, that I saw that the family had been killed not in their
own village but in Livera, now called Sadrazamköy, several miles away in the
Kormakiti peninsula. What was the meaning of omitting this seemingly significant fact? Was it that, for the frightened Turks in 1964, this fact made no
difference? Was it that they knew who had killed them, and that they were

indeed co-villagers, even if the deaths took place away from the village? Was it that they wanted the story to make more of an impact on me?

It seems likely that it was all and none of these reasons. I quickly learned that only the two young men, İbrahim Nidai and Şevket Kadir, had been killed while living in Lapithos, though there were other martyrs that Lapithiotes counted as their own because of their roots in the town. On the day that I went to ask the mayor about these numbers, he gave me a list of sixty-one names, with names of thirty-five Turkish Cypriots in blue and those of twenty-six soldiers from Turkey in red. Yet when I took the list to Hüseyin Amca, the local representative of the Assocation of Martyrs' Families and Disabled Veterans, he recognized only three of the Turkish Cypriot names. Like Salih Usta's assertion that twenty-one Lapithos Turks had been killed, there was clearly a complex relation between knowing and not knowing, between the certainty I sought and the uncertainty the stories represent. There is a diffuseness in the stories, where meaning appears to run beyond the bounds of words or facts and to say, "*It could have been any of us. Or all of us.*" Like the brutal representations of the dead that used to be so common throughout northern Cyprus, these lists of names call upon one simply to accept without question their mute witness.

What these names point to is not a form of certainty but rather an uncertainty, something beyond their bounds. The mute witness of these lists of names seems to point to an unidentified threat, the constant possibility of recurrence. They point to an absent presence, that of their former Greek neighbors, an other that is always there and yet cannot be seen or fully known. This was, in more explicit forms, the argument that former TRNC president Runf Denktaş and official histories made for the permanence of division: namely, the ever-present threat of an absent other whose motives could never be known or trusted. And so in official rhetoric and representations, burned and bloody bodies not only portray their suffering but equally point to a threat beyond the frame.

Perhaps the most famous example is a nondescript house in the Kumsal district of Nicosia that has gained infamy as the Museum of Barbarism. It was the site of what is known as the Kumsal massacre, the famous murder of a woman and her three children as they hid in a bath in their home. The woman was the wife of a Turkish army doctor, and she and her three children were murdered in early 1964. Photographs were projected around the world, the house was turned into a Museum of Barbarism, and the story was repeated as the most horrible instance of Greeks' capacity for atrocity.

Today, as one enters the museum, one encounters a catalog of unspeakable suffering: photographs of partial and burned bodies, destroyed villages, children crying in front of tents. In some photographs, inconsolable women wail. In one room to the right of the entrance is a large slab on one wall on which are engraved the names of martyrs from the 1963–64 period. But anyone entering the house already knows that the museum's centerpiece is at the rear, in the bathroom. For it is there that the bullets and even the blood from the Kumsal massacre have been preserved. Photographs show the three children and their mother huddled in the bath, pieces of flesh torn away by the force of the bullets. The bloodied bathrobe and pajamas that they wore are preserved under a glass case, and the bloodstains, though faded, still form a recognizable pattern on the walls.

"*I refuse to go there*," a friend who lives near the memorial told me. Many people I know clucked over the fact that teachers take their small pupils on visits to the museum. "*It's just breeding chauvinism*," they complained. As a result, a recent book that charged that it was not Greek officers but Turkish ones who killed the army officer's wife and children, was taken very seriously. It was discussed in the Turkish Cypriot newspapers, where the evidence was seriously weighed. Back in Lapithos, Fadime Teyze complained to me, "*Have you heard what they're saying? Those poor little babies, and they're saying we may have had them killed*." Her voice reached a keening wail as she talked about the innocent children, as she asked if I had seen the house. I was able to say that I had. Other people whispered, "*What do you think? Could it be?*" Even most of those who complained of the extremism of the museum could not believe the assertions, and even my friend who refused to visit the museum later told me that she knew one of the survivors and so affirmed that it couldn't be true.

Before the checkpoints opened, such caricatured uses of suffering had already lost their effectiveness, especially for the youth, and were being called into question. One important reason for this was the way that such images froze the past in the present, seeming to prevent them from moving on to the future. And so, paradoxically, these images which aimed at reminding Turkish Cypriots to forget a past with their former Greek neighbors were countered with the claim that it was "*time to put the past behind us*." Until this time, suffering had been emphasized as sacrifice, where Turkish Cypriot dead seemed to be placed on the pyre of the past. In these narratives, the arrival of Turkish troops appeared to be the end of history, the beginning of a new history in which Turkish Cypriots had been "liberated," in which their migration to the north was an *özgürlük göçü*, a "freedom migration." But as Turkish Cypriots began to feel more and more that they lived not in freedom but in what they began to call an "open-air prison," as they began more and more to see the power that had liberated them as an oppressor, they began to see that the past was not finished but in fact threatened to return.

One way in which it threatened to return was through breeding chauvinism that could lead to further conflict. The crude representations of suffering that implied a barbarian other beyond the frame began to seem an old-fashioned nationalism, out of step with the times, and young people were at the forefront of a movement intended to remove from power the *statükocular*, or those who had tried for so long to maintain the status quo. The "status quo" came to signify the unchanging present, the present mired in a past that had been insistently forgotten. Now, many voices said that the only way really to put the past behind was not through forgetfulness but through remembrance. Before the opening of the checkpoints, many people began to call for recognition of the other's suffering, a recognition that would give that other humanity and so allow them finally to forget.

"*Putting the past behind us,*" then, meant acknowledging everyone's suffering and moving toward the future. Indeed, even before the checkpoints opened, Nicosia officials removed photographs at the Ledra Palace checkpoint that showed Turkish Cypriots who had been murdered. Not long after that, Turkish Cypriot educators worked to change the history textbooks, attempting to eliminate elements that might promote chauvinism. Especially after the checkpoints opened, most people expected some form of reciprocity, that Greek Cypriots would also want to "*forget the past*" in the interests of creating a common future. This is what so many people meant when they repeated that "*France and Germany put the past behind them, and we can, too.*" But Turkish Cypriots were soon disappointed to find that their own attempts to forget the past met with no reciprocity, as all the signs and symbols on the other side of the checkpoint remained intact, and schoolbooks remained unchanged. Indeed, in some quarters of Greek Cypriot society, changes in Turkish Cypriot representations of the past were seen as concessions, admissions of the "real" history.

Despite their own weariness with the constant invocation of suffering, many Turkish Cypriots expressed astonishment at Greek Cypriots' inability to "*put the past behind us.*" And by a year after the referendum, they were faced with a new intrusion of the past into the present: a number of Greek Cypriots opened lawsuits against foreigners and Turkish Cypriots for use of their property in the north, using the open checkpoints to deliver summonses. Many

Turkish Cypriots in Lapta began to feel under threat, and almost all of the younger people with whom I spoke complained that "*we've changed, but now we see they haven't changed.*" They soon began to see that forgetting the past and moving on to the future was not possible unilaterally but depended also on the acknowledgment of their former neighbors.

Fadime Teyze's daughter, Emine, lives in Lapta but teaches in a Nicosia high school. She was only a baby when they fled to the Boğaz enclave, and her husband, also originally from Lapta, is only a few years her senior. "*We don't really remember the Greeks,*" she told me. "*We don't remember living with them.*" Like so many of the Lapithos Turks in her age group, she protested for peace and voted in favor of the Annan Plan because she was tired of being mired in the "status quo" and wanted to give her children a better future. But by a year after the referendum, she was brimming over with anger and fear.

"*In this forty-year period, unfortunately, the world has changed so much, but for Turkish Cypriots nothing's changed,*" she complained. "*Nothing's changed! Again today, we said 'yes' to the Annan Plan, we destroyed a lot of the taboos, and still they have us in a vise! They're still squeezing! This is what I don't understand. We've been under this pressure for generations. And there's nothing for us. But I say this is probably the result of our leaders' wrong-headed politics. We couldn't explain ourselves, probably. And I protest this! Why should this Cypriot people always be a victim, always be the trampled upon? At this point, I'm the one who should be screaming to the world [instead of only the Greek Cypriots]. We were born, grew up, and are dying in this cattle pen.*"

Nationalist discourse had been shaken by the time of the checkpoints' opening, but with the visits of Greek Cypriots and especially their rejection of a plan for reunification, Turkish Cypriots began again to emphasize their own suffering, this time as a challenge to what they saw as an attempt to erase it. "*Of course they suffered, but we suffered more,*" I heard repeatedly. And this would inevitably be followed by the conclusion, "*We have to put the past behind us. We don't want to go back.*" It was in this moment that their own suffering was remade and brought back, now not as sacrifice but as struggle.

Fighters' unions again became vocal; large flags and new monuments began to appear. Among the intellectual classes, this revival of nationalism was blamed on the Turkish army, even though it was clear that many of the new monuments and memorials were sponsored by Turkish Cypriots, ones who now emphasized not a nationalism bred in Turkey but a very local Turkish Cypriot nationalism, a dedication to the unrecognized state for which they had fought. An enclave nostalgia developed during this period, as writers in newspapers opined a time when "*everyone had worked together.*" New books appeared, and memoirs by fighters and local histories of enclave life began to give substance to their suffering, now not only as sacrifice but as a struggle that they had undertaken together.

Although symbols that emphasized sacrifice were largely rejected, those that emphasized struggle were reclaimed. This also took the form of defending the everyday symbols of that struggle, such as the houses where they now live and the privileges they now claim. In the face of what they now began to see as an attempt by the "other side" to erase them, a refusal to recognize their suffering, many Turkish Cypriots with whom I spoke began to insist on their own suffering, not as material for chauvinism but as a way of reclaiming presence and a capacity for struggle in the present. It was especially in this moment that "*putting the past behind us*" began to mean preventing the past's return.

In the north, institutionalized traces of violence have encouraged forgetting through a combination of ubiquity and inattention. Although martyrs' names are everywhere, only a few of those names are recognizable, and there has been no systematic attempt to make them recognizable. One may live in a Greek Cypriot home where the traces of its owners are only half erased. Although a new reality was built on the ruins of the past, reminders of the need to forget were visible not only in flags and memorials, not only in pension checks and housing for martyrs' families, but in the reminders of an absent presence visible in half-effaced monuments, the ruins of cemeteries, and the house where one now lives. Like words whose meanings change, even though these symbols may lose the former force of forgetfulness, they may be reinvented as the language of a struggle to prevent the past's return.

In the south, songs and plays celebrating lost villages; memorial services that proceed like funerals; and memory books that attempt to recollect the village in all its quotidian detail suggest a need to remember that in its attention to certain details is inattentive to others. Turkish Cypriots are not a part of memory books, just as they are not a part of most recollections of life before their departure. In those books' descriptions of the town's history, the Ottoman period is one of spilled blood, seized land, and brave Lapithiotes' participation in the 1821 struggle for Greek independence. Turkish Cypriots may have lived in the town, but they are absent from the town's history.

Eleni spends her time painting cypress trees bathed in light, as she remembers them. Anna invests her life in the poetry of the everyday, and in writing children's books that will teach about their lost lands. Many people talked to me about the system for distributing water in the town, a system now in ruins. Others return to their homes to try to find traces of what once was. It is the details that are sustaining, but it is that attention to detail that also masks forgetfulness. The constant reminders of that other life make it seem as though there is nothing else that may have been forgotten.

Not long before the checkpoints opened, Greek Lapithiotes chose to commemorate their town with a memorial near the Ledra Palace checkpoint, just next to where the Kyrenia municipality now stands. Even Greek-speaking Turkish Cypriots usually cannot read the language, and so most are unaware that the statue commemorates the "Lady of Lapithos," a heroine who saved the lives of twelve Greek soldiers during the Turkish military intervention by taking food to them as they hid in a cave in the mountains outside the village. This is seen as an act of incomparable bravery, and her success at it is attributed in part to the fact that she had been a midwife who traveled throughout the surrounding villages and spoke some Turkish. What it erases is the fact that Turkish Cypriots who had already returned to the town saw what she was doing but chose to ignore it, letting her make her trips to the mountain each day where they understood that the soldiers were hiding.

But the statue, inscribed with the other common slogan, "Agonas—Lefteria—Epistrofi," "Struggle—Freedom—Return," stands not only as a memorial to a moment in history but also as a tribute to the power of memory. It is often bedecked with fresh flowers, and it was erected in such a way that the "Lady of Lapithos" looks directly through the Ledra Palace checkpoint and across the ceasefire line to the north. The struggle that the statue represents is against the invader, the Turkish army, and that is still a reason to maintain such a statue even in the presence of Turkish Cypriots who now cross the checkpoints each day and pass the statue on their way to shop or to work. Turkish Cypriots do not seem to notice the statue, and in any case it is not aimed at them. It is another reminder of the struggle, another trace of resistance against the power of forgetting and the possibility of permanence.

Pension checks for martyrs' families; houses that once belonged to others; monuments to Greek heroes; other monuments to victims of those Greek heroes; paintings and poetry; sports teams that bear the names of lost villages; broken tombstones; a Turkish kilim thrown across Cypriot tiles—all these elements of daily life have come to be imbued not only with a pathos but with a politics. They have not only become part of habit; they have become so familiar that they mask the reasons for their own familiarity. They are familiar because we already know and understand the relationship to the past that they describe. It is such a familiar relationship that we do not need to ask why streets are named after martyrs or why statues may testify to a struggle for return.

In the familiarity of that world we learn to feel at home, taking for granted the premises of its politics and the discourse of its disputes. It shapes the landscape of our lives in such a way that other landscapes seem unfamiliar to us. And in such a way we may overlook that remembrance is selective, that forgetting requires recall, and that absence is not loss but rather the specter of that which may yet return.

SIX

The Spoils of History

I HAD BEEN LIVING in Lapta for several months when I got a call from Vasillis one day on my Turkish number. When I heard his voice, my immediate thought was for the expense of the call, which would be billed as international. As far as I could tell, he and Maroulla probably lived off a small government pension, supplemented by their goats and olive trees, and no doubt by a bit of money from their son. I felt guilty when he told me that he had called several times on my other number; I hadn't gone to Nicosia in some time and so hadn't checked it.

He told me that they wanted to come to visit, and we set a date when I would pick them up from a church on the southern side of the checkpoint. I expected to be in Nicosia that day, but the opportunity to interview someone I had been trying to track down kept me in Lapithos the night before. I was about forty-five minutes late to the church; they had been waiting almost two hours.

The day was hot, and I felt that my being late had created an uncomfortable atmosphere. We drove this time in the direction of Morphou, circling around to the west of the mountains and approaching the town from the mouth of the Kormakiti peninsula. Vasillis tried to break the ice by telling me about the villages through which we passed—their histories, the ways in which they had been divided. Although Maroulla was clearly upset with me, Vasillis wanted to put a good face on things, perhaps because this time around we had business together. The Annan Plan had failed, but Vasillis was still determined to return. He would return even if it meant renting a room, or a house. He would spend his small savings to return to the land that was his birthright.

8. Antique shop in north Cyprus.

The home that Vasillis and Maroulla had built together lies on the main road from the sea into the town, a long, narrow stretch fronted by a row of houses, and behind them orchards. Before 1974, the land near the sea had been the most valuable, not because of its proximity to the beach but because of its productivity. According to most accounts, it was at one time covered in productive citrus orchards, and Lapithiotes sold their lemons in markets across Europe. Today many of the fields are barren, many of the trees withered. A 1994 European Court of Justice decision forbidding the import to Europe of citrus bearing the TRNC stamp meant a change of local economic strategy. *"We used to make money selling our citrus,"* one old man, a refugee from Paphos, told me. *"We could send our children to school, get them married. Now all we can do is sell the land."*

When I first lived in north Cyprus in 1995, Greek lands were occupied mostly by Turkish Cypriots and Turks from Turkey, with only a smattering of foreigners renovating the village houses on long-term leases. At that time, north Cyprus was still a sleepy place, full of rattling, ancient cars and shops selling clothes no longer quite in fashion. The fairly small community of foreigners consisted mainly of British and German expatriates, many with ties to the island. Most of these ex-pats were more nationalistic about northern Cyprus than more cynical Turkish Cypriots tended to be. They read books such as Harry Scott Gibbons's *The Genocide Files* and English-language propaganda of the Turkish Cypriot leadership. They were informed, if in a lopsided way, about how the island had come to its current state, and when they began to take over Greek village houses on long-term leases and to restore them, they were taking a gamble that the Cyprus Problem would never be resolved.

By the late 1990s, sleepy northern Cyprus had begun to wake up a bit. In 1984, the government had begun to give what it called *kesin tasarruf*, a deed guaranteeing right to use, to those who presented title deeds for equivalent land in the south. By giving up those deeds, they were guaranteeing that they could pass the property to their children, even that they could sell the property in a limited way. In 1993, in response to pressures from those who had not been able to find the equivalent in "exchange points," the government began to distribute what it called *yükümlü koçan*, a type of title deed that could be gained through adding up other sorts of points, not only exchange points but also "fighter's points." And in 1995, the government allowed anyone living in Greek Cypriot homes to purchase the title for a pittance, finally allowing Turkish settlers and those who had not left property in the south to gain those titles, provoking a rash of sales and a flood of new properties on the real estate market.

Many Turkish Cypriots had long wanted the titles, but the government's decision also happened to coincide with increased tensions between north and south. At the time of the titles' distribution, there was a test case ongoing in the European Court of Human Rights, a case that had been brought by a Greek Cypriot against Turkey. A year later, in 1996, the court would accept the claim of a Greek Cypriot refugee, Titina Loizidou, that the Turkish army had illegally prevented her from returning to her home, and it demanded that Turkey pay compensation. That same summer, two young Greek Cypriot men would be killed as they tried to cross the buffer zone dividing the island, in a protest against Turkish occupation. As though in defiance of both events, the government in the north continued to issue titles that would ultimately have lasting effects both on the face of "occupation" and on any chances for a solution.

By the time I returned to Cyprus in late summer 2001 after a two-year absence, I found that the north of the island had sprouted an estate agent on every corner, many foreign or with foreign ties. Most of them were developers, and in some of the most beautiful areas of the north they had begun to chop down citrus orchards to build row after row of boxy little bungalows and rambling villas. The government in the north was unprepared for this boom, but it also appears to have turned a blind eye to something that would set an ailing economy on its feet again.

Foreigners began to snatch up property at what for them were bargain prices, and only a couple of years later, the announcement of the Annan Plan fueled this real estate explosion because of a clause that allowed persons who had engaged in "significant improvements" to keep the property. Turkish Cypriots appalled by the construction's effects on the environment nevertheless shrugged that as long as they were under embargo, they didn't have many choices. If they couldn't export goods, they could at least import buyers. And so foreigners began to be issued unrecognized titles to land in an unrecognized state. And after the checkpoints opened, Greek Cypriots began to find their dreams of return cluttered with bulldozers and bungalow complexes.

Vasillis and Maroulla were in such a position, and I admired their fortitude in the face of it. Maroulla's childhood home was given to a Turkish family as the spoils of war; Vasillis's childhood home was sold to a British couple that doesn't believe it was Greek; and the house they had built together belongs to a Lapithos Turk known to Vasillis who rents it as a daycare center. On top of it all, the lower lands near the sea where Vasillis had his orchards are now prime development property, since they're within walking distance of the beach. By the day we made this second visit, three bungalows were already being squeezed onto a narrow plot of land down the road from the daycare center. There was, then, a sense of urgency about things, and Vasillis said that he planned to sign on for the large case in the European Court of Human Rights that about fourteen hundred Greek Cypriots were bringing against Turkey. At the same time, he seemed genuinely to believe that going back to live in the town, reestablishing ties there, would be the first step toward full return.

On the day of this particular journey with them to Lapithos, we turned up the main road leading to their home, and Vasillis suddenly signaled that he wanted to stop. It was the house of his old friend Mustafa, he explained. Mustafa, it turns out, was from one of the wealthy Turkish families of Lapithos, and many of his fields were just across the road, several abutting Vasillis's own. The house where Mustafa lives, however, did not belong to him before the war, something I realized when they began to discuss visits from the house's Greek owners. When I later looked it up on Vasillis's map, I saw that it belonged to a member of a prominent Greek Cypriot family.

We sat on the front porch, where Mustafa's bed remained unmade. Mustafa had broken teeth, a dirty shirt, and a thick Cypriot Greek that I had trouble following. The two men had a pleasant enough conversation as we were served lemonade by a blonde Moldovan maid whose role in the house was dubious. The real subject of their conversation was the lower floor of the house, which was then empty. Could Vasillis come sometimes to stay there? Maroulla was taciturn, her face pinched. She didn't like Vasillis's obsession, and they often bickered in low voices about it.

"*Why not?*" Mustafa shrugged, and I was momentarily hopeful, even though there was something about Mustafa that I didn't particularly trust. For weeks I had tried to think of ways Vasillis might return to the town, the most recent of my schemes being an attempt to cut a deal with a Turkish Cypriot developer who advertised plans to build on what appeared to be Vasillis's land. A clean title for a finished house, perhaps?

But this would certainly be better, a renewal of old ties. It was with some swelling of hope that we left Mustafa and his Moldovan and followed the winding road to Ayia Paraskevi, where we once again drove through their old neighborhoods. When we had finished our visit, we descended through the town to the sea for a doleful lunch in a *kentron* that used to belong to Maroulla's cousin. It is now owned by a land speculator who had the sharp look of someone eyeing prey. I racked my brain for places to take them, people to introduce them to. This was supposed to be my role, after all: intermediary, conduit of information. Vasillis had insisted that he wanted to meet the Turkish Cypriots that I knew in the town, but I had a hard time thinking of ones who would be eager to meet him, who wouldn't wonder why I would put them through the imposition.

I finally thought of Şefika and Hamit, whom I had interviewed once. Hamit is a small, wiry, good-natured man, and Şefika is his sweet-faced bride from another village. Before bringing Maroulla and Vasillis to the house, I first made my way through the garden to the porch and asked Şefika's permission, telling her that Vasillis believed he knew Hamit. And indeed, the two men embraced warmly, although the two women were more reserved, ambivalent. Vasillis was very happy, and he told me that Hamit was a hard worker, that he used to work twenty-four hours a day. I recognized this as the supreme compliment that Vasillis intended it to be.

When we sat down to lemonade, Vasillis began again the theme of his scheme to return. Hamit and Şefika nodded but offered no advice. And there was of course the ever-present question of why Hamit and Şefika were not in their own house. "*No, this isn't our house,*" Şefika turned to me in Turkish, her voice tinged with defiance. "*We know it's not our house. But what do they want? Everyone can't just pick up and move again. Do you see this garden? Do you know how many hours went into this garden?*"

As we left, Şefika kissed me and gave me walnuts in sweet syrup that she had just made. She offered them to me, not to Maroulla, and I noticed the dour expression on Maroulla's face as we climbed back into the car. I knew then that I would not tell either one of them what Şefika had said.

A number of Turkish Cypriots I know have begun wryly to call the place where they now live a *ganimet ülkesi*, a country built on spoils. Indeed, I had only been in the town a short time when I began to hear them again and again—the stories of Turkish Cypriots' return to the town, and of the *ganimet*, or plunder, that followed. And it still remains hard for me to imagine this moment of what the Turkish Cypriots with whom I spoke seemed to perceive as their triumphant return: a moment when the fighting had barely paused, when many older Greek Cypriots unable or unwilling to leave still hid in their homes, and when the Turkish Cypriots returning from a decade lived in squalor claimed empty houses as their own and ransacked others for refrigerators and furniture. Were they at all concerned about the older Greek Cypriots they knew, who must have observed this frenzy with fear from behind half-closed curtains? What stories would the Greek Cypriots then enclaved there tell once they were forcibly sent to the south?

For most people, this period when they claimed their neighbors' homes appeared as the completion of a history, one that had begun with their own departure from their villages and the looting of their own homes. Indeed, in the north of the island, a new lexicon developed after the war to talk about what their fleeing neighbors had left behind. Listening to people describe the period, I soon began to realize that *ganimet* had a slightly different meaning from *yağma*, which also was used for spoils, but usually in the sense of "to pillage." So while Greek Cypriots had pillaged Turks' homes (*yağmadılar*), the word was less often used for what Turks themselves did in the wake of their neighbors' flight. *Ganimet* has the connotation of booty, the spoils of war. It is something that is *helal*, lawful or legitimate, in popular interpretations of Islam.

Ganimet is given context not only by the destruction of their own homes but also by the deprivation of the enclaves. So many people repeated to me that they had "fled naked," with little more than the clothes on their backs, and that in the enclaves they struggled to survive. According to Fadime Teyze, they were empty-handed when they left Lapithos, and when I asked her to try to describe their life in the enclaves, she cried, "*How did we manage to eat? How did we hold up? A three-month-old baby, it didn't know anything! How did we feed it? How did we bring it up? The* gavur *didn't know anything. Turkey sent everything, may Allah give Turkey strength. We got everything in shares— our lamb, our sugar, everything in shares. On the one hand shoes, on the other hand . . . beds—always beds of straw. Beds, blankets, we didn't take anything.*"

The story has a way of breaking down. Fadime Teyze's daughter Emine remembers that they struggled. "*It's not that we were starving—I don't remember starving. But it was always what we could get in sacks—dried foods. Beans, rice. Sometimes potatoes. At home we had our garden, we had every kind of fruit. Do you know how long I went without eating fruit? It wasn't that we were starving, but there was malnutrition. Some of us children started getting dark spots on our skin from the malnutrition.*" Others told me that they remembered eating nothing but potatoes for a month. Then a month of beans.

For more than a decade, they felt the loss of their homes not only as nostalgia but as an everyday struggle. So when they heard that Turkish troops had landed in July 1974, the Turks of Lapithos were overjoyed. And with the flight of their Greek neighbors, they began quickly to return to the town. There, they settled in abandoned Greek property, their own homes unlivable. They returned to find war-ravaged neighborhoods, gutted houses, bodies rotting in the orchards. Plates of food had been left on tables, clothes still hung in closets, photographs were still on the walls. "*My son said, 'Don't come back yet, Mama. There're still Greeks here,'*" Fadime Teyze told me. "*He was a policeman, so he came and had a look. We wanted to come back, but he told us to wait. We came back in October, and people were already moving in.*"

What followed their return was a frenzied period of plunder, as Turkish Cypriots returning to their villages and others fleeing from the south scavenged and squatted. The lottery system for distributing property held up only as long as people didn't simply find houses they liked and move in. One Lapithiote woman who spent her twenties in the enclaves told me of being allotted a house in the neighboring town of Karavas. Semra was then almost nine months pregnant and had endured three days of hiding under a cot in the Boğaz enclave as intense fighting and bombing continued in the surrounding mountains. When she and her husband arrived in Karavas, they searched all day for the house with their number, but when they found it, there was already someone there. It had been a nice house, a large house, and the man occupying it pointed across the street to a much smaller house with a half-built upper floor. "*That's your house*," he told them, and his rough appearance compelled them to feign belief.

Indeed, the looting of Greek property was thorough; it was also thoroughly normalized. Fadime tells me in a matter-of-fact way that the house they were given was completely empty when they found it, plundered by the Turkish military. "*There was nothing. Nothing. It was completely empty. Wooden cabinets, everything was empty! We brought these four chairs from Boğaz* [the camp where they had lived]. *I didn't want anything else!*" She points to several pieces of furniture, then to a daybed in the corner. "*My son made that in Boğaz, he took the pieces from a chicken pen, and he made a bed out of it for the children. We left one for the soldiers, but we brought one here, as a souvenir.*"

As with the old woman who occupied the house of the official who had destroyed her own, some plunder was reciprocal. But much of it appears to have been either necessity or simple enjoyment of the spoils of a war that they felt they had finally won. Turkish Cypriot refugees from Paphos soon arrived in Lapithos, and quite a few told me that they had fled to the north on foot across the mountains. Because the Turkish Cypriot administration made efforts to settle communities together, in villages that resembled their places of origin, many Paphos refugees who had lived in the mountainous areas near the sea were settled in Lapithos, some arriving early enough also to claim houses that they liked.

Moreover, while Greek Cypriots had fled from the advancing Turkish army, Turkish Cypriots had fled from their own neighbors and so harbored few hopes of return. Rather, they saw their new homes as the "last stop," the last flight, and they wrangled among themselves to secure property equivalent to what they had left behind, or in many cases even better. Along with new village and street names, new statues and flags, the landscape of the north was remade in this period through intimate acts of plunder.

Today, Greek Cypriots return to find their former neighbors in the houses that they know as their own. Like Vasillis, many Greek Cypriots returning ask, "*Why don't they just go back to their homes, and let me go back to mine?*" Even more, they wonder about changes in the homes, about the remnants of their lives that they had left behind in flight. They wonder about letters in their drawers, a special dress in a closet, the table where they used to eat. They wonder about the pieces of their lives that have now been scattered.

A broken wall and a mansion at a crossroads. Dried beans in shares and food left on tables. Shattered glass and broken tombstones. This history of plunder describes yet another remaking of reality in the Cyprus conflict, one in which communities were recreated from the ruins of others, and a new territory was imagined through the claiming of property. It is a history in which landscapes of loss are turned into topographies of violation.

Özker Yaşın, best known as a nationalist poet, wrote a novel immediately after the war that already describes the invasion and its aftermath, and in it he discusses another word that emerged in the Turkish Cypriot lexicon after 1974 to refer to plundered property: *buluntu*, "found things." Yaşın's novel, *Girne'den Yol Bağladık*, takes its title from the popular song of the time, "Girne'den Yol Bağladık Anadolu'ya," "We Connected a Road Between Girne and Anatolia." But although the author was known at the time as a staunch nationalist, the book is not one that simply lauds the invasion and its aftermath. The center of the story is a young couple, Oktay and Aysel, with their small daughter Oya, and their adventures on the way to being given a Greek house. What is important about the book is that the author is able to express through this story many of the contradictions of the period.

In a scene near the beginning, Oktay encounters on the street an old friend, Ali, whom he knew when he was fighting in the mountains. Ali is from Limassol, where Greek soldiers held him prisoner for ninety days. When he was released, he managed to cross to the north and be reunited with his family.

> "Three days have passed since I was released," Ali tells Oktay. "I've been in Nicosia three days. And in these three days do you know the word I've heard the most, Oktay?"
>
> "I know, Ali ağabey."
>
> "Okay, so tell me what's the word I've heard the most."
>
> "*Ganimet!* (Spoils!)"
>
> Ali stared in astonishment. "How did you know?"
>
> "Was I right?"
>
> "Yes, you were right."
>
> "Now certain circles are trying to prettify this 'spoils' word. They don't say 'spoils.'"

"What do they say, then?"

"Found items (*buluntu*)!"

"So, found items."

"Jean-Paul Sartre had a novel, Nausea (*Bulantı*). It resembles that."

"*Buluntu, bulantı.* They both lead to the same thing. They make a person sick to the stomach in the end."

"Right you are, Oktay. If you only knew the stories we've heard in these three days. It's impossible to control it all at this point. People we know as honorable, virtuous—people are even saying they've looted."

At that moment a friend of Ali's enters the room, and they greet each other. The acquaintance, Fuat, explains that while he was held prisoner, his own home in the south was looted, which leads Oktay to ask if he was unable to bring anything with him.

"I brought some things," Fuat replies. "I filled a suitcase with the most important belongings and clothing, and I brought it. They stole that suitcase here."

"What on earth?" said Ali. "How did that happen?"

Fuat laughed. "That's our situation. . . . It's good that I didn't wait too long for the housing allotment. They gave us a house in Girne. We went and looked, most of the furniture had been taken. I put the suitcase in a corner and thought I'd go get a broom, some soap and detergent. I went to the store. I wasn't gone even half an hour. When I got back, I looked and saw that there was dust blowing where our suitcase had been."

"You mean they mistook your suitcase for loot?" Ali asked.

"I don't know," Fuat replied. "You shouldn't ask me, you should ask the ones who took my bag."

What is important about Yaşın's novel is that it both documents the period and expresses many of the ambiguities that would become important later. The postwar period of *ganimet* was one in which almost everyone seems to have engaged. In this period, it acquired the connotation of right or revenge, after the previous decade of deprivation. The period of *ganimet* appeared as the completion of a history, one that had begun with their own departure from their villages and the looting of their own homes. It was also a period that at the time was described as the writing of a new future, starting with a blank slate. In this new marking of territory, the property that they found there would also legitimately be theirs.

Looting was something that "everyone" did, and it was given legitimacy through the new state's distribution of Greek Cypriot property. In order to prevent everything from breaking down into disorder, the new government began collecting movable property and redistributing it to those who needed or requested it, keeping it in what were popularly known as *ganimet ambarları*, "loot depots." In the early years, there were many complaints of unfair distribution, as Turkish Cypriots arriving from the south of the island protested that they had left behind more valuable property than they had been given. The plunder of Greek Cypriot property, then, was normalized, even naturalized, by assimilating property to a new "national" territory. Greek Cypriots had been sent to the south, they would not return, and the problem was the division of the spoils.

Looting was normalized, but it was also something that was questioned, even portrayed as a kind of social illness that corrupted the community. And the naturalization of this claim on Greek property depended on the legitimacy of one's own claims to self-determination. Within a decade or so after the war, it became clear that there was to be no international recognition of a state in the north. Discontent began to ferment, as Turkish Cypriots remained unable to have direct trade or direct flights into their "pirate" country and were unable to travel with its passports. Such discontent increased in 1996, with the Loizidou case, which demanded that Turkey pay restitution for preventing the Greek Cypriot refugee from returning to her property. Even after that, many people were able to ignore the decision for several years, until Turkey finally decided in 2001 that it would have to pay the compensation as part of its EU accession bid. In the wake of that decision, the property that many Turkish Cypriot "owned" or occupied in north Cyprus no longer seemed *helal* or *meşru*, legitimate.

And at this point it became quite common to hear Turkish Cypriots wryly refer to the country where they now live as a *ganimet ülkesi*, a country built on spoils. By this time, as well, the real estate boom had taken hold, as shrewd investors who had bought up Greek Cypriot land on the cheap in the mid-1990s now began to profit from the global real estate boom by building bungalow complexes to sell to foreigners. Until that time, there had been very little building on Greek Cypriot land, and one of the ways in which

Turkish Cypriots had maintained a sense of legitimacy was by not developing, by simply keeping Greek Cypriot property in anticipation of a final solution.

But the real estate boom was something quite different, as it plundered Greek Cypriot property a second time, jump-starting an ailing economy and making a small group of investors quite wealthy. At the same time, almost everyone benefited in some way from this plunder, as it created new sectors in building materials and interior decoration. This became known as the *ikinci ganimet dönemi*, or second period of *ganimet*. And it was in this period that people began to feel that not only was the state that governed them unrecognized, but the very homes where they lived had become illegitimate. It was in this period that the word *ganimet* lost its meaning as "spoils of war" and gained the meaning of "plunder."

The difference, of course, is that while "the spoils of war" appear to draw history to a close, to signal the completion of a history, "plunder" has no such connotation of right. And while it may be a truism to say that every state is founded on theft, to call the place where one lives a *ganimet ülkesi* is wryly to acknowledge that one's own theft lacks legitimacy. Unlike a view of *ganimet* that sees it as the "spoils of war," a view of *ganimet* as plunder calls history into question. Unlike calls to "forget the past," to "put the past behind us," it emphasizes the entanglement of past and present, indeed the transformative nature of the past for the present. It emphasizes not that history has come full circle, that it has reached completion, but that it remains incomplete. It emphasizes the unfinished nature of history, which may yet find its completion in unexpected ways.

I had been living in Lapithos for several months before I again went to see Eleni. I had run into her at the celebration of Lapithos crafts, and she had wondered why I hadn't been to visit. It was a hot spring day, and even in the early morning the sun was showing the first signs of a summer clarity. In the garden behind Ozan's house the apricots were ripe and hanging full from the trees. The ground under the trees was covered with them, browning and dotted with fruit flies. I took a plastic bag and began to gather fruit, taking some from the lower branches of the trees and some from the ground around. I hadn't asked Ozan before taking the fruit and so didn't want to take too much, or to pluck too many from the trees. But in the mind of someone with little experience in these things, many of the apricots that had recently fallen to the ground looked just as enticing as those still on the branches.

I arrived at Eleni's house at around noon and presented her with my bag. I had heard so many nostalgic stories of refugees going to pick fruit from their orchards, and I had been at Maroulla's side when she drank water from the spring of Koufi Petra and handed me a cup. A refugee from the village of Karmi, not far from Lapithos, had been arrested for trespassing when she entered the garden of her father's coffeeshop to pick flowers. And so when I presented Eleni with my bag, I explained that I had been in Lapithos. "*I brought these for you*," I said.

Instead of the pleasure I had expected, her warm greeting froze into a disapproving glare. "*You should know I can't accept these*," she reprimanded me.

"*But so many of the refugees go and pick fruit*," I began. I realized my mistake and was fumbling for an explanation.

"*But you should know by now that I couldn't accept them*," she repeated. "*I don't want anything from Lapithos until we're all able to return*."

Nevertheless, she kept the bag in her hand. She glanced at Kostakis, who was sitting listening, then into the bag. "*In any case, they're overripe*," she remarked, retreating into the kitchen, I assumed to throw the bag away.

And she was right to reprimand me; by then, I certainly should have known. I had memorized the refugee association slogans: *Struggle— Freedom—Justice. We want a solution that is workable and just. We are against invasion and occupation and in favor of human rights.* And the one that hangs at the checkpoints: *This is not the road to return.* To taste the apricots I had brought her would have been for Eleni to taste the bitterness of her own absconded past.

Eleni's rejection was not simply a refusal but also a denial. It was not only that she refused to take the apricots; her manner of refusing was one that denied the possibility of crossing to the north, of picking this fruit. It was an insistence on holding the past in place and a denial of the transformative capacity of the present. Like Anna's remark that "*either everything will go back to the way it once was or we'll continue to live in our dreams*," Eleni, too, preferred to deny not only the bitter reality of the open border, but also the reality of the different history that was suddenly visible in the form of occupied houses, damaged cemeteries.

For Eleni, to inhale the scent of lemons or bite into the sweetness of an apricot would have been like opening the locked room of someone one has loved and lost. As long as the room remains locked, one is confronted neither with the truth of the past nor with the truth of its loss. But when one enters the room permeated with his odor, filled with the half-completed pieces of a life, one is confronted once again not with the person one had thought one knew, but rather with the pieces of that person, pieces that may not fit the whole one had known. The accumulated objects of a life point to thoughts to which one is not privy, fantasies one cannot know, dreams that are half-realized. One is confronted with the incomprehensibility of the other, the incomprehensibility of history itself, visible in pieces that cannot be made to fit one's image of the whole. Those remains of a life become remainders, pieces that stubbornly insist that the other can never be fully known. For Eleni, then, to taste the apricots would have represented a form of mourning, an acknowledgment that perhaps it is only the taste of an apricot that is left.

Perhaps in order to understand the significance of plunder one would have to go with Greek Cypriots as they return to their former homes and point out, *"This was mine, and this."* As they search for traces and wonder why certain things have survived and others have been lost. As they cut oranges from their orchards and timidly ask for mementos. As they face the new knowledge, available to them only since the 2003 opening of the border, that the ones who plundered their homes and occupy them now are not only foreign Turks but also their former neighbors.

Perhaps in order to understand the significance of plunder one would have to live with the traces of violation—a table cleared of the food that had been left there, sheets that one scrubs to remove their owners' traces, clothes that persist in retaining their owners' scent. Walls and doors, tables and beds, all carry the traces of their former owners. They carry the traces of one's violation, and of acts of violation that one has committed.

The muhtar of my neighborhood lives at a crook in one of the main roads, across from what is now a swampy gully and was in the past a clear stream that gushed with the winter rains. The house is above a workshop, at the edge of the former Turkish quarter and near the municipal offices. But this was not where Salih Usta originally lived. His own home was down the street, he told me, though he had not lived there since he was a youth. It was then that he began working as an apprentice to a Greek master carpenter, but in 1955, he said, things changed. *"They came one day and told the master he couldn't hire a Turk anymore. They threatened to kill him. So I left."*

He left for Nicosia, and a Turkish master, eventually graduating to become a master carpenter himself. Because he was already settled in Nicosia before 1964, he became responsible for protecting large numbers of relatives when they fled in that year. By that time, he was already married with his own home, and as so often happened in that period, they came to him. "*That's the way it was for about ten years,*" he said. "*About twenty of us in the house, one on top of the other.* "

His family finally returned to the town immediately after the war, but he remained in Nicosia. "*It was another two years before we came back,*" he told me. They found a house where they could settle, with a workshop, and because they didn't need anything, he says, he saw no reason to loot. "*I'm a carpenter, I make everything—tables, cabinets, chairs. But one day my wife, she said, 'Let's go look in that house over there.' Mind you, everybody else had come back two years earlier, so there wasn't much left. But we went, and we found a dowry chest. My wife liked it, so I brought it home, and I sanded it and fixed it up, and we put it in a corner.*"

Until this moment, Salih's story resembled that of so many others that I had heard—the stories of *ganimet,* or spoils, and the frenzy of looting that had followed the war. "*Then one day,*" he told me, "*my mother came to the house, and she looked at the chest. She said, 'Where did you get that chest?' And I said, 'From so-and-so's house.'*" Here he mentioned a Greek Cypriot name. "*She looked at it some more, and she said, 'That was my chest. Look inside, there's an inscription in Ottoman that my father wrote to me.' So I opened up the chest, and there it was, right there.*"

"*And you knew this man?*" I asked, referring to the owner of the house where he'd found the chest.

"*Of course I knew him,*" he answered. "*He was our neighbor.*"

In this story, the old carpenter is not only telling of reciprocal plunder; he is telling a history of the conflict through a history of its objects. He is telling a history of retribution, but he is also telling a history that remains strangely unfinished, in the sense that the man from whom he gained retribution is unaware, doesn't know that in the old carpenter's mind things have come full circle, been set right.

In fact, objects themselves and their circulation have the potential to embody the unfinished nature of the conflict. Because unlike the violence, which ended long ago and has the potential for resolution, objects remain: they age, they're bought and sold, they're thrown away. They circulate, tainting everyone—creating a "country built on spoils," where all are affected. Unlike violence, violation continues in the form of looted churches and plundered homes, of cabinets that stand in a corner or a chest emptied of its dowry.

Indeed, in Cyprus plunder is not only a sordid chapter in the history of inter-communal relations; it shapes those relations even now.

Like the Cyprus problem itself, objects remain. And so in the encounters of the opening, these *remains* of history became history's *remainders*, pieces of a past that do not fit, and hence *reminders* of a past that is unfinished and so capable of molding the present in new and unexpected ways.

When the ceasefire line that divides the island was still closed, it was possible to imagine the pre-conflict past as a lost wholeness, represented in many people's minds by the homes and lands that they had lost. But in visiting their homes what many people encountered instead was a fractured wholeness, in which pieces of the past re-emerged in the form of objects, reminders of a past that does not entirely fit the narratives one has wanted to believe for so long. Questions appear in the form of tables and chairs, clocks and photographs, that remain in what other people now claim as their homes. And they were visible in the objects that people encountered or failed to find in their homes, objects that appeared stranded in the wreckage of a lost wholeness. They were objects that carried both one's own and others' memories, and in the space between those memories, new questions emerged.

These intimate objects become uncanny reminders of the intimacy of conflict, an intimacy that larger narratives have suppressed. This is what, in his own analysis of the Uncanny, Lacan describes as the persistent presence of a real that cannot be subsumed in the categories available to us. This is the irruption of the real into the reality that we believe we know. These objects point to remainders of history, and as such become reminders of moments of history that have not been incorporated into one's own narrative. Objects, then, pointed to unanswered questions of an unfinished past that return to press insistently on the present.

Birol showed me photographs of herself from the enclave period, in her wedding gown or sewing uniforms for the *mücahitler*. The photographs are important to her, and yet she tells me that when they returned to the town, she burned the photographs that she found in the house where she now lives. "*I took them out into the garden, and I burned them all,*" she tells me. She burned intimate items, but she kept certain pieces of furniture that she found. "*Now the Greeks of this house come,*" she tells me, "*the* cira *brings her grandson. And they walk through the house, and she says, 'This was ours, this wasn't. This was ours, this wasn't.'*"

Many people destroyed or rid themselves of personal items that they found in houses; others, like Fadime Teyze, saved them but were glad when they had an opportunity to return them to their owners. Some people told me that they had special rooms or closets that had been closed off and that contained personal items. Most saw the return of items as a form of closure, much as Turkish Cypriot refugees from the south appear to have viewed their own visits to their homes. With the presence of those personal items, or a lingering curiosity about the state of one's house, there was something in the past that remained unfinished, and returning photographs or visiting a village now in ruins became a way to "put the past behind us."

But what was less expected was the way that objects came to represent stories, and hence pieces of the past that appeared in the wake of a fragmented whole. Like Birol, many people had been able to make a separation between objects that were personal and those that were usable, between objects that seemed to represent their owners and those that bore traces that might be erased. Birol burned photographs but kept tables and chairs, and now the Greek owner of the house returns and points to them as her own. While Birol had tried to erase traces of the other, what she had not anticipated was that the other might return and trace her right to belong through the objects that remain.

For many Greek Lapithiotes returning to their homes, questions appear in the form of battered cabinets and lost letters, in the form of broken tombstones and looted churches. They appear in the form of Greek houses for sale and dowry chests in the windows of antique shops. They appear in the form of a present built on the ruins of a looted past. And these traces of violation and ways of living with them both recall unresolved pieces of the past and raise new questions about the other. And it was these new questions about the other that would arise to shape the present in unexpected ways.

I had been living in Lapithos for a couple of months when I invited a close Greek Cypriot friend to stay with me. I had tried hard to find Turkish Cypriot property in which I could stay, but in the end had given up and rented the apartment from Ozan. As if it wasn't bad enough that my landlord was in the business of restoring and selling Greek houses, the part of the house where I lived was filled with antiques whose origins were unclear. I knew that many of them must be from Greek houses, and yet after thirty years it is difficult to know the provenance of any particular object. In the period after the war, furniture and valuables were taken from homes and brought to others, some of which themselves have subsequently fallen into disrepair. Items have been sold and circulated, some as "souvenirs" that have made their way to homes in England.

Although my friend said nothing about the wrought-iron bedstead or the intricately carved sofa, she noticed a painting hanging above the sink in the kitchen. It was one that had also caught my attention—a naïve oil painting of farmers reaping wheat. I hadn't thought that it could be valuable and had paid no attention to the signature. But when Ozan dropped by as my friend was preparing to leave, she turned and asked him, "*Would you be willing to sell this painting? It's by a painter I really like.*"

Ozan turned dark and looked confused. "*No, I don't want to sell anything,*" he said uncertainly. He insisted that his wife had chosen everything for the house.

After Ozan left, my friend explained to me that the artist was Mihail Kkasialos, Cyprus's best-known naïve painter. And I would learn later what anyone who knows Kkasialos also knows: that he was from the small Mesaoria village of Assia, which has more missing persons than any other place in the north apart from Nicosia. Kkasialos had been enclaved there for a short time before being sent to the south with injuries that would cause his death only a week later. Had the painting been taken from Assia and made its way to Lapithos? Had someone in Lapithos or one of the neighboring villages bought it before the war?

And I was reminded of my meeting with Anna, when she had told me of an aunt who had been enclaved in Lapithos. In her books written before the opening, and even in other stories that she told me about her own life, she had insisted then that there were never problems between Turks and Greeks in the town, that Turks were forced to leave by their own leadership, and that many Turks who left in 1964 gave the keys to their homes to their Greek neighbors. One of her books, for instance, describes the secretive return of a young girl to Lapithos two years after their flight. The girl, Eleni, makes her way to her house, where she finds a Turkish Cypriot family living. The family take the girl in while they try to find a way to return her to the south, and in that period Eleni discovers that she feels quite comfortable with her protectors, even begins to love them:

> She felt now how much until the day before she had hated these people who saved her, who helped her, who showed her love and gave her protection, these people of another race and another religion, because they had taken her home and her inheritance.

Now, though, she finds that they are just like her own people, and just like all simple people. Kamil and his wife, she finds,

> worked the land, poured out their sweat, and endured. They endured until the time of the return of their friends, the owners of the land, their co-villagers. They knew that they lived in the home of their friend only temporarily, and they knew and believed that their friend would return, just like all of their fellow-villagers.

In Eleni's eyes, then, Kamil and his wife become humanized as she also perceives them as enduring, awaiting the moment of "the return of their friends," the land's real masters, *ton idhioktiton*, its owners or proprietors. Anna explains Turkish Cypriots' presence, then, as a form of waiting, expecting the moment of return.

At the end of this story, as the little girl is preparing to leave, the wife calls Eleni to their bedroom and climbs up on a chair to take a small bundle from the top of a wardrobe. The girl opens the bundle carefully, revealing letters and family photographs: "She looked and looked, and she didn't know what to say. The good woman. . . . With how much care she had collected and preserved these. And now she was giving them to those to whom they belonged." At the end of the scene, we find them "embracing and kissing like mother and daughter."

This is a scene that foreshadows other such scenes that were replayed again and again after the checkpoints' opening, stories intended to show the humanity of the other. And yet the cracks in this seemingly seamless narrative appear in the contrast between the stories that Anna writes and the ones that she tells. When I met with her, Anna told me the story of an aunt who had been enclaved after 1974, because she had been unable to flee. The Turkish army herded Greek Cypriots into the Ayios Theodoros quarter, preparing to expel them to the south. In preparation for expulsion, Anna's aunt returned one day to her home in the Ayia Anastasia quarter to try to collect some belongings, and she found that Turkish Cypriot refugees from Paphos had already settled there.

Women had gathered and were drinking coffee in the entryway. When Anna's relative approached and said that it was her house, the Turkish Cypriot woman who had settled there replied, "*No, it's our house now.*" Anna's relative looked up and saw that her dead brother's photograph was still hanging on the wall in the entry. She asked to take it. But when she climbed onto a footstool to take it down, one of the women drinking coffee knocked the footstool from under her. Anna concluded the story with the lesson that Turks are not to be trusted.

Moreover, this story of Anna's relative was brought back to her by events in the present. Anna had told me of her father's emigration to Egypt, where he earned enough money to build their house and furnish it lavishly. And it is now her belief, since the opening of the border, that the Paphos Turk who possesses her childhood home is hiding their paintings and furniture in a locked room in the house. While Anna has refused to go herself to Lapithos, her sister went and found a family of foreign tourists renting the house for the week. Apparently, the Paphos Turk who took over the house installed a swimming pool in the garden and advertises the house on the Internet. Her sister toured the house, but there was one room that remained locked, and that has now become the object of Anna's fantasies.

In the absence of the other, Anna had sought answers to the question of what the other wanted, of how the other could do what he had done. But in the wake of an encounter with an other who stubbornly refused to be encapsulated in one's own narrative, new questions have arisen, now posed in different forms and braided into other narrative strands from the past. Anna remembered her aunt's encounter with the Turks living in her house. Others remembered what Turks had said to them when they departed the village in 1964. Ten years earlier, neighbors who knew that I crossed to the north had asked me, "*Do they have enough to eat? Do they miss their homes?*" But now, along with Maroulla, they had begun to ask, "*We'll never go back, will me?*" Or, as Maroulla asked on another day, "*Why would anyone living in Lapithos ever want to leave?*" And so while the desires of the other remain the realm of fantasy, now for Anna they are envisioned not as an imprisoned land but as a room behind a locked door.

While I was living in Lapta, a gruesome murder occurred that became the subject of whispered conversations for many days. A young man of about eighteen, the son of a settler family from Turkey, stabbed the English couple for whom he worked, bringing out many of the town's social cleavages. People were perplexed, because the boy had been born in Lapta, even if his parents were settlers, and his family had worked for the English couple for more than a decade. The couple were even paying for his older sister to study at university in Turkey. Most people remarked that the boy had learning difficulties, perhaps psychological problems. "*We might've expected it from the workers,*" many people remarked, referring to immigrant workers from Turkey's south and southeast who had come to work in the construction industry, who often slept on site, and who crowded one of the coffeeshops in the main square in the evenings. "*But we knew this boy,*" they would say, referring to the gradual integration of persons from Turkey who had arrived after 1974 with different habits and ways of living. Their children now speak the Cypriot dialect and are often hard to distinguish from Cypriots, while immigrant workers are looked upon with suspicion.

Şükriye, the woman who today lives in the house of the man who destroyed her own, remarked that from the terrace of her house she can see all the workers going by. "*We don't know any of them,*" she commented. Many of them live down the road from her, in the house of a Turkish Cypriot now living in London. "*They keep coming and going. Ten people sleep in a room.*" She laughed at a famous remark of former president Rauf Denktaş, "*Giden Türk, Gelen Türk,*" "The ones going are Turkish, the ones coming are Turkish," referring to emigration of Turkish Cypriots in the 1980s and 1990s and the arrival of immigrants from Turkey in their stead. "*It's because of Denktaş that things are in the state they are now,*" she insisted. "*That's why Talat was elected, because he doesn't want the Turks.*" Mehmet Ali Talat, who became president in 2004, had led the north's campaign in favor of the Annan Plan and against the "colonization" of Turkey. He had been a main proponent of "peace" and as a result had overthrown the man who had led the fight for an independent state.

But when I looked up from the terrace where we sat, I saw that on the wall of Şükriye's entryway hung a photo of Denktaş in his youth, along with photos of her brother Ibrahim, who was murdered, and her brother-in-law, who had gone to study in Turkey to become a teacher but had then returned and was killed during the famous battle at Erenköy, Greek Kokkina, now a Turkish Cypriot exclave in the island's southwest. "*We still love Denktaş,*" Şükriye insisted.

Greek Cypriot nationalist narratives told a story of Turkish Cypriots pushed into enclaves by their leaders and a Turkey that always wished to divide the island. But those narratives could not take into account what they encountered when the checkpoints opened: Turkish Cypriots who insisted on a version of the past that seemed by necessity to imply a separate state. Before the checkpoints' opening, they had read of immigrants from Turkey who, reports said, had begun to outnumber Turkish Cypriots and whom their former Turkish Cypriot neighbors didn't like. Many people believed that it was the "settlers," or immigrants from Turkey, who kept Denktaş in power, while their former Turkish neighbors wished for a return to *the way things once were.*

The opening of the checkpoints showed that the political landscape and Turkish Cypriots' political will were considerably more complicated than that. Ironically, the one house I saw where leftist materials were explicitly displayed belonged to a Turkish immigrant from the Black Sea coast who had fought as a conscript during the 1974 war. During the war, he had met his first wife, a Turkish Cypriot from a village to the west of the island, and he had returned to the island to marry her. Afterward, they had divorced, and he had married his current wife, a refugee from Limassol with whom he has two grown daughters. Inside his house hang the emblem of CTP (Cumhuriyetçi Türk Partisi, Republican Turkish Party), the party that had most explicitly supported the Annan Plan, and a poster for the Bu Memleket Bizim Platformu, the This Country Is Ours Platform, a coalition that had formed to oppose Denktaş, support reunification, and end Turkish "colonization" of the island. "*I was a leftist when I was a kid,*" he tells me. "*That didn't change when I came to Cyprus. Now we go to Limassol. I have a lot of Greek friends there. We sit in the harbor and drink and curse the state of the country.*"

But many of the Turkish Cypriots' houses in Lapta are today filled with political paraphernalia of a different sort. Photographs of Denktaş or Atatürk or Bülent Ecevit, the Turkish prime minister who had ordered the military intervention, occupy spaces in living rooms. Photographs of persons who have died, become *şehit*, or martyrs, occupy special places apart from the usual family wedding photos. Many homes have only a few books, among them the three-volume list of Turkish Cypriot martyrs published by the Association of Martyrs' Families and Disabled Veterans. The same association gives out calendars, as do many of the political parties. Some people hang Turkish or Turkish Cypriot flags of varying sizes in their homes, while those same flags may decorate posters or other paraphernalia that are not explicitly political.

Hüseyin Amca's daughter Nadime told me her father suffered a serious crisis after the checkpoints opened. The house where he now lives had belonged to a priest, a man they believe was murdered in 1974 by one of his Greek neighbors who supported the coup against President Makarios. After the checkpoints opened, they kept expecting the family of the priest, but no one arrived. Finally, after some months, a man claiming to be the priest's brother arrived. When they asked about the priest, he said that he was living in Nicosia, but he wasn't well enough to come. They invited this man inside and seated him in the living room. But as he looked around the room, she said, he suddenly jumped from his seat as though burned. Hanging directly behind him was a large Turkish flag, and he was taken aback. According to Nadime, he couldn't sit any more and left not long after.

Such small, visceral encounters open the way for larger fantasies, or for the return of pieces of the past that may provide meaning for the present. Nadime told me, for instance, that the brother came with someone else and that *"they crept up on the house." "We found them in the garden,"* she said. *"They were creeping around in the orchard. Why would you do something like that if you didn't have bad intentions?"* Moreover, they were suspicious of the fact that before the priest's brother arrived, they had asked a number of former neighbors why the family hadn't come, and they all claimed not to know the family. Nadime commented, *"We thought maybe they were trying to hide the fact that he was killed by the EOKA man across the street."*

Although almost all the older Turks in Lapta voted against the Annan Plan, most of their children and grandchildren appear to have voted in favor. The overall "yes" vote in the town was 57 percent, though it's hard to know how many of those were last-minutes changes of heart, when it became clear that their former neighbors would defeat the plan. One of those who voted in favor was Nadime, though she would later ask, *"What did we do it for? We thought we wanted peace. But I remember from my childhood when our neighbor came and said, 'We're going to kill you all, right down to your cats and dogs.' I thought we could put the past behind us, but it seems they still want it all."*

Such encounters tend to be framed by visible signs that are "read" through what one already "knows" about the other. For Greek Cypriots, the sight of their occupied homes, looted churches, and demolished cemeteries was a visceral encounter with occupation. For many Turkish Cypriots visiting the south, the sight of villages in ruin or homes bulldozed for parking lots, as well as the comparative wealth on display, were signs of a life that had gone on without them, as well as of the "occupation" of the Republic by their Greek partners.

But those signs are also complicated by encounters that don't fit, and by small events that recall other pieces of the past. Questions about the motivations of the other, then, are raised by events in the present where people read large meanings into small things. A Turkish Cypriot from Paphos who rents the house he occupies to foreigners; Vasillis's encounters with Lapta Turks who are polite but reticent; a villa built by a Turkish Cypriot on top of a Greek cemetery—all of these pieces of the present become as inscrutable and as open to fantasy as a room behind a locked door.

In the film *Çamur* (*Mud*), Derviş Zaim, a Turkish Cypriot director who has made a name for himself in Turkey, uses mud as a metaphor for the buried past. The mud of the film's title refers to the muddy edge of a salt lake, minerals in which are thought to have healing powers. But we also discover that buried at the edge of that lake are Greek Cypriots who were killed by a young Turkish Cypriot during the 1974 Turkish military intervention in the island. The film's claustrophobic atmosphere becomes increasingly oppressive as, almost thirty years later, the man is more and more haunted by this past, until the final scene in which he commits a reckless act that he knows beforehand will lead to his own death. Like struggling in quicksand, the more the protagonist flails, the more he's dragged under.

The film is part of a new rethinking of the past, a call to confront the destructive power of denial. And yet the title of the film also points to a lack of clarity in the past, to an element of unknowability. As I was completing these chapters, a new book appeared, the first of its sort for Turkish Cypriots from Lapta. Called *Göç Destanı* (*Chronicle of Displacement*), it collects the stories of Turkish Lapithiotes until the moment of their flight from the town. Like Greek Cypriot memory books, it aims at locating persons in place, and because the author is himself from Lapta, it does so both by providing a map of where they lived prior to 1964 and several pages tracing their genealogies. The map itself, unlike Vasillis's, makes no attempt to include Greek Cypriots and so only sketches the areas where Turks had lived until that time.

As I read the testimonies that the book collects, I pieced together the houses where they had once lived, along with the various ties by marriage, some of which had until then remained opaque to me. But it also gave me another way to tie together stories. Until then, I had pieced together such stories using only Vasillis's map and had discovered, for instance, that the carpenter's workshop in which Hüseyin Amca had worked and from which the EOKA thugs chased him away now belongs to Salih Usta. I had discovered through Vasillis's map that it was unlikely that Meropi had no experience of Turks, given how close they lived to her own home. But now I began to piece the two maps together.

The second map was drawn roughly in a circle, and it was crowded with names. Unlike Vasillis's map, which stretched over twenty-six pages, this map was encapsulated in one page, with abbreviated names, or names written over each other. I had to turn the map again and again to understand its orientation, and I had first to find some familiar names and identify them with particular houses in order to comprehend their relation to each other. I then began tracing out not only people with whom I had spoken, but also their relatives, and their vicinity to each other in those years.

No sooner had I oriented myself in the map than one name stuck out—that of İbrahim Nidai, former head of the town's TMT organization and one of the two men who disappeared on Christmas Day, 1963. His house was on a small lane above the upper mosque. When I returned to Vasillis's map, I saw that there were two pages with that same small lane on them, but I had not realized until then that Vasillis's Greek entry, "Nitais," was the same Ibrahim Nidai who had become a şehit and whose name now graces the main street of the town. Not only that, but as I looked more carefully now, turning the pages of Vasillis's map and comparing it to the book, I saw that Salih Usta's father's home had been on that same lane, the home from which the dowry chest that Salih later recovered had been stolen.

But turning the pages I found not only this, but something more: at the bottom of the lane was the animal pen of Vasillis's story, the pen Vasillis's uncle had gone to check when he saw that the Turks' houses on that street had been looted. Until that moment, the looted homes of Vasillis's story had remained abstract, could have been any homes in the town. Now they condensed in the form of a dowry chest that had come to stand for a history come full circle.

And in the moment of this realization I remembered Salih Usta's startled glance when he saw the map, and his remark that people would think I'm a spy. I realized then that in the closeness of these neighborhoods, he must have known Vasillis much better than he was willing to say. I thought, as well, about one of my last days in Lapta, when Vasillis had come to see me on his own, insisting that we go speak to the mayor of the town. It was a very hot late June day, and Vasillis came to get me in his pickup, immediately identifiable as Greek by the license plates from the south. As we drove in the late morning heat toward the mayor's office, we passed Salih Usta's workshop. I saw him then, standing outside. He stood quite still as we drove by in Vasillis's pickup, watching us carefully until we turned the corner.

The maps spread out on my desk, Salih Usta's inscrutable gaze in my memory, I realized that it is from such small moments that histories may be made.

Just as in the postwar period Turkish Cypriots developed a new lexicon to refer to the objects that they found, so in the months following the opening of the checkpoints many Turkish Cypriots sought new ways to talk about the houses where they lived, the tables from which they ate. Many people began to speak of the houses where they lived and the objects that they had found as parts of a history in which they were caught up. So, when Greek Cypriots began to visit, many Turkish Cypriots would refer to them as "the Greek (Cypriot) of this house" (*bu evin Rumu*). It was a way of pointing to a form of belonging while at the same time putting stress on the house rather than its owner, on the property that was contested rather than the person contesting it. Such new ways of speaking point insistently to the past in ways that also indicate its unfinished nature.

This became clear to me when talking to Aris, as well as to the couple who now live in his house. Long before the checkpoints opened, Aris had participated in bicommunal workshops that at one point brought him to the north. He described to me with excitement the day that a bicommunal group of architects in which he participated brought him as far as Lapithos. He told me of how on that afternoon he escaped from the group in order to find his house. He ran away from them and made his way through the winding footpaths that he had known as a child, coming to the house among lemon orchards that his family had abandoned.

Aris soon discovered that Bulut's family had taken over the house. Bulut is a man of my own age who had been born in the enclaves and who saw the town for the first time when they returned there in September 1974. After they returned, his father opened a coffeeshop on a corner near their house, the house that had belonged to Aris's family. I heard the same story from both men: how Bulut's father saw Aris passing the coffeeshop and flagged him down, asking him, "*Are you related to Aris?*" "*He was my grandfather,*" the younger Aris replied. "*I knew it,*" the old man said to him. "*You look just like him. Come home with me now and let me give you some things I've saved.*"

Bulut's father had known Aris's grandfather before they left the town, and when they moved into Aris's house, Bulut's father had saved the photographs, hoping to return them one day. In a sad irony, by the time Aris was able to return to the town, he was probably the age that his own grandfather would have been when Bulut's family fled in 1964. Both young men told me this story as an example of the ways personal ties could transcend communal rifts. Bulut was in favor of the Annan Plan and curses the nationalists, talking freely about the bodies that he saw as a boy when they returned to the town, about a mass grave near the sea. Aris, in turn, was a long-time participant in the bicommunal workshops that were supposed to have given Turkish and Greek Cypriots a common language for speaking about their problems.

Yet one of the persistent problems is literally one of language. Unlike their parents, many Turkish Cypriots of Bulut's generation speak no Greek, and many have minimal or no English. Few Greek Cypriots have ever learned Turkish. As a result, Bulut and Aris communicated indirectly, through Bulut's wife Hanife. Ironically, Hanife is from a settler family that arrived from the Black Sea coast of Turkey, near Trabzon, and she grew up hearing Pontic Greek at home. Hanife, then, is the one who facilitates communication, and she was the one who told me about the problem of the clock.

"*They came one day, and he looked up and saw the clock*," she told me, pointing toward a chiming clock perched on a ledge high in the sitting room corner, above the entertainment set. "*The only thing left in this house when we found it was this clock. One day he came, and he looked up and noticed it. And he said to me, 'Why don't you let me take that clock?' And I told him no. He protested, 'But it's our clock!' 'No,' I said, 'it's the house's clock.'*"

Fadime returned photographs but lived in a house not her own. Birol burned photographs but kept the furniture that the house's owner now points out to her grandson as theirs. While photographs had to be returned or destroyed, furniture and other belongings might be cast as *buluntu,* "found things," what belonged to the house rather than to its owner. But notably, in saying that "*it's the house's clock,*" Hanife does not claim the clock as her own. Instead, she claims her right to use it until this unfinished history ends, until the conflict reaches a conclusion.

An Ottoman chest, a locked door, and a clock that beats out endless days all stand as reminders of a life that was truncated but not terminated, a past that was ruptured but not concluded. Unlike the violence that divided the communities and which ended long ago, violation continues in the form of looted churches and plundered homes, of photographs stashed away and chests emptied of their dowries. Indeed, in Cyprus plunder is not only a sor-

did chapter in the history of intercommunal relations; it shapes those relations even now. The visible remains of that past today are the ever-present
reminders that history is never linear, that victims may also violate, and that
resolving the past also requires us to tell a story whose ending we may never
know.

SEVEN

The Pieces of Peace

O NE DAY ABOUT a year after the referendum, a Greek Cypriot friend asked me to meet him in Nicosia in order to take him to the National Struggle Museum of northern Cyprus. The museum, erected in 1978 to honor the struggle for Turkish Cypriot survival and independence, stands near one of the Venetian gates leading into the walled city of Nicosia and is enclosed by a Turkish Cypriot army base. To enter, one presents an identity card to a young soldier, and passes a line of rusting tanks to enter the modernist structure through large glass doors. The several times that I've visited the place, I've always been the only person apart from the small staff, who occasionally rearrange the exhibits. The dim, dusty museum seems a sad reminder of a history of intercommunal violence that for many years Turkish Cypriots have struggled to forget.

Unlike its counterpart in the Greek Cypriot south, few Turkish Cypriots visit the museum. In the south, the Greek Cypriot National Struggle Museum sits inside the grounds of the archbishopric, a reminder of the central role of the church in the bloody struggles that divided the island. Visits to that museum have often been part of school curricula, enforced by the Minister of Education and Culture, who in the past has been named by the archbishop. Taking children to their own struggle museum would be anathema in the changed climate of the north, where Turkish Cypriots have begun openly to discuss their "occupation" by Turkey and the adverse role played by nationalist histories.

The arrangement of the museum is roughly chronological, chronicling a history of Turkish Cypriot suffering between 1958 and 1974 that is virtually unknown in the south. The exhibits are arranged in a spiral, taking one from

9. "Nai," or "Yes," rally in favor of the Annan Plan,
with a large "Oxi," "No," banner in tthe background.

outside to in. The museum is also set at varying levels, moving from lower to higher. The lowest point records the massacres of 1963 and 1964; the middle point the organization of defense and eventual Turkish military intervention; and the highest point the establishment of an independent state. The museum is covered with modernist paintings of mustachioed Turkish Cypriot fighters, children hiding in fright, and village massacres. There are also many, many photographs of the dead. Mutilated bodies and burnt corpses appear side by side with some of the antiquated guns used by the guerrilla forces for defense. The intended effect of these guns placed alongside the photographs in the museum is clearly to show the justification and inequality of the fight. In these representations, the blood of the dead blends into the blood-red of the Turkish flag, so that as one moves into the room that shows the establishment of a new state, one can understand the slogan inscribed there: "*Vatanı vatan yapan şehit kanıdır,*" "*What makes a homeland a homeland is the blood of martyrs.*"

At the end of the visit, my friend was near tears. I happened to know the director of the museum, a bureaucrat who had himself been a fighter, as had all young men at the time, but who showed no support for this political use of the dead and little stomach for his job. While my Greek Cypriot friend was educated in England and speaks perfect British English, the museum director spoke only Turkish and a smattering of village Greek. In a halting combination of Turkish, Greek, and English, and as I provided some translation, the two proceeded to have a political discussion about hopes for the future. The museum director emphasized that he wanted peace, that almost all Turkish Cypriots wanted peace.

Barış in Turkish and *irini* in Greek—these were the words on everyone's lips during the referendum campaign. Those in support of the United Nations plan spoke first of peace, but soon it was possible even for those on the Turkish right who favored partition, or even those on the Greek right who wanted a unitary state under Greek control, to say that they wanted "peace." By the time of the referendum, "peace" had become such a widely used word that new businesses sprang up in its name: Peace Market, Peace Kebab, even a Peace Barber. In the weeks leading up to the referendum, even after it had become clear that Greek Cypriots would vote "no" to the plan, tens of thousands of Turkish Cypriots gathered on several occasions in the squares of north Nicosia to shout, "*Kıbrıs'ta barış engellenemez*": "*Peace in Cyprus can't be impeded.*"

By the time of the referendum, Turkish Cypriots had gotten used to turning out in the tens of thousands for meetings protesting the actions of their long-time president Rauf Denktaş, a man who had emerged as one leader of the struggle in the 1960s but had ultimately prevailed over his competitors because of his firm allegiance to Turkey. He remained in power for thirty years, but that same allegiance to Turkey was what ultimately turned many Turkish Cypriots against him. The tens of thousands who turned out for rallies in the squares around the presidential palace called for "peace"—something vaguely understood as a federal solution to the island's division that would also allow them to enter the European Union along with their Greek compatriots. It was only with the sobering effect of the referendum that those in the camp favoring the UN plan stopped to ask if these various uses of "peace" were really mutually translatable, if they really meant the same thing.

When I first arrived in Cyprus in 1993, the language of "peace" was beginning to gain momentum. It was gaining momentum through groups that came to be known as "bicommunalists," or Turkish and Greek Cypriots who met in workshops intended to create dialogue about the past and possible futures.

Supported by international organizations, bicommunal groups met for more than a decade in the bullet-pocked Ledra Palace Hotel in the buffer zone, where they tried to graph their differing views of the past with red and blue markers. Among a small group, friendships developed, and these core bicommunalists were among the few Greek Cypriots who turned out for the rally in the north.

Many of those who participated in the workshops came to be known as "peace activists," or persons working for something that they abstractly called "peace." It was a language that was easy to use and hard to pin down, as though keeping things vague might make their realization possible. Certainly, it was a language that spread contagiously after the opening of the checkpoints, because, as so many people put it to me, "*War is a terrible thing. Who wouldn't want peace?*"

During the time of the referendum, the word "peace"—*barış* or *irini*—was on everyone's lips even as it became more and more clear that the same word in different languages didn't and couldn't mean the same thing. While Greek Cypriot and Turkish Cypriot diplomats wrangled over security issues and the workings of a federal state, most average people found their visions of peace bound up with hopes for return or long-suppressed fears. "Peace activists" could speak a vague language of unification in fluent English while sitting in Brussels or Berlin, showing to European observers that the "real" problems of Cyprus were not between the people but in the leadership. To the outside world, they presented an alternative voice precisely because they spoke in a "universal" language that was not anchored in the problems of the island. It seemed as though if only people could mingle, could see each other and talk, the island's problems would be solved.

But a year after the checkpoints opened, only a handful of these core "peace activists" from the Greek side turned out to support the thousands of Turkish Cypriots who rallied in favor of the Annan Plan. And on the lips of many of the Turkish Cypriots present there were the same questions: "*Where are the Greek Cypriots? Why have they not come?*" These were questions that echoed through the past, stirring other questions that had been only partially buried. In the enthusiasm to work for a new future, many Turkish Cypriots had said that it was time to "*put the past behind us.*" "*The Europeans did it,*" friends kept telling me. "*The French and Germans fought two wars, but now they cooperate together.*" I would hear this same example again and again, as it pervaded a certain strand of media in the north that was in search of a "European" solution. It was a call to confront and resolve the past, to move on to a different sort of future.

On the day of our visit to the museum, many months after the disappointment of the referendum, it had become clear that things were not going to be as easy as sitting down and working out a few fine details of history textbooks. It had become clear that it was not a matter of resolving history, or of writing a narrative that was acceptable to most, but of dealing with a history that was still incomplete and that still impinged on and shaped the present and its politics. On that day, my friend became visibly upset by the museum director's insistence that they wanted peace, that everyone wanted peace. "*No, don't say barış,*" my friend insisted emotionally, and the museum director turned to me in puzzlement. "*Barış simainei dichotomisi,*" my friend explained in a combination of Turkish and Greek. For my friend, *barış*, or peace in Turkish, means partition—at least in Greek.

For more than three decades, Greek Cypriots have couched their demands regarding a "solution" in a language of rights: the right of return, the right to freedom of movement, the right to know the fate of the missing, the right of the majority not to be dictated to by a minority. What became clear during the referendum was that, when translated into local rather than abstract, universal language, these demands amounted to a return to a unitary state that would also entail a denial of Turkish equality. Turkish Cypriots, in contrast, have asked for respect: respect for their culture, respect for their language, respect for their past, respect for their humanity. This has meant, for them, maintaining a separate space, a zone of protection where their equality is ensured. These are the differing expectations of how a history that everyone has experienced should be completed, how a history of conflict might be resolved. These demands, then, lie behind the words *barış* and *irini*. Nowadays, in the period after the referendum, it is quite common for Greek Cypriots to say that "peace" in Turkish means partition, while Turkish Cypriots remark that "peace" for their Greek partners means the right to control it all.

While in one sense obvious, this difference was consistently put aside by the groups who worked for something that they abstractly called "peace" in the almost fifteen years before the ceasefire line opened. And so in the period after the opening of the Green Line, bicommunal leaders who had gone through years of conflict-resolution training and had led hundreds of hours of workshops suddenly found themselves without a constituency. At first, everyone was simply sitting in the harbors, drinking with their newfound friends from the other community. And after the referendum, there suddenly seemed nothing more to discuss.

Certainly, the thrill of the forbidden had vanished. But even more than that, the specter of an incomplete history returned to haunt the political present. It had been fine to sit in a timeless hotel, lost somewhere in a border zone, and to argue about a past that seemed long gone in a language that reserved politics for the politicians. The unresolved past seemed then possibly resolvable, by finding a narrative on which all could agree. But the opening of the checkpoints made it clear that the past was not only unresolved but unfinished, that it would continue to shape the present in unexpected and perhaps unwanted ways.

The opening of the checkpoints made it clear, also, that the stalemate that is the Cyprus Problem was not only a diplomatic impasse but was present in interactions between people. Fadime would offer coffee to "*the Greeks of her house*," while Vasillis would take the Turkish family living in his own house a Greek version of Turkish delight. Newfound friends would eat and drink in the Kyrenia or Limassol harbors. And yet very few would talk politics, which led to the same impasse: Greek Cypriots demanded their rights, and Turkish Cypriots wanted recognition of their suffering. And so, even as the unfinished past returned, it did so in ways that reinforced senses of communal and national belonging because of the felt need for recognition of one's right to belong.

The languages of rights and recognition, then, pointed to an unfinished past that would return to shape the political present as soon as a plan for reunification was put on the table. For even more than questions of security or a federal state, people wanted to know if they would be able to return to their parents' land, to claim their inheritance, to reconstitute their communities. Suddenly, the lemons from a lost garden acquired more political significance than any attempts to narrate a past that very few expected ever to reclaim.

If you go onto any internet search engine and enter "Lapta" or "Lapithos," most of the sites the search returns are either those of various lobby and refugee groups based in the south and in London, or those of estate agents selling and renting property in the town. One of the most sophisticated of the former is the website of Lobby for Cyprus, which now includes a large segment on property. According to the Lobby website, "Not content with having occupied the northern part of Cyprus, Turkey is now engaging in the systematic concreting over of stolen Greek Cypriot land and selling it to foreigners." But if you hit the "back" button and return to the search results, you may scroll through page after page of property developer and estate agent websites, all either British or from known Turkish Cypriot families. Not only do the latter have no links to Turkey, but many Turkish Cypriot developers were among the foremost supporters of reunification and "peace."

In the period before the open checkpoints, it was easy to believe that the north was a place under military occupation, where generals controlled every aspect of Turkish Cypriots' lives. Especially because of the experience of invasion and flight, so sudden and so powerful, it was not hard to believe that Turkish Cypriots might also be victims of occupation, that they longed to reunite the island and needed Greek Cypriots to help them evict the occupiers. So when I first arrived in the island in the early 1990s, Greek Cypriots who learned that I crossed to the north often asked me is I wasn't afraid, if their former Turkish Cypriot neighbors didn't long to return.

Although those questions died away with the opening of the checkpoints, the narrative that framed those questions and gave them meaning has not disappeared, demonstrating once again what the journalist Peter Gourevitch calls "the peculiar necessity of imagining what is, in fact, real." Yet in the past few years many of these ways of narrating the conflict have acquired an ideological vagueness, one that attempts to patch over questions from the past. On the same Lobby for Cyprus website, a woman now living in London had visited family graves in Morphou and Lapithos and wrote a brief statement about it:

> I felt equally upset to see the destruction and the desecrated graves. We searched for the graves of our loved ones. At the first cemetery of Ayios Mamas all that was left from our uncle was a broken cross, thrown with others inside the ruined small church. There was no grave to go to and lay some flowers. Sadly all we could do was light a candle on the broken cross. Half of the cemetery was desecrated and the other half taken over by luxury villas. We were determined to find the graves of our family members. The second cemetery of Archangelos is high on the hills. We found the family grave of our great-grandmother and great-grandfather.

But when the website showed a photograph of her in the church of Ayios Mamas, among the broken tombstones, the caption read, "Greek Cypriots who have visited their homes and lands in the occupied north have been shocked and outraged at the wanton systematic deliberate destruction of Greek heritage by the Turkish occupiers." Here, the label "Turkish occupiers" allows for the continuation of a politics aimed solely at Turkey even as it keeps open the possibility that those "occupiers" are in fact one's former neighbors. Although many people still believed that the destruction of churches and cemeteries had been the work of the Turkish army, they nevertheless asked me, regarding their former neighbors, "*Why have they left it this way?*"

Talking vaguely of "Turkish occupiers" is primarily a political strategy, one that puts the blame on Turkey and demands the withdrawal of that country's troops from the island. But at the same time, the vagueness of the phrase elides a gap between what one knows and what one is able to explain. This is the space where one's imaginations of the real begin to reveal their limits and fray at the edges. And it is at this point that one may try to patch the gap, talking about "Turkish occupiers" or insisting that it would be better "*if we could just go back to the way things were.*" Some in Cyprus have begun to decide that this tear in the social imagination may be irreparable and indicates that the society has outgrown its imaginary clothes. In any case, many people have begun to say, those fashions are outmoded. But even for those who find them outmoded, change is never an easy thing. And so many people still insist on retaining these increasingly fragmented scraps of the social imagination, even as it becomes more and more difficult to patch them all together.

In Cyprus, as in other divided societies, much has been invested in the meaning of particular words. What many Turkish Cypriots call a border, Greek Cypriots insist is a ceasefire line, possibly a Green Line, sometimes the Attila Line. While Turkish Cypriots claim to have a state, Greek Cypriots invariably call it a "pseudo-state," with a "pseudo-president," "pseudo-laws," and "pseudo-police" to enforce them. For Turkish Cypriots, the south of the island is *Rum kesimi*, the Greek part, while Greek Cypriots call the north *ta katexomena*, the occupied lands, and insist that the cause of the Cyprus Problem is *eisvoli*, or invasion.

All these words made sense in the worlds that existed before the checkpoints opened, when there was little in people's experience to contradict them. Then, those words seemed given, so that to talk about "occupied lands" was a simple naming, like talking of a table or a chair. What the opening of the checkpoints made clear was how arbitrary those phrases were, how much they depended on the structure of imagination that held their meanings in place. For instance, *epistrofi*, or return, had always had the meaning not only of a human right but also of return to an idealized time before conflict. *Epistrofi* was not only a return to a place but a return to a lost past. What the opening made clear was how much that idea of return depended also on a denial of the present.

For Turkish Cypriots, one of the words whose implications subtly changed with the checkpoints' opening was *tanıma*, or recognition, the thing that they had never been able to gain. *Tanınmak*, or being recognized, had for decades been the goal of Turkish Cypriot political leaders, especially long-time president Rauf Denktaş. But by the time the checkpoints opened, most Turkish Cypriots had become weary of this frustrating struggle and had begun to understand that political recognition wasn't on the horizon. At best, a Taiwan model; at worst, incorporation into a federal state without ever being recognized on one's own. Denktaş's failure to recognize that no one was going to recognize him was one of the things that made him so outmoded in an age when most Turkish Cypriots wanted incorporation into a borderless EU.

But what the opening of the checkpoints made clear was that the demand for recognition, *tanınma*, was more than the international acknowledgement of a right of self-determination. Even more than a right, what recognition implied was an acknowledgment of their suffering, and a recognition of a history different from that told by their Greek neighbors. What *tanınma* implied after the open checkpoints was their ability to make their voices heard, this time to the Greek neighbors who worked so hard to deny that recognition.

One of those who had been caught between these forms of recognition was Aziz Kent—also known as John, or Con, Aziz—owner of the first Turkish-owned hotel, the Celebrity, on the Lapithos coast. I went to visit him one day in his thickly carpeted office and found a small, portly man with a neat polo shirt who immediately began explaining to me that he has suffered for years because of false propaganda in the international press saying that his hotel was confiscated Greek property. He is a self-made man who had left the isolation of his Tylliria village in the 1950s, he says because of Greek pressure, and had risen from busboy to millionaire in London. He decided in the early 1970s to return to and invest in his homeland, bringing an English wife, fluency in the English language, and the idea that he would help the Turkish Cypriot economy by putting a foot into the growing tourist industry.

He originally found a piece of land in Kyrenia, which he offered to buy from a Greek friend. But, he says, "*the land registry office which was in the control of the Greek authorities—only the Greek authorities they could issue titles—they wouldn't allow the Greek to sell to me. I had to find land that belonged to Turkish people.*"

He found land in Lapithos, but then the authorities held up his permission for more than two years, insisting that he had to have a Greek partner. He found a friend who would make no claims on the property, and they resubmitted the papers. But when he went to his appointment with the district officer, he was made to wait for hours. Finally, as the officer was leaving the office, John Aziz approached him. "*I went and approached him and said, 'Excuse me, sir, I'm John Aziz, inquiring about the Celebrity Hotel building permission.' He turned around and said, 'Wait, you dog.' And he just walked away and left me there.*"

He eventually got the permission, but the tale that he tells is a familiar one from that time, one of obstruction of Turkish businesses and Turkish attempts to buy land. Instead, Turkish sales of land to Greek buyers were facilitated, as were applications for passports by Turks wanting to leave the island. At the same time, he claims Greek Cypriot friends and says that he wants "peace," having written a book on building bridges to peace through tourism. Yet even his expressions of the shape of "peace" are contradictory.

> *If we let people mix—there are a lot of good people. And the freedom of everybody's movement, including the long-suffering 200,000 Cypriot Turks, I think we should have some rights, as well. Human rights. We're talking about human rights, and the European human rights, where are they? I ask them. . . . I'm a European citizen, being a British subject, where are my rights? How are you going to protect me? Your websites, because now you're a European, your website is stating false information, that my hotel, that everybody knows is Turkish, is still on the website in Greek. They say that they're going to remove it, but what about all the suffering it's caused me all these years? It stopped people coming to the Celebrity Hotel and Chateau Lambousa. They're all on Turkish land, it's all Turkish property, it's my design!*

His own losses as a businessman are assimilated to other forms of discrimination to which he was a somewhat distant witness. When he says, "*I think we should have some rights, as well. Human rights,*" he echoes a common strand of discourse among Turkish Cypriots that questions the call among Greek Cypriots for human rights that ask for their own displacement. "*Don't we have human rights, too?*" I heard so many people ask.

And so, even as pieces of the past returned to haunt the political present, many people seemed to assimilate their own unanswered questions to the unfinished history of the island. That unfinished history was represented by the themes of rights and recognition, what each side claimed that it had never been able to gain. But now for many people those unattained goals returned in new and more concrete ways, in the form of a house, a garden, and the bitterness of unplucked lemons.

Immediately after the referendum, a friend told me something that was very prescient but that I didn't believe at the time. She said to me, *"The Cyprus Problem is really all about property. Now everyone's going to start suing each other. You just wait and see."* I laughed, but only a few months later her prediction came true. And it came true in the most unexpected way, in the form of an acquaintance, a friend of friends, a quiet, earnest architect by the name of Meletis Apostolides, a refugee from Lapithos.

The house from which Meletis's family fled is in a lower neighborhood of the town as the land flattens out toward the sea. This is the fertile land where few people lived but where many had orchards. The house itself was relatively new in 1974, a square, flat-roofed structure that now boasts aluminum shutters. It's on a wide stretch of busy road, what was once the main road from Kyrenia to the west, before the two-lane highway near the sea was built. The house is now shared by two Turkish Cypriot brothers, one married who lives on the ground floor and the other still unmarried, who lives in a half-basement.

The first time I spoke to Meletis it was in the presence of one of his childhood friends, and the two had speculated on Lapithiotes' attachment to the place. *"Have you ever seen a place so beautiful?"* his friend asked. I had to admit that I hadn't. *"It's the combination of mountain and sea,"* Meletis added. I commented that the dramatic steepness of the mountain as it falls to the sea was also one explanation that some people had given me for the history of madness in the town. They laughed and agreed that it was possible. *"And it's the light,"* Meletis remarked in his quiet way. *"The clarity of the light. I only realized it much later, when I was in London. The skies were so gray there, and I had to carry a compass to find my way."*

He had gone to London to university and had planned to return to the town after graduating, but he was never able to do so because his family was displaced. Before the war, they had grown lemons in their orchards, exporting them abroad. His mother's health suffered as a result of the invasion, and he talks about how she refused to buy lemons afterward. *"We are a family that's exported millions of lemons, why should we go and pay for lemons now?"* she would say. Meletis participated in some of the bicommunal workshops, and so had Turkish Cypriot friends who would sometimes bring him lemons from Lapithos. He would give them to his mother. "She would never eat them," he would tell a journalist, "She just wanted to keep them. She wanted them there, to see, to touch, to smell. In her old age, each time she would see me, she would ask 'When are we going back to Lapithos?'"

When Meletis returned to Lapithos after the checkpoints opened, he found that an English couple had bought part of his land and a half-finished villa from a relative of the Turkish Cypriot who lives in his house now. The couple then finished the villa, which stands in what used to be his orchard. The English woman, Linda Orams, would later tell me, "*He thinks we chopped down the orchard, but that's just not true. We bought the villa half-finished, and the trees were already gone. In fact, we were disappointed that there weren't more trees, and we began planting.*"

The villa is larger than Meletis's own house, and it partially blocks the view from the back patio to the sea. But the patio itself is small, really only a landing with steps leading into the garden. Clearly, the orientation of the house was not to the sea but to the road, and to the orchards that surrounded it. The low stone wall that surrounds the new villa is only about thirty feet from the back door of Meletis's house. And in comparison to the arched terraces, the marble walkways, and the swimming pool of the Orams' villa, Meletis's house seems a bit shabby and worn. And the peculiar location of the villa, almost abutting Meletis' house in the middle of open fields, is a reminder of the haste with which so many villas have been constructed and sold, or half-constructed and half-abandoned, in the past few years. At the same time that they've devastated the landscape, these new developments have begun to crowd out Greek Cypriots' dreams of return.

"*I thought about it for several months,*" Meletis told me. "*But I just couldn't let them get away with it.*" When he says that he couldn't let them get away with it, he means that he couldn't let the English couple get away with a breach of what he considered to be just international conventions. And so he sued.

The fact that he was able to sue at all is a reflection of the incredible legal and political tangle into which the Cyprus Problem has become knotted since the opening of the checkpoints, and since the Republic's entry into the EU. Prior to this time, cases had been brought against Turkey in the EU Court of Human Rights. The test case brought by Titina Loizidou had been considered a monumental victory, and other Greek Cypriots had signed on for more such cases. Around the time of the checkpoints' opening, the number of suits queued in the European court had swelled to fourteen hundred.

But the opening of the checkpoints changed the legal frameworks. Meletis decided to sue in the court of his own country, which claims sovereignty over the north. And now that the Republic of Cyprus is an EU member, Meletis knew that the decisions of the Republic's courts would have to be enforced by the EU. Moreover, because of the open checkpoints Meletis's lawyer was able to cross to Lapithos and watch as a bailiff issued the summons to the English couple in person. Not surprisingly, when the case came to court in the south, Meletis won, and the sixty-odd-page judgment demanded that the villa be demolished and compensation paid. The case was later remanded to Britain, where Meletis hoped to seize the couple's properties in England. A new twist was added to the case when Tony Blair's wife, Cherie Booth, announced that she would represent the English couple.

Meletis told me that his motivation in bringing the suit was to prevent the destruction of Greek Cypriot land. *"How can there be a solution if nothing's left for Greeks to return to?"* he asked. But when one sets a precedent, it's hard to control what will happen afterward. At the end of April 2005, the first lawsuit against a Turkish Cypriot for use of Greek Cypriot property was brought against a restaurateur in Famagusta, using information obtained when he applied for an identity card in the south. Indeed, much evidence began to emerge that the government in the south was tacitly supporting, if not encouraging, such suits. Very quickly, such suits piled up, and it was soon estimated that several hundred lawsuits to be brought by Greek Cypriots against their Turkish compatriots were queued in the courts of the Republic. This was, of course, a divisive step that created much ill will.

I was living in Lapta when news of these lawsuits first hit the newspapers, the extent of them also exaggerated by rumor and false information in the press. Simultaneously, the Republic passed a law making the use of Greek property in the north illegal. They threatened that anyone using that property would be subject to arrest and that those arrest warrants would be valid throughout Europe and enforceable by Interpol, which also operates in Turkey. Persons using Greek Cypriot property, then, were threatened with being unable to leave the north of the island.

Tensions mounted as more lawsuits were filed, as rumors spread that summonses were being issued to Turkish Cypriots in Nicosia and other areas of the island. Fadime's daughter Emine lives on her family's ancestral land, where they've built three bungalows side by side. But when I went to see her, even she expressed the anxiety that many people had begun to feel:

Why is that we can't live like other people in the world, more happily, more content, able to go wherever we want? It was the same in the 60s, it's the same today. The gates opened, people went and got a European passport, we said yes, and still people can't leave the island. They have Greek property, they're going to be arrested. So what about Turkish Cypriot freedom, what about human rights? The Greeks' rights are violated, and the world stands up in protest. And what about our violated rights? There's nothing for us. . . . Today because of the threat of being arrested, they can't even go to Turkey! We changed our administration, we destroyed the status quo, and nothing's changed!

My landlord Ozan was in a constant state of anxiety over his own position, not only because of his business but also because his entire family lives in Greek property. Ozan's mother has been pestered by "the Greeks of her house," who come and tell her that they're going to take it back and force them to leave.

I heard first from Ozan about the man who came to his office, claiming to be an architect. "*Three of them came,*" he told me. "*Two men and a woman. I invited them to have coffee, and the woman said, 'We don't drink coffee in our churches.' But it's not a church! It was just a place where people would go to make wishes. And I said to her, 'In Europe, they turn churches into museums, and cafes.' And then the man who* claimed *to be an architect started saying how I was ruining all the village houses. I don't believe he's an architect, because he didn't understand anything about renovations. We started arguing, and I told them to get out, or I was going to call the police.*"

When I met Aris and his wife and their friend Nikos, they told me about an encounter that had put a damper on their visits to the village. "*We saw a Turkish flag over the chapel, and we went in,*" Nikos said. The rest of the story is as Ozan had related it, though Aris explained that he had accused Ozan of cannibalizing some of the old houses to find building materials for others. They tell me he became enraged. "*He picked up a large stone and threatened us with it! He chased us away. He was shouting, 'You come and threaten us. Don't come any more!'*"

When I later told Ozan that the person he had chased away was making plans to open a lawsuit, he was quite pleased. Like John Aziz's story of his hotel, or Emine's complaint that the world sees only certain human rights and not others, for many Turkish Cypriots the language of rights has by necessity implied a denial of their own recognition. This seemed to become clearest in the lawsuits, which were a struggle for rights that also revived a past that Turkish Cypriots remember as a struggle for existence. And in turn, the struggle for recognition, to claim a place and insist on it, has meant, for Greek Cypriots, a continuing denial of their rights to their homes, their rights to their trees, their rights to the graves of their ancestors.

The languages of rights and recognition that recurred at the time of the referendum, then, represented more than political positions. They represented pieces of the past that had never been fully incorporated into communal narratives and that returned with the desire to pick flowers from one's childhood garden. They represented those parts of the past that could not be brought to completion and that obstinately recalled unanswered questions. They represented the political potency of the past, not as narrative but as unreconciled memory. A locked door or the taste of an apricot was not only a symbol of the past but a way of thinking about it that also braided it into their lives today. They represent new stories, new ways of thinking about the past, that interweave with choices in the present.

It was toward the end of my stay in Lapta that I first began to hear the remark that "*if we solve the property issue, the Cyprus Problem is finished.*" Indeed, it was soon clear both from the way the press treated the issue and from the way people had begun to talk about it that many Cypriots, both Greek and Turkish, seemed to believe that property was the key to "finishing" the Cyprus Problem, whether they liked that solution or not. Although many Turkish Cypriots were initially anxious, with the escalation of the suits, many also began to hope that once their Greek neighbors were compensated for their properties they would have no more claims on the north. Many Greek Cypriots, on the other hand, feared exactly the same consequence.

And it was around this time that Turkish Cypriots began talking about their own legal options, about what they could do to retaliate. Some began again to raise the issue of *vakıf* lands, lands that had belonged to religious endowments before they were expropriated and redistributed in the British period. The most disputed territory in the island, the decaying seaside town of Varosia, was always said by former Turkish Cypriot president Rauf Denktaş to be built on *vakıf* land. Others began to sue for their own land in the south that was expropriated by the Republic of Cyprus in the post-1974 period. In the largest suit for compensation so far, Hüseyin Helvacıoğlu produced title deeds saying that a large portion of the international Larnaca Airport was built on his land, and he asked compensation of £100 million. When the suit was announced, journalists had a field day.

"I thank Hüseyin Helvacıoğlu," wrote one. "And I hold him forth as a hero who is protecting the honor and dignity of the Cypriot Turk. . . . [W]hether you like it or not, the Cypriot Turk owns this land. Both in the south and in the north the richest lands belonged to the Cypriot Turks. In the English period, the Turks' inherited lands were given to the Greeks; and later they were seized by the Republic of Cyprus. And you see after 1974 the Larnaca Airport was built. Without asking anybody, without paying compensation, completely illegally."

And, just to complicate matters further, in February 2006 Arif Mustafa, from Episkopi in the south, finally had enforced a suit that he had won almost a year before in the courts of the south for restitution of his property. That property was then occupied by Greek Cypriots, who had to be rehoused by the Republic. This of course caused immediate panic among Greek Cypriot refugees, since estimates indicate that there are about fifty-five hundred potential cases exactly like Mustafa's. In addition, there are another eight thousand possible cases where housing for Greek Cypriots was built on Turkish Cypriot land, and another thirty-five hundred cases of former Turkish Cypriot businesses being used by Greek Cypriots.

In an interview with the Turkish Cypriot newspaper *Kıbrıs*, Arif Mustafa argued that the courts in the south were forced to rule in his favor or risk being sent themselves to the EU human rights court. "Because," he said, "on the one hand you're against invasion, and on the other hand you're an invader. How can that be? The Greeks say, 'Turkey occupied the north,' but then they occupied my land in the south. If I can't enter my property, that means they've occupied it. How can a state that's entered the EU do something like that?"

Arif Mustafa claims, moreover, that it's the refugees who are going to solve the Cyprus Problem through their lawsuits. "I wrote a petition to the government to get my house back, and eight months later the housing director called me and said, 'Did you write a petition to get your house back?' 'Yes,' I said. 'In that case, show me the house,' he said. After that he told me that the house wouldn't be given to me. We argued. I said to him, 'Whatever conditions you say your refugees came here under, we went to the north under the same conditions. You were afraid of the Turkish army, but the forces of the Greek coup and Makarios chased us from our land,' I said."

For Greek Cypriots, on the other hand, the escalation of the suits began to present individuals with an opportunity for justice that seemed to be at odds with the "justice" for which, as a community, they had worked for so long. Although the Greek Cypriot government tacitly encouraged individual suits or cases in the European Court of Human Rights, the ambiguities of the situation became clear when the ECHR decided, in 2006, to allow a local remedy for the fourteen hundred cases queued on its docket. The Annan Plan that Greek Cypriots rejected would have provided a universal solution for the property issue, and as a result of Turkey's support for the plan and Greek Cypriots' rejection of it the ECHR offered Turkey the option of implementing a local solution to the property problem. By the end of 2006, the government in the north had set up a reparations commission, and cases began to trickle in, despite the Republic's dire threats that application to the commission in the north constituted recognition of that government's legitimacy.

By June 2007, more than 180 Greek Cypriots had applied to the commission, and several cases had been decided—in some cases for compensation, in others for restitution. Although the applicants' names were to be kept confidential, they were leaked to the south, causing an uproar and accusations of treason in the Greek Cypriot parliament. Despite this or perhaps because of it, by one month later the number of applicants had risen to more than 230. By the end of December 2007, that number had increased to more than three hundred.

Many of the applicants had never financially recovered from their 1974 losses; others wanted to make a political statement. But in all discussions there was the hope or fear that if only the property issue would be resolved, the Cyprus Problem would be "finished." For many of those who declared the applicants traitors, what was at stake was not only their application to a commission in a state that they consider illegal. More important, just as refugee organizations had claimed that return to one's village would be an impediment to "real" return, so a legal solution to the property problem was soon perceived as an impediment to a "real," or a political, solution.

Property, then, is at the intersection of the personal and the national, at the point where "human rights" are realized. Attempting to gain a judgment for reparations is both a personal matter and, as Meletis's and Arif's cases show, a patriotic act. One asks a transnational legal body to recognize one as the "real," the legitimate owner, and the suits treat property as an inalienable possession, what the former Greek Cypriot minister of the interior called a "sacred and inviolable right." However, the only way to turn property into an inalienable possession, or legally to make a claim of absolute right, is also to make a claim about territory, and therefore about history and politics. Indeed, respondents in the civil suits have remarked that those suits were treated like criminal cases and that they were really trials of history.

Putting history on trial is in some sense every wronged person's dream, especially when the legal cards are stacked in one's favor. But the effect here is that one asks transnational courts not only to recognize the legality of one's existence, but to recognize that *only* oneself has a legal existence. Lawsuits such as Meletis' or Arif's effectively attempt to legitimate a territorial claim through reducing it to a legal dispute over a property regime. Some commentators have called this continuation of conflict in the courts "lawfare," or the pursuit of strategic ends by judicial means. Just as war is supposedly the means to which one resorts when diplomacy fails, "lawfare" may be the struggle to which one resorts when war also fails to reach a conclusion. This is, then, the juridical equivalent of conquest.

At the same time, even in the suits themselves, one can see differing versions of the way in which "peace" should come about, or differing versions of how the conflict should be resolved. For while Greek Cypriots have systematically pursued a "justice" that they believe has heretofore eluded them—either because of the Turkish invasion or, in some cases, because of the obtuseness of their own government—Turkish Cypriots have rather half-heartedly engaged in a search for recognition and respect. "*Whatever conditions you say your refugees came here under, we went to the north under the same conditions,*" Arif tells the minister of the interior, who refuses to accept his claims. Turkish Cypriots have so far been limited by the need first to pursue their cases in the courts of the Republic, since they must first exhaust "local remedies" before taking cases to the ECHR. But even the few suits that have been opened in the south appear to be aimed less at "justice" than at forcing the recognition of another history.

Even though the lawsuits represent such a struggle, no one seems to expect that they will result in something as clearcut as a victory in battle. Rather, when people say that the Cyprus Problem will be "finished," they simply mean that it will end, that there will be nothing left to argue over. For with the opening of the checkpoints, the unfinished past had returned for very many people in concrete ways, in the form of occupied houses, unkempt fields, and demolished churches—and, for Turkish Cypriots, villages covered in concrete or left in ruin. The lawsuits appear to represent an opportunity to finish the matter, even without resolving the problems that lie at its essence. And so when Arif Mustafa claimed that the refugees would "solve" the Cyprus Problem with their lawsuits, or when many people told me that soon the problem would be "finished," there was the hope, or the fear, that an unfinished history would draw to conclusion, even if it would not be resolved. If a lost orchard had come to represent a ruptured life, then the mundane, judicial compensation for that orchard might also represent a form of peace with the past in the absence of anything that one might call real "peace."

As I was nearing completion of this book, I boarded a plane from Cyprus to London. It was August 2007, four years since the opening of the border, four years since my project had begun. A couple sat next to me, and behind them their teenage children. The man was clearly Cypriot, and although the woman occasionally spoke to him in broken Greek, it was with an American accent. I would soon learn that she was Cypriot but had grown up in America, while her husband had arrived at the age of twenty-two, four years after the war that had made him a refugee. They had been visiting relatives, as they said they do quite frequently. I told them that I had been staying in north Nicosia for personal reasons, and they told me that they had visited the north only once.

"*We went to his village, but his mother's house isn't there anymore,*" the woman told me. "*His mother won't go, because her house was destroyed. We've only gone once, because it's too sad to go and see things like that. I hope that someday there will be peace. We just want peace.*"

I asked about her husband's village. "*Vadili,*" he told me. "*It was three thousand people, one thousand Turks. We never had any problems there.*"

I asked him if the Turks were still there in 1974, but he didn't understand me at first. When he realized that I was asking if the Turks had left in 1963, he became agitated. "*The Turks didn't leave, that isn't true. That's just propaganda that they tell.*" He began to tell me that TMT tried to force Turks to leave, in order to divide the island. But, he insisted, there were no problems in his village. "*There were three or four Turkish villages near ours, and none of the Turks left.*"

I tried to say that in not every case they left, but in many cases they did. And when they didn't, it was often because they were already in villages with a Turkish majority or where they could defend their neighborhoods. The following day, I would look up Vadili and find that it was in what was then a stronghold of TMT activity and that the Turks of Vadili had set up a perimeter around their neighborhood. "*The Turks would come to work for us,*" he told me, "*but we couldn't go into their villages. They were all guarded.*"

Only the day before, a woman had explained to me, as had so many women, the humiliation of the searches at the Greek checkpoints before 1974. It was for this reason that many women remained in the enclaves, not even leaving to work. And many women told me that they still feel a shiver of fear whenever they come to a police barricade or a crossing.

I wanted to tell the man this but didn't know where to begin. "*You know, I've been doing research on this,*" I tried to explain to him. "*I haven't met a single Turkish Cypriot who says that they left their villages because of TMT. Everyone says that they were scared. And when they didn't leave, it was because they were in villages that they could protect. They would arm themselves.*"

The woman clucked her tongue in commiseration at the thought that they were frightened. The man was frustrated. I saw him turn dark and shuffle in his seat. He looked out the window, but I could see him thinking.

He turned to me again. "*A lot of them have Cyprus passports now.*"

"*They don't have much other way to travel,*" I commented, and his wife nodded agreement.

"*But you can't enjoy the benefits without the responsibilities,*" he insisted. "*A lot of them come to work in the south now, just like they used to work for us before.*"

The conversation had begun to peter out in the frustration of politeness. The wife related a story from when she was seven and visiting her grandmother, who had a house near the Green Line in Nicosia. Her older brother was out riding a bicycle and got too close to the Turkish soldiers guarding the line. The soldiers began to shout, and her grandmother ran in fear to collect the boy. "*But I'm sure that someday there will be peace,*" she repeated. "*There has to be.*"

Her husband, by the window, had donned a baseball cap and stared at the passing clouds as the plane veered to the right. There were many things that I wanted to say to him, and many that he clearly wanted to say to me. Instead, he clenched his fists as he stared out the window. There was silence between us, but it was not anything that I would call peace.

EIGHT

Betrayals of the Past

MORE THAN A year after the referendum, I drove the two hours from Lapithos to the Paphos village where Maroulla and Vasillis now live. It was late May, and past the concrete chaos of Limassol the land was cracked and dry. They offered me coffee and preserved bitter oranges at a plastic table outside the kitchen door. Locusts hummed, and Vasillis fretted. We sat under grape vines that were beginning to bear fruit, and a trickle of breeze stirred the heat.

"*I was willing to settle for one-third of my land*," Vasillis told me, the part that he would have received had the Annan Plan passed at referendum.

Vasillis asked me again about the Turks in the town, about the ones I had met, and about the mayor, who is from the Paphos area, not far from where Vasillis lives today. He clenched and unclenched his hands as we talked. The Turkish Cypriot who lives on his property had begun building a house, he told me. He suspected that he might be trying to sell other parcels of the land.

As we were speaking, Maroulla, who had been standing slightly behind Vasillis, suddenly leaned toward me and rested her hands on the table. "*Why should anyone now living in Lapithos ever want to leave?*" she wanted to know.

As she said it, I imagined whitewashed houses that tumble to the sea. A stone church resting in the curve of mountain like a child in its mother's arms. I looked down at her wrinkled hands resting on the table, and I found it impossible to reply. There had been a sinking in my stomach that grew as I crossed into the Paphos hills, my own dislike of this dry, prickly landscape after the lushness of the town to which they cannot return. A sadness welled up inside me like an illness.

10. Destroyed cemetery in Lapithos (May 2009).

Vasillis snapped at her that she knows nothing of how these things work, and I felt something constricting in my throat. There was much that I could have said to him—much that I had learned, but much, I thought then, that it would have been pointless for him to hear. Why should I be the one to dampen his dreams? I thought, and I maintained my silence.

By the time I left them, the sun had set, and I drove back toward Nicosia in the dark. Loyalty, even honesty—the most human of responses—had been impossibly suspended inside me for months, and that impossibility finally released itself in a stream of tears. For the two-hour drive back to the city, alone in the car, I finally allowed myself to cry.

Much has been written about the ethics of research, but nothing had prepared me for the demands of loyalty and the inevitability of betrayal. I had read and even taught about the necessity of creating rapport with people, of gaining their trust. It is a basic tenet of anthropology that this can be a dangerous matter, described in most introductory textbooks. According to one,

> The fieldwork process is based largely on overcoming the boundaries which exist between the personality of the researcher and that of the informant. We call this breakdown of protective boundaries "rapport building." Through the building of rapport, we erode the informants' tendency to protect their private personalities. It is possible, even probable, that with the development of rapport, the informant provides information that could be damaging to them, if not properly protected.

Many such books even today have a condescending tendency to assume an unequal power relationship between the educated, "Western" anthropologist and his or her "native informants," and they warn of the dangers of extracting information on that basis, information that must be carefully protected.

"One might even argue," continues the textbook quoted above, "that 'rapport-building skills' are the most insidious deception." I couldn't agree more, though not for the reasons the author gives. In a place like Cyprus, with one of the highest literacy rates in the world, there is considerable understanding of what it means to do research and write a book, especially since writing is a familiar pastime of many people in the island. Many people want to write their own books, to make themselves heard, though the foreign researcher has a special status, and one bounded by a healthy measure of distrust. Cyprus is also, per capita, a highly researched society, at least in terms of survey data. So few people reacted with surprise when I wanted to talk to them, though they often felt that they should lead me to people who "really know."

I also gained some advantage from being a woman, and in many people's eyes a relatively young one, who seemed to pose little threat. Women, especially, took me in, leading me into their own worlds shaped not so much by conflict as by catastrophe, intimate worlds that had been overturned. But what most defined my work and set its parameters was the choice from the beginning to work on "both sides"—a choice that was fraught from the start with problems of definition but that soon acquired layers of meaning that would in the end become a burden. Because even as I struggled to give meaning to this phrase, *both sides*, even as I insisted to myself that the idea of "sides" in Cyprus is a construct, an effect of the island's division etched in our language, I also found myself being pulled to *take* sides, to show that one side or the other was right. I found myself caught in a space *between* sides, a space that I soon recognized as untenable. That space between, I soon saw, was a space of relativity that was impossible to maintain when the basis of the gap itself is one of historical right.

Because that space between is untenable, I soon found myself being pulled *across*, sympathizing first with one side and then with the other, in an equally untenable ping-pong of empathy that in the end could lead to only one conclusion: violation of trust, or the perception of it. For I soon began to realize that for very many people the division itself, the gap into which I had fallen, was a rupture defined by betrayal. There had been a violation of trust, a social contract destroyed. In its wake, communities had been scattered, peoples uprooted, new loyalties defined. I had chosen to do research, then, on the betrayals of the past and their traces in the present.

Unfortunately, I soon realized that betrayal would inevitably be its result.

In many of the stories that people told me, betrayal gained its just reward.

On the first day that Hüseyin took me to meet his sister, Birol seated me in her living room, the shutters closed tight in the middle of the day, and began: "*The old woman insisted on going home. We were all afraid, but she wanted to go home.*"

She sat on the edge of her seat, her hands on her knees, leaning forward, rocking slightly. "*Her sons were in the mountains fighting,* she continued, *and she came to the village alone. And of course the Greeks came to her and wanted to buy her land. That's what they would do then: try to buy our land. It was summer 1974, they say. Just two weeks before the Operation. She sold some of her land and put the money under her pillow. And the Greeks came in the night and killed her and took the money. They chopped up her body and threw it off the cliff at Five Mile beach. When her family came to look for her, they told them, 'Go look at Five Mile beach.' And only two weeks later the Operation happened and our army landed at that beach. Allah took his revenge."*

"*You got this on tape?*" her brother Hüseyin asks me.

Yes, I got it on tape.

"*It's an important story.*"

Birol insists: you must tell the Americans, you must make them listen. They must recognize us.

Her brother Hüseyin tells her: "*Don't talk to her about the Americans.*"

"*No,*" she says. "*The Americans must listen. I did beautiful embroidery, I would've been a teacher in the villages, teaching the girls embroidery. I was only eighteen. Eleven years! The best years of my life, in a tent. That's why I can't keep house now. And they took my embroidery, and they used it for their daughters' dowries. And now they come here, and I have to make coffee for them.*"

You make them coffee?

"*Yes, I make them coffee. But I don't speak Greek, so we can't talk, just a few words. And the Greek of this house comes, and she brings her grandson.*" Birol jumps up now, running about the room. "*The cira, the Greek woman, she points to things, 'This was ours, this wasn't ours. This was ours, this wasn't ours.' And what about me? I wake up in the night and recite prayers until dawn. I turn on the television, and if there's something against Turkey, or against northern Cyprus, I pray. My husband thinks I'm crazy, but I pray until dawn.*"

How long have you done this?

"*Since the border opened. Since they started coming here.*"

Birol's brother Hüseyin is insistent that I must document their suffering, and he is disappointed to learn that I speak to Greek Cypriots, as well. "*Well, what do they tell you?*" everyone would ask me. They were thirsty for news that was not constrained by the demands of hospitality.

Hüseyin Amca was twelve, he tells me, when he left school "*because the Greeks were causing too much trouble.*" He began work as an apprentice ironworker, first for a Turkish master, then for several Greek ones. "*I got tired of this one, and I left. I got tired of that one, and I left,*" he told me, laughing. He was sixteen, he says, when he was finally working regularly for a master whose shop was in the center of the village, between the municipal offices and the Turkish school. But one day a group of seven or eight Greek youths attacked the shop and him. The reason, he claims, is that his family had a parcel of land in the upper quarters, and a Greek woman had wanted his father to sell it to her. "*They were pressuring him. They wanted us to sell and leave.*" His father refused, and he claims that the attack was at her bidding. "*The rich people would make an investment in EOKA,* he claims, *and after that they'd use EOKA to get Turkish property for cheap.*"

Hüseyin's daughter whispers to me, "*I know he's too much. He's a bit fanatical. But he feels betrayed, you see. He won't admit it now, but he speaks Greek like a Greek. All his friends were Greek. They used to go drinking and carousing and chasing women together. They danced for days at his wedding, and then those same friends took up guns and said to him, 'We're going to kill every one of you, right down to your cats and dogs.' He feels betrayed.*"

Who said that?

Hüseyin's wife Ayşe rises and points out the window. "*They lived there, and there,*" she says.

Those who return to Lapithos say, "*The village seems dead.*" It seems a ghost of itself. They've chopped down the trees, and it seems naked. The houses seem smaller, and the paths that once joined neighbors and relatives are amputated by fences. There used to be commerce, festivals, bustle in the streets. Life and noise. Why have they not cared for things?

Greek Cypriots from Lapithos agree with me that the village seems to have some special significance among refugees. It's the light, some tell me. It's the contrast of sea and mountain. It was a commercial center. It was civilized, they say.

Turkish Cypriots from the village laugh. "*I think the reason it's so symbolic for the Greeks is sheer pride,* an old mason told me. *They had worked so hard to cleanse it of the Turks, and now they can't stand to see it in Turkish hands.*"

On a road near the outskirts of the southern part of Nicosia sits a small house that ten years ago had housed a union of EOKA fighters. I had gone there then to interview former teachers; today that house belongs to the Greek Cypriot municipality of Lapithos. I went there one day to meet the mayor, and as I waited for him, I fell into conversation with a woman also sitting in the anteroom, and I asked her which part of the town she's from. She told me that she's from Ayios Theodoros, the neighborhood where I was renting a house. It was one of the poorer neighborhoods of Lapithos, and one that bordered and overlapped with the two main concentrations of Turkish houses. Like many refugees, she pointed to an old photograph of the town that hung on the wall above a desk, and observed that it was much greener before. "*They've chopped down the trees,*" she said, a complaint I heard often. Her father had planted many lemon and fruit trees in their orchards, she told me, but they're gone now. And, she said, everything looks much smaller than she remembered.

She was around my age, old enough to remember but young enough to have those memories shaped by everything she would have heard since. She told me that she's visited only once, and it seemed crowded and dirty to her. Different. When I asked her if she wanted to return, she said that she definitely does, and she wiped tears from her eyes. Yet there was something wistful in her answer, like an acknowledgment of a dream better left deferred. She paused before adding, "*But only if we can all return.*" And there was uncertainty in her voice, something left unsaid. And a portion of fear.

Birol does not sleep. Eleni's husband smokes incessantly. High blood pressure, cancer, eccentric obsessions. Everyone takes pills; illness seems an integral part of life. A friend's sixteen-year-old daughter takes medication for hypertension, a sad inheritance. Betrayals are traced in the body. And it's the women who say it to me most: "*It's because of our suffering,*" they tell me in Turkish. "*We'll die far from our homes,*" they tell me in Greek.

And then the Turkish family from Vassilia, the neighboring village. Parents and five children who had gone to visit relatives some miles away. It was the end of 1963, and they were stopped on the road. They were killed by being thrown into a well.

Parceled bodies, unretrievable lives. Wells beyond the village, beyond the community of the human.

Legend tells of a place in Pano Lefkara whose name in ancient Greek means "disgusted by blood." "*It is called that because when the Ottoman armies came to Cyprus, there was a battle against the Lusignans in which so much blood was spilled that the ground was saturated and could drink no more.*" The earth was revolted, sick with blood.

I go to have coffee in Nicosia with a friend who paints as catharsis and who takes a rainbow of pills to relieve her various illnesses. A new grave has been discovered in Alsancak/Karavas, the village so close to Lapithos that they are like a small urban sprawl. A woman had been digging in her *avlu*, her inner courtyard or garden, when she discovered bones, human bones.

"*Oh, but I had a friend*" Özden says. "*She moved into Ayios Georgios after the war.*" Ayios Georgios is a village on the sea a short drive from Lapithos. The first two Turks of Lapithos killed by Greek special forces were murdered there. And during the war, the village, like Lapithos, was the sight of fierce battles; Greek Cypriots claim many missing. It is the home of Five Mile Beach, the site of the first Turkish military landing, and the place where, in Birol's story, the old woman's body was thrown. The largest monument in the island was built over that site, a giant modernist hand stretching from the sea to seize the land.

"*They planted vegetables in their garden, she tells me, and they were always boasting about the size of the vegetables. Then one day she called me and told me to come over. It was incredible: There had been a heavy rain, and it had washed up the skeletons buried in the garden.*"

Water bitter with murder, soil satiated with blood. A land imbued with betrayal.

I heard rumors of a mass grave on the coast of Lapithos. "*Oh, yes,*" a young man tells me. "*It's right past those hotels.*" We stand in his kitchen doorway, which faces toward the sea. The house officially belongs to an acquaintance of mine, Aris, who now lives in Nicosia. The young man, Bulut, was only seven when they returned to the village, but his child's mind was imprinted with the images of bodies littering the orchards. They had returned early, before the Turkish army swept through in a clean-up operation that dumped the corpses near the sea. "*When I was a teenager I would go to fish in that cove,*" he said. "*If it had rained, bones would wash up and float on the water.*"

The Committee of Missing Persons had made an abortive attempt a year earlier to find the Lapithos mass grave. "*Everyone knew they were digging in the wrong place,*" Bulut insists. *Everyone knew.*"

When I try to find someone to take me to the grave, everyone demurs.

Betrayal seeps into the present, remains washed up by a flood.

I hear first from Ozan about the man who came to Ozan's chapel-cum-office, claiming to be an architect, and of the way that they argued about Ozan's renovations. "*I don't believe he's an architect,*" he insists, "*because he didn't understand anything about renovations. We started arguing, and I told them to get out, or I was going to call the police.*"

Ozan's mother is being pestered by *"the Greeks of her house,"* who come and tell her that they're going to take it back and force them to leave. Ozan told me that he had nightmares, that he's been agitated.

When I meet Aris, Maria, and their friend Nikos, they told me themselves about the encounter. *"He picked up a large stone and threatened us with it! He chased us away."*

There is no statute of limitations on the traces of trauma, especially when one constantly irritates the wounds. Even though it's difficult, I admitted to them that Ozan was my landlord, that I was living in a Greek Cypriot house. *"The owners of his mother's house have been pestering her,"* I tried to explain.

Aris had been one of the first to promote ecotourism and the restoration of village houses. They lament the hundreds of villas that now clutter the village, and the loss of their orchards. I laugh and try to joke with them. *"The ironic thing,"* I say, *"is that on that issue you and Ozan would agree."*

They laugh, as well, and Maria jokes that perhaps Aris and Ozan should go into business together. But her humor cannot mitigate my own sense of betrayal. The inevitable betrayal of being between.

"Salih Usta thinks you're a spy, Ozan laughs. *I tried to explain to him what you do, but he doesn't understand about research."*

The last time I saw him before Ozan mentioned this, Salih had told me the story of a young Greek man who visited the village after the opening of the border. The young man claimed that his grandmother was buried under an orange tree in what used to be their garden, and he wanted the help of Salih, as muhtar, in exhuming the bones. *"I had to ask him, 'Was she killed?' Because if she was, I wouldn't want to get involved. 'No,' he said to me. 'It was during the invasion, but she died of natural causes.' They didn't have time to bury her properly, so they buried her under the orange tree. 'What you're asking is complicated,' I said to him. 'I'll have to ask the mayor, probably the Minister of the Interior. It's going to be a lot of trouble for me. So I'll do it on one condition.'"*

And then Salih explains to me about a man whose name Turkish Cypriots had repeatedly whispered when discussing incidents in the town. *"He's probably got hundreds of murders on his hands,"* Salih tells me. He was an official in the town, and everyone knew that he was the one who followed İbrahim Nidai and Şevket Kadir on the day that they disappeared, and that he stopped their car outside Ayios Georgios. Most people told me that he killed them by throwing them into a furnace.

"*So I said to the boy, 'You go to so-and-so, and you ask him what he did with my uncle's body. Then I'll help you.'*"

And according to Salih, the boy went, and he found the sergeant, and he asked him about the bodies. "*And you know what he told me? That they buried them at Five Mile Beach, right under the monument. That's what he told me. You see what he was saying? He was saying, 'Go take down the monument if you want their bodies.' That's the way things are.*"

I ask Salih if he still helped the boy exhume his grandmother from the base of the orange tree. He just laughs.

While renovating a Greek house near the main square of the village, builders knocked down a wall and found a large arms cache. Many people had told me that the man Salih blames for his uncle's murder had a stockpile of weapons in his basement. And the women talked about guns aimed at their children, mostly by young men who were neighbors. "*They would sit in the café,*" Fikriye Teyze tells me, "*and they would take aim at the children from there. I had a neighbor—we worked in the fields and shelled beans together. Her son took out a rifle and used to aim at my boy from their house.*"

I mentioned this one day to Vassilis, and he laughed sheepishly. "*They got scared because we'd go to the mountains and shoot off rifles,*" he shrugged. And he made a motion of firing into the air. But there was embarrassment in his voice.

Later, Anna told me that Vassilis is a true patriot, that he had been a hero of EOKA. I had known that there was something in his past that he hadn't disclosed, but then I confronted him about this. "*Absolutely not,*" Maroulla answered for him. "*He was never in EOKA. He was arrested by the British once, that's all.*"

But I understood that some parts of the past will always remain murky in the present.

The Greek Cypriot mayor of Lapithos, the mayor "in exile," comes to his office for a few hours once a week. Although I offered to arrange it, he refused to have contact with the Turkish Cypriot mayor, the one actually in the village, the one who does the hard work. Even though the "exiled" mayor is a leftist and works in a union that has bicommunal roots, he rejected my suggestion a year earlier that perhaps it was time to bring the Greek and Turkish people of Lapithos together and force them to talk politics. "*That's not how things get decided,*" he replied.

He was only a boy when the Turks left the village, but he remembered a neighbor, Tamer, with whom he used to play. Tamer's family stayed longer, he said, because the father hadn't wanted to leave.

I wanted to check this story and, through a circuitous route, found myself returning to Hüseyin. It turned out that Tamer was a nephew of sorts, but they knew nothing about whether or not the family had stayed on in the village. "*His grandmother was Greek*," Hüseyin remarked, implying that if it was true, it was probably because their loyalties were tainted.

But it also reminded him of his own problems when he tried to join TMT. "*They didn't want me at first*," he complained. "*I had too many Greek friends.*" Instead, it turns out that they recruited his sister Birol, who was only fourteen at the time. That was 1960, the year of the Republic's birth.

Old Christodoulos's coffeeshop is now a grocery, run by a Turk from Paphos. It was one of the few mixed coffeeshops, since it bordered the Turkish quarter. "*The EOKA men didn't like it*," he chuckled. And he told me the story of the old Turk with a limp, who spoke Greek like a Greek and would come to the coffeeshop every evening. Some of the men warned him not to come, but his limp prevented him from walking further, so he continued his visits, even though the EOKA men began to accuse him of being a spy. Then one day his body was found.

Much later I learned the story from the old Turk's niece: "*I heard it in the night, the sound of a motorcycle going back and forth, back and forth. They wanted it to look like an accident, you know. But if you saw his body, you'd know it was no accident.*"

Old Christodoulos now lives in dilapidated refugee housing in Lakatamia, as do several of his children and grandchildren. He has not visited the village and has no plans to do so. "*I can't afford a passport*," he explained. "*And besides, why visit if we're not going back? Even if we went back, what would we do? We're too old now, we can't work the land.*"

It seems that time itself slips into betrayal.

I had heard from others that there may have been one old Turk who never left Lapithos in 1964 or who later returned, and who kept a kebab stand near the shore. The grocer who remembered playing under a fig tree has his shop on the coast road, and I asked him about this rumor. He claimed to know nothing about the man with the kebab stand. He knew of only one old woman who returned to the village, but she died just before the invasion.

His wife interjected to ask, "*Did she die? Or was she killed?*"
"*She died naturally*," he said. "*My father found the body.*"

Some time after my visit to them in Paphos, Vasillis came to see me, and I offered him coffee in my rented house, which he commented must be a good place for writing. He was clearly trying hard, struggling to understand. After the coffee, we were to go talk to the mayor about whether or not they would permit Vasillis to stay in the village sometimes, if they would perhaps let him rent a room. He was putting his hope in Mustafa.

But only a few days before this visit I had returned to speak to Mustafa and had found him alone in the house, the Moldovan gone to town. He had insisted on sitting too close to me, and I left early. But in our brief conversation, I had asked him what he intended to do about Vasillis. He had laughed; he had no intention of renting him a room. "*This all used to be ours,*" he had remarked, letting his arm sweep across the orange groves across the road. And I had asked if he meant that it belonged to his family, which was one of the wealthiest in the village. "*Oh, yes, but the whole village belonged to the Turks.*" And he had told me the story of their Ottoman forefathers who were fond of Greek women, but then had leaned forward to warn in the low voice of someone who knows, "*Anyway, the* ciras, *the Greek women, they're not clean, you know.*"

Mustafa had told me that day that he had been one of the core group of TMT fighters who had organized in the area in the early 1960s, meeting in the house of the schoolmaster, a man now known throughout the island for his writings and his principled anti-Turkey stance. At the time, the schoolmaster was a military commander trained by Turkey.

Vasillis finished his coffee, and I realized that I had to decide. If I kept silent, I would betray him; if I told him, I would betray Mustafa.

"*Don't trust Mustafa,*" I finally said. "*He was in TMT all along.*"

Vasillis didn't reply, just bowed his head.

And I wanted to say to him, "*You claim he was your friend. How could you not know?*"

The words formed on my lips, but the moment passed. And I sensed then that the secret to all our betrayals must be found somewhere in a question that I could not bring myself to ask.

Reading the Future
(In Lieu of a Conclusion)

NOT LONG BEFORE leaving Lapithos, I went one last time to drink coffee with my neighbor, Sevgül. She is the wife of one of the local coffeeshop owners, both refugees from Paphos, and she has a network of relatives in the village. She is a pert, pretty woman of about fifty, with blond hair, blue eyes, and an abundance of freckles. But like most women her age, she complains of her health, attributing her high blood pressure and other problems to the years spent in the enclaves. She also has told me that although they have nothing against the Greeks, after all they've suffered she wouldn't want them to come back. She wouldn't trust them to live near her as neighbors.

On this last meeting before my departure, one of her relatives by marriage, Tomris, and her brother, Mehmet, arrived and began talking of their trips to the south, where they still have relatives. The brother and sister are also related to my landlord, and they're all from the same Paphos village, where some of their uncles remained with their Greek wives after the island was divided. As we sipped our coffee, Tomris complained of the difficulties her uncle's young son has had, especially in school.

As we talked, everyone finished their coffee and turned over their cups in the saucer to allow the coffee grounds that remained at the bottom to trickle down the sides. As the thick grounds slowly slide to the bottom, they create shapes that Sevgül was going to read in order to tell the future. She said that she would begin with Mehmet's cup, and she took it up, turning it into the light. She began rapidly reciting, using the practiced formulas of someone for whom reading coffee cups is like a memorized incantation. A dark spot predicts a period of trouble; numbers indicate days, or weeks, or months.

In the middle of her reading, she turned the cup and said in a naïve and serious way, "There's a map of Cyprus. That means that you have an unsolved problem, but it will be solved."

Tomris, sitting on the sofa opposite, glanced at me, and we laughed. Sevgül seemed surprised at our laughter. "We look at the shapes," she turned to me and said by way of explanation.

"Oh, I know," I said, smiling. "I just liked the interpretation."

Tomris was trying to suppress her own laughter. "You should put that in your book!" she exclaimed.

I promised her that I would.

Notes

The Sorrow of Unanswered Questions

Page vii. *Our Valuable Properties Remaining in the South*: Hasan Fehmi, *Güney'de Kalan Değerlerimiz* (Nicosia: Özyay Matbaacılık, 2003).

Chapter 1. Paths of No Return

Page 1. *has it withstood last winter's rain or has it yielded?*: Yiorgos Moleskis, "The House and Time," in *Step-Mothertongue: From Nationalism to Multiculturalism: Literatures of Cyprus, Greece and Turkey*, ed. Mehmet Yashin (London: Middlesex University Press, 2000), 109.

Chapter 2. The Anxieties of an Opening

Page 42. *if the past is, as one historian called it, a foreign country*: David Lowenthal, *The Past Is a Foreign Country* (Cambridge: Cambridge University Press, 1985).

Page 55. *was once well known and had long been familiar*: Sigmund Freud, *The Uncanny* (New York: Penguin Classics, 2003), quotes on pages 124 and 132.

Chapter 3. A Needle and a Handkerchief

Page 78. *they connect a great many people*: Georg Simmel, "The Stranger," in *The Sociology of George Simmel*, trans. Kurt H. Wolff (Glencoe, Ill.: Free Press, 1950, 1964), 405.

Chapter 4. Geographies of Loss

Page 85. *I can stand it no more*: Meropi Karatzia-Siakidhou, *Istoria Trion Gheneon* (Nicosia: Meropi Siakidhou, 1998), 1.

Page 89. *service of his village*: Chrysanthos S. Kyprianou, ed., *To Pankyprion Ghimnasion kai i Laografia*, 3 vols. (Leukosia: Aragennisis, 1968), 152.

Page 90. *never saw him again*: Mustafa Kemal Sayın, *Efsane Toprakları* (Nicosia: Kıymet Kültür ve Sanat Yayınları, 2003), 17.

Page 98. *Ah, Kyrenia, my mother!*: Because of subsequent interviews with the women who appear in this book as Eleni and Anna, and because of sensitive information that both women discuss, I have chosen to treat two of their writings as interview material and therefore to suppress citations.

Chapter 5. In the Ruins of Memory

Page 110. *forces of civilization of the Earth*: Fokas Fokaidis, *Lapithos: Istoria kai Paradhosis* (Nicosia: Kyrenia Municipality, 1982), 110.

Page 110. *the water and the gardens*: Fokaidis, *Lapithos: Istoria kai Paradhosis*, 117.

Page 114. "I Do Not Throw Up," *Enosis*, September 28, 2008, http://www.yialousa.org/downloads/Enosis_200809.pdf.

Page 114.*hear anyone mentioning it*: "Tales from the Coffeeshop," *Cyprus Mail*, August 6, 2006.

Page 116.*invasion and occupation*: Municipality of Lapithos, *Imepoessa Lapithos: 3000 Chronia* (Nicosia: Municipality of Lapithos, 2001), 276.

Page 117.*gained by such a visitor*: Municipality of Lapithos, *Imepoessa Lapithos*, 274–75.

Page 118.*much more frightening*: Joyce Dalsheim, "Settler Nationalism, Collective Memories of Violence and the 'Uncanny Other,'" *Social Identities* 10, 2 (2004): 165.

Page 128. *was taken very seriously*: Costas Yennaris, *From the East: Conflict and Partition in Cyprus* (London: Elliot and Thompson, 2004).

Chapter 6. The Spoils of History

Page 143. *people are even saying they've looted*: This paragraph and the next from Özker Yaşın, *Girne'den Yol Bağladık* (Istanbul: İtimat Kitabevi, 1976), 21–23.

Page 143. *kissing like mother and daughter*: Please see note for Chapter 4, p. 98, above.

Chapter 7. The Pieces of Peace

Page 167. *selling it to foreigners*: www.lobbyforcyprus.org.

Page 168. *imagining what is, in fact, real*: Peter Gourevitch, *We Wish to Inform You That Tomorrow We Will Be Killed with Our Families: Stories from Rwanda* (New York: Farrar, Straus, Giroux, 1998).

Page 173. *When are we going back to Lapithos?*: Sevgül Uludağ, "Yeraltı Notlar," March 11, 2005, http://www.stwing.upenn.edu/~durduran/hamambocu/authors/svg/svg2_11_2005.html.

Page 177. *without paying compensation, completely illegally*: Ismet Kotak, "Kıbrıs Türkü çulsuz çaputsuz değildi!" İsmet Kotak, *Halkın Sesi*, June 6, 2005.

Page 177. *and Makarios chased us from our land*: Interview with Arif Mustafa, "32 yıl sonra evinde," *Kıbrıs Gazetesi*, February 19, 2006.

Chapter 8. Betrayals of the Past

Page 184. *If not properly protected*: John Van Willigen, *Applied Anthropology: An Introduction*, 3rd ed. (Westport, Conn.: Greenwood, 2002), 51.

Main Sources and
Suggestions for Further Reading

The works listed below are ones that were useful in the research and writing of this book. This is not an exhaustive bibliography but rather a list of suggestions for further reading. Those readers interested in a more complete bibliography of works related to Cyprus may consult my *Imagining the Modern: The Cultures of Nationalism in Cyprus* (London: I.B. Tauris, 2004).

On History and Anthropology

For the reader wishing to gain a broad but nuanced view of the Cyprus conflict, I recommend Michael Attalides, *Cyprus: Nationalism and International Politics* (New York: St. Martin's Press, 1979) and Zenon Stavrinides's daring *The Cyprus Conflict: National Identity and Statehood* (Nicosia: author, 1975). An introductory chapter in Cynthia Cockburn, *The Line: Women, Partition and the Gender Order in Cyprus* (London: Zed Books, 2004) is one of the best summaries to date of events leading to the division. Yiannis Papadakis, *Echoes from the Dead Zone: Across the Cyprus Divide* (London: I.B. Tauris, 2005) is an excellent introduction to the histories that have arisen around division and to the misunderstandings that differing narratives produce. An excellent volume of interdisciplinary work that represented a first attempt at exploring the politics of Cyprus's past is Vangelis Calotychos, *Cyprus and Its People: Nation, Identity, and Experience in an Unimaginable Community* (Boulder, Colo.: Westview Press, 1998). A volume published several years later, Yiannis Papadakis, N. Peristianis, and Gisela Welz, eds., *Divided Cyprus: Modernity, History, and an Island in Conflict* (Bloomington: Indiana University Press, 2006) provides one of the best anthropological introductions to current issues in the island.

The issue of Cypriot displacement that is central to this book has its own small but growing literature, to which I refer in references to specific chapters. For an introduction to the issue, Peter Loizos, *The Heart Grown Bitter: A Chronicle of Cypriot War Refugees* (Cambridge: Cambridge University Press, 1981) is indispensable; it provides a powerful account of Greek Cypriot displacement in 1974 and attempts to rebuild lives in the island's south. His follow-up work on the health effects of long-term displacement, *Iron in the Soul: Displacement, Livelihood, and Health in Cyprus* (Oxford: Berghahn, 2008), is an especially valuable resource because of its study of one village community over more than four decades.

A Prelude to Mourning

The best work on the conflicts of the 1960s and Turkish Cypriot displacement during that period is Richard Patrick, *Political Geography and the Cyprus Conflict, 1963–1971*, Department of Geography Publication Series 4 (Waterloo, Ont.: Faculty of Environmental Studies, University of Waterloo, 1976). For an understanding of life in the enclaves during that period, see Vamık Volkan, *Cyprus: War and Adaptation: A Psychoanalytic History of Two Ethnic Groups in Conflict* (Charlottesville: University of Virginia Press, 1978).

In thinking about the particular contested history described here, especially the Greek Cypriot belief that Turkish Cypriots voluntarily uprooted themselves, I found works on Palestinian displacement particularly useful, especially Rosemarie M. Esber, "The 1948 Palestinian Arab Exodus from Haifa," *Arab Geographer* 6, 2 (Summer 2003): 112–41; Walid Khalidi, "Why Did the Palestinians Leave, Revisited," *Journal of Palestine Studies* 134, 2 (Winter 2005): 42–54; and a number of the essays in Ahmad H. Sa'di and Lila Abu-Lughod, eds., *Nakba: Palestine, 1948, and the Claims of Memory* (New York: Columbia University Press, 2007), esp. Sa'di, "Afterword: Reflections on Representation, History, and Moral Accountability," 285–314 (esp. 298).

Chapter 1. Paths of No Return

I found Sarah F. Green, *Notes from the Balkans: Locating Marginality and Ambiguity on the Greek-Albanian Border* (Princeton, N.J.: Princeton University Press, 2005) and Daphne Berdahl, *Where the World Ended: Re-Unification and Identity in the German Borderland* (Berkeley: University of California Press, 1999) especially important for thinking about local practices of border-making.

In the past three decades, there has been a proliferation of work on memory that makes it necessary for the researcher to be highly selective. The most useful works for me were Paul Antze and Michael Lambek, eds., *Tense Past: Cultural Essays in Trauma and Memory* (London: Routledge, 1996), especially Lambek's chapter, "The Past Imperfect: Remembering as Moral Practice," 235–55; Mieke Bal, Jonathan Crewe, and Leo Spitzer, eds., *Acts of Memory: Cultural Recall in the Present* (Hanover, N.H.: University Press of New England, 1999), especially Carol Bardenstein's chapter, "Trees, Forests, and the Shaping of a Palestinian and Israeli Collective Memory" (148–68); Jonathan Boyarin, *The Storm from Paradise: The Politics of Jewish Memory* (Minneapolis: University of Minnesota Press, 1992); Marianne Hirsch, *Family Frames: Photography, Narrative, and Post-Memory* (Cambridge, Mass.: Harvard University Press, 1997); Renee Hirschon, *Heirs of the Greek Catastrophe: The Social Life of Asia Minor Refugees in Piraeus* (Oxford: Clarendon Press, 1989); Elizabeth Jelin, *State Repression and the Labors of Memory* (Minneapolis: University of Minnesota Press, 2003); Dominick LaCapra, *History and Memory After Auschwitz* (Ithaca, N.Y.: Cornell University Press, 1998); and Liisa Malkki, *Purity and Exile: Violence, Memory, and National Cosmology Among Hutu Refugees in Tanzania* (Chicago: University of Chicago Press, 1995).

Keith Brown, *The Past in Question: Modern Macedonia and the Uncertainties of Nation* (Princeton, N.J.: Princeton University Press, 2003) and Jennifer Cole, *Forget Colonialism? Sacrifice and the Art of Memory in Madagascar* (Berkeley: University of California Press, 2001) were useful for thinking about locality and memory-making and the practices of local memory-making. On embodiment and memory, I recommend Tim Ingold, *Perceptions of the Environment: Essays in Livelihood, Dwelling, and Skill* (New York: Routledge, 2000); C. Nadia Seremetakis, "The Memory of the Senses, Parts 1 and 2," in *The Senses Still: Perception and Memory as Material Culture in Modernity*, ed. Seremetakis (Boulder, Colo.: Westview Press, 1994), 1–43; and David Sutton, *Remembrance of Repasts: An Anthropology of Food and Memory* (London: Berg, 2001).

Specifically on the question of space and memory I was influenced by Gaston Bachelard, *The Poetics of Space*, trans. Maria Jolas (Boston: Beacon Press, 1969) and Emmanuel Levinas, *Totality and Infinity: An Essay on Exteriority*, trans. Alphonso Lingis (Pittsburgh: Duquesne University Press, 1969). Other works that were very helpful in thinking about the question included Joelle Bahloul, *The Architecture of Memory: A Jewish-Muslim Household in Colonial Algeria 1937–1962*, trans. Catherine du Peloux-Menage (Cambridge: Cambridge University Press, 1996); Pierre Bourdieu, *Outline of a Theory of Practice* (Cambridge: Cambridge University Press, 1977); Henri Lefebvre, *The Production of Space*, trans. Donald Nicholson-Smith (Oxford: Wiley-Blackwell, 1992); Simon Schama, *Landscape and Memory* (New York: Vintage, 1995); and Yi-Fu Tuan, *Space and Place: The Perspective of Experience* (Minneapolis: University of Minnesota Press, 2001).

On subjectivity in the context of social change, I found useful Arthur Kleinman and Erin Fitz-Henry, "The Experiential Basis of Subjectivity: How Individuals Change in the Context of Societal Transformation," in *Subjectivity: Ethnographic Investigations*, ed. João Guilherme Biehl, Byron Good, and Arthur Kleinman (Berkeley: University of California Press, 2007), 52–65; Philip Gourevitch, *We Wish to Inform You That Tomorrow We Will Be Killed with Our Families: Stories from Rwanda* (New York: Farrar, Straus, Giroux, 1998); and Carol J. Greenhouse, Elizabeth Mertz, and Kay B. Warren, eds., *Ethnography in Unstable Places: Everyday Lives in Contexts of Dramatic Political Change* (Durham, N.C.: Duke University Press, 2002).

Chapter 2. The Anxieties of an Opening

On the issue of Turkish settlers in Cyprus, see two reports by Mete Hatay, *Beyond Numbers: An Inquiry into the Political Integration of the Turkish "Settlers" in Northern Cyprus*, PRIO Report 4/2005 (Oslo: International Peace Research Institute, 2005) and *Is the Turkish Cypriot Population Shrinking? An Overview of the Ethno-Demography of Cyprus in the Light of the Preliminary Results of the 2006 Turkish-Cypriot Census*, PRIO Report 2/2007 (Oslo: International Peace Research Institute, 2007), as well as Christoph Ramm, "Assessing Transnational Renegotiation in the Post-1974 Cypriot Community: 'Cyprus

Donkeys,' 'Black Beards,' and the 'EU Carrot,'" *Southeast European and Black Sea Studies* 6, 4 (2006): 523–42.

On the notion of the uncanny, see Sigmund Freud, *The Uncanny* (New York: Penguin Classics, 2003) and Jacques Lacan, *The Seminar Book VII: The Ethics of Psychoanalysis, 1959–1960*, trans. Dennis Porter (London: Routledge, 1992). In thinking through notions of the uncanny and place, I found Lévinas, *Totality and Infinity*, as well as Mladen Dolar's article, "'I Shall Be with You on Your Wedding-Night': Lacan and the Uncanny," *October* 58 (1991): 5–23, especially useful.

Sevgül Uludağ's important work in *Yenidüzen* newspaper has brought to light much information about missing persons and other victims of conflict-related violence in the island. Her book *Oysters with the Missing Pearls* (Nicosia: Ikme Bilban, 2007) was one of the first attempts to bring to light stories that had been suppressed and denied on both sides of the island.

In thinking about the relationship between shame, denial, and cultural intimacy, I referred especially to Emmanuel Lévinas, *On Escape*, trans. Jacques Rolland (Stanford, Calif.: Stanford University Press, 2003) and Stanley Cohen, *States of Denial: Knowing About Atrocities and Suffering* (Cambridge: Polity Press, 2001). Other works I found useful were Laurence J. Kirmayer, "Landscapes of Memory: Trauma, Narrative and Dissociation," in *Tense Past: Cultural Essays in Trauma and Memory*, ed. Paul Antze and Michael Lambek (New York: Routledge, 1996); Annette Kuhn, *Family Secrets: Acts of Memory and Imagination* (New York: Verso, 1995); Renata Salecl, *On Anxiety* (London: Routledge, 2004); Yi-Fu Tuan, *Escapism* (Baltimore: Johns Hopkins University Press, 2001): and Bernard Williams, *Shame and Necessity* (Berkeley: University of California Press, 1993).

The best explication of cultural intimacy appears in Michael Herzfeld, *Cultural Intimacy: Social Poetics in the Nation-State* (New York: Routledge, 1997).

Chapter 3. A Needle and a Handkerchief

The case of Palestinians is perhaps the best comparison of a group whose displacement has been misrepresented. For documentation, see Walid Khalidi, *All That Remains: The Palestinian Villages Occupied and Depopulated by Israel in 1948* (Washington, D.C.: Institute of Palestine Studies, 1992). For a comparison of the experiences of Palestinians and Israelis over a fifty-year period, see Dan Rabinowitz and Khawla Abu Baker, *Coffins on Our Shoulders: The Experience of the Palestinian Citizens of Israel* (Berkeley: University of California Press, 2005). Dan Rabinowitz, *Overlooking Nazareth: The Ethnography of Exclusion in Galilee* (Cambridge: Cambridge University Press, 1997) also provides important insight into the everyday workings of exclusion in mixed towns and villages.

The classic text on reciprocity is Marcel Mauss, *The Gift: Forms and Functions of Exchange in Archaic Societies* (1922; London: Routledge, 1990). On the refashioning of community in the wake of violence, see Maurice Blanchot, *The Writing of the Disaster*, trans. Ann Smock (Lincoln: University of Nebraska Press, 1995); Judith Butler, *Precarious Life: The Power of Mourning and Violence* (London: Verso, 2004); Veena Das, *Life and Words: Violence and Descent into the Ordinary* (Berkeley: University of California Press, 2007); and Neni Panourgia, *Fragments of Death, Fables of Identity: An Athenian Anthropography* (Madison: University of Wisconsin Press, 1995).

Chapter 4. Geographies of Loss

The most important anthropological work to date on mapping and memory is Susan Slyomovics, *The Object of Memory: Arab and Jew Narrate the Palestinian Village* (Philadelphia: University of Pennsylvania Press, 1998). In addition, Rochelle Davis, "Mapping the Past, Re-Creating the Homeland: Memories of Village Places in pre-1948 Palestine," in Sa'di and Abu-Lughod, eds., *Nakba*, 53-76, provides interesting points of comparison with the Cyprus example.

Please see Chapter 1, above, for further references on place and memory. For initial thoughts on the relationship of property and territoriality, see Robert David Sack, *Human Territoriality: Its Theory and History* (Cambridge: Cambridge University Press, 1986). I found the most useful comparison to be with the case of Israel/Palestine, for which there is a growing literature. See especially Baruch Kimmerling, *Zionism and Territory* (Albany: State University of New York Press, 1983); Dan Rabinowitz, "An Acre Is an Acre Is an Acre? Differentiated Attitudes to Social Space and Territory on the Jewish-Arab Urban Frontier in Israel," *Urban Anthropology* 21 (1992): 67–89 and "To Sell or Not to Sell? Theory Versus Practice, Public Versus Private, and the Failure of Liberalism: The Case of Israel and Its Palestinian Citizens," *American Ethnologist* 21 (1994): 823–40; as well as Oren Yiftachel, *Ethnocracy: Land and Identity Politics in Israel/Palestine* (Philadelphia: University of Pennsylvania Press, 2006).

Chapter 5. In the Ruins of Memory

There are several works dealing specifically with the question of collective memory and refugee identity in Cyprus. Antonios Maratheftis, "Den Ksechno, I Do Not Forget: The Greek Cypriot Refugee Experience as Oral Narrative," Ph.D. dissertation, University of Texas at Austin, 1989), provides a self-reflexive account of these processes. Tasoulla Hadjiyanni, *The Making of a Refugee: Children Adopting Refugee Identity in Cyprus* (Westport, Conn.: Praeger, 2002) was one of the first attempts to deal with the question of post-memory, or the ways parents' memories are transmitted to children. However, Stefan Ege, "Re/producing Refugees in the Republic of Cyprus: History and Memory between State, Family, and Society," M.A. thesis, University of Zurich, 2007, suggests that the adherence of children to refugee identity is highly situational.

Roger Zetter has dealt specifically with the ways Greek Cypriots were resettled after their displacement and the relationship of this resettlement to the reproduction of refugee identity. See especially his "Rehousing the Greek-Cypriot Refugees from 1974: Dependency, Assimilation, Politicisation," in *Cyprus in Transition: 1960–1985*, ed. John T. A. Koumoulides (London: Trigraph, 1985), 106–25, and "Reconceptualizing the Myth of Return: Continuity and Transition Amongst the Greek-Cypriot Refugees of 1974," *Journal of Refugee Studies* 12, 1 (1999): 1–22.

On the uses of the slogan "Dhen Xechno," see Miranda Christou, "A Double Imagination: Memory and Education in Cyprus," *Journal of Modern Greek Studies* 24 (2006): 285–106, and Christalla Yakinthou, "The Quiet Deflation of Den Xehno? Changes in the Greek Cypriot Communal Narrative on the Missing," *Cyprus Review* 20, 1 (2008): 15–33.

On the politics of commemoration in north Cyprus, see Moira Killoran, "Nationalism and Embodied Memory in Northern Cyprus, in Calotychos, ed., *Cyprus and Its People*, 159–70, and "Time, Space, and National Identities in Cyprus," in Mahmet Yashin, ed., *Step-Mother Tongue: From Nationalism to Multiculturalism: Literatures of Cyprus, Greece, and Turkey* (London: Middlesex University Press, 2000), 129–46. Other useful works for thinking about the refashioning of reality after conflict in Cyprus include Paul Sant Cassia, *Bodies of Evidence: Burial, Memory and the Recovery of Missing Persons in Cyprus* (Oxford: Berghahn Books, 2005), and Costas Constantinou and Yiannis Papadakis, "The Cypriot State(s) *in Situ*: Cross-Ethnic Contact and the Discourse of Recognition," *Global Society* 15, 2 (2001).

I found some of the most useful works on the social efficacy of commemoration and memoralization to be Paul Connerton, *How Societies Remember* (Cambridge: Cambridge University: 1989); the classic text by Maurice Halbwachs, *On Collective Memory* (Chicago: University of Chicago Press, 1992); John Gillis, ed., *Commemorations: The Politics of National Identity* (Princeton, N.J.: Princeton University Press, 1994), and especially the article by Claudia Koonz in the same volume, "Between Memory and Oblivion: Concentration Camps in German Memory"; Pierre Nora, "Between Memory and History: *Les Lieux de Mémoire*," *Representations* 26 (1989): 7–25; and James Young, *The Texture of Meaning: Holocaust Memorials and Meaning* (New Haven, Conn.: Yale University Press, 1993).

On the everyday political practices of memory-making, Jelin, *State Repression and the Labors of Memory*, is especially important. On the relationship between space and time in the politics of memory, see especially Jonathan Boyarin, ed., *Remapping Memory: The Politics of Timespace* (Minneapolis: University of Minnesota Press, 1994), especially Boyarin's chapter, "Space, Time, and the Politics of Memory," 1–38. Michel de Certeau, *The Practice of Everyday Life* (Berkeley: University of California Press, 1984) is very helpful for thinking about the everyday fashioning of reality, while Elaine Scarry, *The Body in Pain: The Making and Unmaking of the World* (Oxford: Oxford University Press, 1987) is helpful for thinking about the making of worlds after war.

The final reference to absence and loss is influenced by Dominick LaCapra, "Trauma, Absence, Loss," *Critical Inquiry* 25, 2 (1999): 696–727.

Chapter 6. The Spoils of History

Once again, the Israel/Palestine case provides one of the best opportunities for comparison. Both Ted Swedenburg, *Memories of Revolt: The 1936–1939 Rebellion and the Palestinian National Past* (Minneapolis: University of Minnesota Press, 1995) and Nadia Abu el-Haj, *Facts on the Ground: Archaeological Practice and Territorial Self-Fashioning in Israeli Society* (Chicago: University of Chicago Press, 2002) describe the normalization of a territory reshaped after violence.

The growing literature from the subcontinent on everyday life after violence was very helpful in thinking about Cypriots' encounters with the remainders of violation. Important works in that literature include Veena Das, *Life and Words*; Deepak Mehta, "Writing the Riot: Between the Historiography and Ethnography of Communal Violence in India," in *History and the Present*, ed. Partha Chatterjee and Anjan Ghosh (New Delhi: Permanent Black, 2002), 209–41; Deepak Mehta and Roma Chatterji, "Boundaries, Names, Alterities: A Case Study of a 'Communal Riot' in Dharavi, Bombay," in *Remaking a World: Violence, Social Suffering, and Recovery*, ed. Veena Das, Arthur Kleinman, Margaret Lock, Mamphele Ramphele, and Pamela Reynolds (Berkeley: University of California Press, 2001), 201–49; and Gyanendra Pandey, *Remembering Partition: Violence, Nationalism and History in Contemporary India* (Cambridge: Cambridge University Press, 2002).

In thinking about this chapter, I also made use of the large literature on trauma, of which I will mention here only Cathy Caruth, "Recapturing the Past: Introduction," in *Trauma: Explorations in Memory*, ed. Caruth (Baltimore: Johns Hopkins University Press, 1995), 151–57 and "Unclaimed Experience: Trauma and the Possibility of History," *Yale French Studies* 79 (1991): 181–92; and Dominick LaCapra, *History and Memory After Auschwitz* and *Writing History, Writing Trauma* (Baltimore: Johns Hopkins University Press, 2001).

The suggestion that objects become remainders of history is influenced by Slavoj Žižek, *The Sublime Object of Ideology* (London: Verso, 1989).

For a rather different take on the issue of plundered property, and one that appeared after this chapter had already been written, see Yael Navaro-Yashin, "Affective Space, Melancholic Objects: Ruination and the Production of Anthropological Knowledge," *Journal of the Royal Anthropological Institute* 15, 1 (2009): 1–18.

Chapter 7. The Pieces of Peace

For more on the national struggle museums, see Yiannis Papadakis, "The National Struggle Museums of a Divided City," *Ethnic and Racial Studies* 17, 3 (1994).

Property has recently become a subject of increasing anthropological attention. Examples include Jessica Allina-Pisano, *The Post-Soviet Potemkin Village: Politics and Property Rights in the Black Earth* (Cambridge: Cambridge University Press, 2007); C. M. Hann, ed., *Property Relations: Renewing the Anthropological Tradition* (Cambridge: Cambridge University Press, 1998); Katherine Verdery, *The Vanishing Hectare: Property and Value in Postsocialist Transylvania* (Ithaca, N.Y.: Cornell University Press, 2003); and Katherine Verdery and Caroline Humphrey, eds., *Property in Question: Value Transformation in the Global Economy* (London: Berg, 2004).

Acknowledgments

I AM INDEBTED TO all the people of Lapithos who gave their time, shared their stories, and allowed me to enter their lives. I hope that I have done them justice, and the reader should know that all infelicities are my own.

This work would not have been possible without the institutions that supported it over the five-year period of its research and writing. A New Century Scholar Fulbright Scholarship from the Council for International Exchange of Scholars and a John D. and Catherine T. MacArthur Foundation Research Grant from the Program on Global Security and Sustainability funded the initial research. The National Endowment for the Humanities provided funding for writing, and the Institute for Advanced Study in Princeton gave me an invaluable opportunity to complete much of the book's first draft in an ideal environment.

I am grateful to the late Clifford Geertz for supporting my membership at the IAS, and to the many colleagues who read and commented on the work while I was there, though especially to Marianne Constable and Michael Peletz. Parts of the work were presented at the Department of Anthropology at Princeton University, St. Andrew's College at Oxford University, and at various venues in Cyprus. Many colleagues have heard or read parts of the manuscript and given their comments on it, and I would especially like to acknowledge James Boon, John Comaroff, Elizabeth Drexler, Carol Greenhouse, Susan Slyomovics, and David Sutton for engagements that provided me with new insight. They will no doubt find places where I have incorporated their remarks, and I ask forgiveness for those places where I was unable to do so.

I completed much of the final version of the manuscript while on leave in Cyprus, and I am grateful to George Mason University for the several months that allowed me to refine the text. During that period, Costas Constantinou and Christalla Yakinthou read the entire manuscript with care, correcting errors and pointing out places where I might be misunderstood. My editor, Peter Agree, supported the project almost from its inception and has been a great source of encouragement.

Special thanks are due to my friend Filiz Naldöven, who was with me from the beginning of the research, introduced me to many of the persons who appear as characters in the book, and sat up long nights with me as we talked about what it all meant.

My husband Mete Hatay arrived in my life while I was in the process of writing, and his steadfast encouragement and boundless support pushed me both to work harder and to stay true to the integrity of the project. He read this work countless times in its many versions, always with equal enthusiasm, putting up with bouts of bad humor and assuring me of the importance of the project. *Sensiz olmazdı.*